Hellenism and Homosexuality
in Victorian Oxford

HELLENISM AND HOMOSEXUALITY

IN VICTORIAN OXFORD

LINDA DOWLING

Cornell University Press

Ithaca and London

First published 1994 by Cornell University Press.
First printing, Cornell Paperbacks, 1996.

Portions of Chapter 1 are reprinted by permission from *Raritan: A Quarterly Review*,
Vol. XIII, No. 3 (Winter 1993). Copyright © 1993 by *Raritan*, 31 Mine Street,
New Brunswick, N.J. 08903. Quotations from Greek Lyrics, translated by
Richmond Lattimore, 2d ed. (Chicago: University of Chicago Press, 1960), copyright
© 1960 by the Trustees of the University of Chicago, are used by permission of the
University of Chicago Press.

♾The paper in this book meets the minimum requirements of the
American National Standard for Information Sciences—Permanence
of Paper for Printed Library Materials, ANSI Z39.48-1984.

Library of Congress Cataloging-in-Publication Data

Dowling, Linda C.
    Hellenism and homosexuality in Victorian Oxford / Linda Dowling.
        p.   cm.
    Includes bibliographical references and index.
    ISBN 0-8014-2960-9 (cloth)
    ISBN 0-8014-8170-8 (paper)
    1. English literature—19th century—History and criticism.   2. Homosexuality and
literature—England—Oxford—History—19th century.   3. Greek philology—Study and
teaching—England—Oxford—History—19th century.   4. Classicism—England—
Oxford—History—19th century.   5. Gay men—England—Oxford—History—19th
century.   6. Oxford (England)—Social life and customs.   I. Title.
PR468.H65D68   1994
480'71'141—dc20   93-32781

FOR WCD

καὶ πᾶς ἂν δέξαιτο ἑαυτῷ τοιούτους παῖδας μᾶλλον γεγονέναι ἢ
τοὺς ἀνθρωπίνους καὶ εἰς Ὅμηρον ἀποβλέψας καὶ Ἡσίοδον καὶ
τοὺς ἄλλους ποιητὰς τοὺς ἀγαθοὺς ζηλῶν, οἷα ἔκγονα ἑαυτῶν κα-
ταλείπουσιν, ἃ ἐκείνοις ἀθάνατον κλέος καὶ μνήμην παρέχεται αὐτὰ
τοιαῦτα ὄντα.

CONTENTS

ILLUSTRATIONS

PREFACE

"In political thought and analysis," declares Michel Foucault in *The History of Sexuality*, the charter for so much current writing about homosexuality, "we still have not cut off the head of the king." His point, that a certain rudimentary conception of power continues in unrecognized ways to dominate modern cultural theory, bears with a special urgency on this last great project of Foucault's career. For *The History of Sexuality* is precisely an attempt to develop a theory of human sexual identity in terms that become available only when one has broken free of what Foucault calls the model of law and sovereignty, the errors and illusions involved in imagining sexuality merely as some realm of free or natural desire reduced to silence by an oppression imposed from above. In relation to sexuality, and in particular, today, to homosexuality, the law and sovereignty model yields what Foucault famously denominates the repressive hypothesis, the history of sexuality as successive scenes in a single drama in which sexual desire struggles to liberate itself from the oppressive weight of law and prohibition and taboo.

There are a number of reasons why Foucault goes to such lengths to dissociate himself from the repressive hypothesis, but the most important, I think, concerns the enormous loss of explanatory power that occurs when the various transmutations of sexual desire are conceived according to the law and sovereignty model — the monarch, the state, the police as agencies of repression and intolerance, the body and its desires as the realm of nature and freedom. Against this impoverishment Foucault then counterposes his own immensely more complex vision of *pouvoir-savoir*, of "discourse" and "law" and "desire" and "sexuality" as belonging to a simultaneous set of relations sustained by power as a ceaseless flow of social energy, as well as those impedances to its flow, built into the system and its operations, to which Foucault gives the name "resistance." This is resistance as envisioned throughout *The History of Sexuality*, as a ruse or strategy through which power expands its operations, ceaselessly generating new "forbidden" or "illegitimate" categories of experience that are then reabsorbed into the larger social structure through their equally ceaseless struggle for legitimation.

If nothing else, such an analysis serves brilliantly to explain why so much writing on homosexuality that today purports to honor Foucault's work nonetheless persists in ignoring his rejection of the repressive hypothesis. For the way in which power silently expands its circumference is always on Foucault's account through the promise of an ever-retreating freedom lying just beyond its reach. Even when one is convinced that this is a sham freedom, its temptations are, one sees, overwhelming:

> If sex is repressed, that is, condemned to prohibition, nonexistence, and silence, then the mere fact that one is speaking about it has the appearance of a deliberate transgression. A person who holds forth in such language places himself to a certain extent outside the reach of power.... Something that smacks of revolt, of promised freedom, of the coming age of a different law, slips easily into this discourse on sexual oppression.... What sustains our eagerness to speak of sex in terms of repression is doubtless this opportunity to speak out against the powers that be, to utter truths and promise bliss ... to pronounce a discourse that combines the fervor of knowledge, the determination to change the laws, and the longing for the garden of earthly delights. (1:6–7)

This is, above all, the perspective I have sought to avoid in the following chapters, in favor of Foucault's own alternative conception of power as the name given to a complex strategical situation in a particular society (1:93), together with his injunction that one must never "imagine a world of discourse divided between accepted discourse and excluded discourse ... but as a multiplicity of discursive elements ... the things said and those concealed, the enunciations required and those forbidden" (1:100). For though the particular society I examine is Victorian England, and though the specific strategical situation I analyze is the Oxford university reform movement, my larger point is always that "homosexuality" eventually emerged as a positive social identity only through a slow process of cultural transformation taking place over centuries, one having as much to do with English classical republican thought in the eighteenth century or the concept of *virtù* in sixteenth-century Florence as with events during the reign of Victoria. This is the level of deep structural transformation, it seems to me, with regard to which Foucault's theory of *pouvoir-savoir* remains wholly indispensable.

In specific terms, my focus in this book is on the way Greek studies operated as a "homosexual code" during the great age of English university reform, working invisibly to establish the grounds on which, after its shorter-term construction as a nineteenth-century sexual pathology (Krafft-Ebing, Havelock Ellis), "homosexuality" would subsequently emerge as the locus of sexual identity for which, today, such late-Victorian figures as Walter Pater and Oscar Wilde are so often claimed as symbolic precursors. As regards Victorian Oxford, my argument is that (1) such leading university reformers as Benjamin Jowett were seeking to establish in Hellenism, the systematic study of Greek history and literature and philosophy, a ground of transcendent value alternative to Christian theology — the metaphysical underpinning of Oxford from the Middle Ages through the Tractarian movement. But (2) once they had done so, Pater and Wilde and the Uranian poets could not be denied the means of developing out of this same Hellenism a homosexual counterdiscourse able to justify male love in ideal or transcendental terms: the "spiritual procreancy" associated specifically with Plato's *Symposium* and more generally with ancient Greece itself.

In the immediate background of the Oxford reform movement, I argue, there lies a specific and overwhelming cultural anxiety within Victorian liberalism, a fear of stagnation and paralysis threatening to leave England isolated within a system of dying or outmoded ideas even as other European nations were beginning to register the stirrings of new movements in scientific and historical thought. In this context England's advances at the level of material progress not only provided no consolation to such liberals as J. S. Mill and Matthew Arnold, but, insofar as they led to commercialization and the complacencies of a mass society, the advances were a source of additional dismay. At Oxford such liberal reformers as Jowett and Arthur Stanley, Mark Pattison, and Goldwin Smith would thus seek in the study of Greek culture nothing less than a surety for England's future life as a nation, a life that would be, as Arnold so insistently repeated, determined by the quality of its *ideas* rather than by the mere quantity of its railways or factories or people.

As we shall see in Chapter 2, a crucial strategy of such leading spirits as Jowett and Pattison was to commandeer for reform purposes certain institutional structures originally developed by the Tractarian generation of J. H. Newman and Hurrell Froude in a specifically religious interest — the revival of the college tutorial as a pastoral and therefore intimate personal relationship, a recent Tractarian tradition of intense undergraduate male friendship — for the secular purpose of producing a new civic elite to lead Britain out of sociocultural stagnation and into a triumphal age of imperial responsibility: Britain as a world civilization, with Oxford as its intellectual center. In this context Jowett and others would call upon Greek studies, and in particular the philosophy of Plato — "the greatest uninspired writing," Jowett called it — as an alternative source of transcendent value to replace the basis previously provided by Christianity. Thus would the course of classical studies known as *Literae humaniores* or "Greats," with Plato's works as the central object of study, undergo a crucial transformation at the curricular heart of Oxford.

The Plato of Jowett and the Oxford reformers, as scholars like Richard Jenkyns and Frank Turner have so ably demonstrated, was in most important respects the Plato of George Grote's *History of Greece* and J. S. Mill's *On Liberty*, the philosopher of a healthy and productive skepticism and a fearless determination, in the phrase from *On Liberty* that was to prove so massively influential on two generations of Oxford men, "to follow one's intellect to whatever conclusions it may lead." Yet this same Plato could then at the same moment and by an identical logic be taken as the tutelary spirit of a movement never foreseen by Jowett or Stanley or Pattison, in which such writers as Walter Pater and John Addington Symonds would deduce from Plato's own writings an apology for male love as something not only noble but infinitely more ennobling

than an exploded Christianity and those sexual taboos and legal pro-
scriptions inspired by its dogmas.

The single most revolutionary consequence of this hidden or "coded"
counterdiscourse was conclusively to sweep aside the deep fears of
"corruption" and "effeminacy" associated with male love by a classical
republican discourse that, as J. G. A. Pocock has shown, had exercised a
powerful hold over the English cultural imagination for over two hundred years, a body of political theory always identifying the health of the
polity as a whole with the *virtus* or virility of an ancient warrior ideal. For
the reformed *Literae humaniores* course at Oxford, meant to move
the university into the mainstream of progressive nineteenth-century
thought, was dominated by a German-inspired revolution in historiography which in the fearlessness of its "scientific" objectivity had
made the crucial discovery that *paiderastia* or Greek love was itself
martial in origin.

Greek antiquity as studied in the school of *Literae humaniores*, in
short, belonged to history as newly conceived by B. G. Niebuhr or
Theodor Mommsen, the past "as it really was," Ranke's *wie es eigentlich
gewesen.* As Pater and Symonds read a work such as K. O. Müller's
Dorians, with its unembarrassed account of the pedagogical, military,
and social centrality of Greek *paiderastia,* or Plato's *Symposium,* with its
ideal of "spiritual procreancy" (209a) — that pure intellectual commerce
between male lovers which brings forth the arts, philosophy, and wisdom itself — they saw that the whole idiom of "effeminacy" which had
generated such fear and loathing of male love could now be suddenly
reversed in its moral implications. The language of male love could be
triumphantly proclaimed the very fountain of civic health in an English
polity imperatively in need, precisely as liberal theorists such as Mill and
university reformers such as Jowett had all along been insisting, of some
authentic new source of ideas and intellectual power.

The following pages attempt to reconstruct the complex conditions
under which the counterdiscourse associated with Pater's *Renaissance*
and Symonds's *Greek Poets* would emerge from within the otherwise
orthodox confines of Victorian university reform and the *Literae humaniores* school, as well as the invisible warfare fought out between this
counterdiscourse and an older inheritance of religious prohibition and

cultural taboo. For the immemorial dread of male love as "corruption" and "effeminacy" would erupt spectacularly in the trial of Oscar Wilde for sodomic indecency — the criminally carnal relations between males, the specter of which had so darkly overshadowed the careers of Pater and Symonds before reappearing in 1895 to destroy Wilde's life and work. My account begins, then, with a certain anomalous and signifi- cant moment in Wilde's trial for homosexual practices. Its argument will ultimately be that it is only at something like our present distance from those same events, when we are at last able to trace even in such records of Wilde's abjection as *De Profundis* the serious claims of that Platonic "spiritual procreancy" earlier developed by Pater and Symonds and the Uranian poets, that we are in a position to grasp the role so crucially played by Oxford Hellenism in the modern emergence of homosexuality as a positive social identity.

I wrote this book as a fellow of the Center for Historical Analysis at Rutgers University, and its argument owes a great deal to conversation with others at the Center — George Chauncey, Rhys Isaac, Claudia Koonz, Robert Nye, Dorothy Thompson, and Edward Thompson — and especially to John Gillis, who as director of the Historical Construction of Identities project did so much to establish the atmosphere in which such conversation might flourish. I thank as well John Pocock for inviting me to several sessions of his Folger Institute seminar which bore on my argument in Chapters 1 and 2, and James Eli Adams and David Riede for timely advice in the revision of the final manuscript. I am grateful to Paul Cartledge for sharing with me his knowledge of the Spar- tan traditions of warfare and paiderastia, and for making many valuable suggestions for the paperback edition of this book.

Other friends and colleagues — David DeLaura, Lowell Edmunds, Thomas Edwards, Richard Howard, George Levine, Richard Poirier, Hugh Witemeyer, Susan Wolfson — have been in various ways involved with the book almost since the beginning, and without their advice and encouragement it could scarcely have been written. I am grateful to them all.

LINDA DOWLING

Princeton, New Jersey

Hellenism and Homosexuality
in Victorian Oxford

CHAPTER ONE

AESTHETE AND EFFEMINATUS

Amphibious thing! that acting either part,
The trifling head, or the corrupted heart,
Fop at the toilet, flatterer at the board,
Now trips a lady, and now struts a lord.
— Alexander Pope, *Epistle to Arbuthnot*, 1735

In the final week of April 1895 Oscar Wilde stood in the prisoner's
dock of the Old Bailey, charged, in the dry words of the indictment,
with "acts of gross indecency with another male person" committed
"against the peace of our said Lady the Queen her Crown and dignity"
(Hyde, *Trials* 179). The prosecutor for the Crown explained to the jury
in more vivid terms just what this meant: Wilde and his co-defendant
had joined in an "abominable traffic" in which young men were induced
to engage in "giving their bodies, or selling them, to other men for the
purpose of sodomy" (190). These same filthy practices, the prosecutor
darkly proclaimed in his final summation, posed a deadly threat to
English society, a moral infection, "a sore which cannot fail in time to
corrupt and taint it all" (253). Wilde answered these charges, as is well
known, in a speech of sudden and eloquent energy. Passionately defending male love as the noblest of attachments, a love "such as Plato made
the very basis of his philosophy, and such as you find in the sonnets of
Michelangelo and Shakespeare," Wilde called it "pure" and "perfect"
and "intellectual" (236), his superb self-possession and ringing peroration so electrifying that the courtroom listeners burst into spontaneous
applause.[1]

1. Wilde was involved in three trials during the period April–May 1895. In the first
he charged the marquess of Queensberry — the father of Lord Alfred Douglas — with libel,

I

To those familiar with Wilde's career as a writer and public personality, his eloquent composure would have come as no surprise. For Wilde
had long since grown accustomed to facing large and hostile audiences
as a dramatist, and some four years before at the Crabbet Club he had
already rehearsed this very defense of male love in virtually the same
words. The extraordinary element in the Old Bailey scene is thus his
listeners' sudden storm of applause. With it this audience of courtroom
spectators would signal a wholly unanticipated assent, momentary and
emotional as it may have been, to a view of love between men that had
always before been proscribed with all the rigor commanded by English
social and religious prohibitions. The applause of Wilde's listeners marks
the sudden emergence into the public sphere of a modern discourse of
male love formulated in the late Victorian period by such writers as
Walter Pater and John Addington Symonds and Wilde himself, a new
language of moral legitimacy pointing forward to Anglo-American de-
criminalization and, ultimately, a fully developed assertion of homosexual rights.

In this sense Wilde's peroration on male love signals a moment of
cultural discontinuity or rupture. For in speaking about Wilde's criminal
activities the Crown prosecutor had been compelled to employ a legal
language conceiving sodomy in what Alan Bray has called "directly
physical" terms (17), that is, as belonging to a forbidden range of merely
genital practices having no essential connection to personal identity.
Against this older discourse of the English common law, so visibly
bearing the sedimented traces of an immemorial village or agrarian past,
Wilde deploys a new and powerful vocabulary of personal identity, a
language of mind, sensibility, and emotion, of inward and intellectual
relations. These are the relations of which male love, as the "noblest
form of affection," represents the most exalted type, with "that deep,
spiritual affection" between an elder and a younger man seen as so global
in its reference to the full individuality of each as to involve the

---

and lost the case. On the basis of evidence produced in that civil trial, however, Wilde
himself was charged with gross indecency between males and subsequently underwent
two criminal prosecutions — a second being called for when the first ended in a hung jury.
I am quoting from the record of the first criminal prosecution.

underlying and invariable substratum of personality traditionally re-garded as constituting identity. Wilde's triumph in the war of discourses symbolized by his exchanges with the Crown prosecutor was to have equated this thoroughly modern notion of personal identity with the ideal of male love surviving in the writings of ancient Greece.

In Wilde's invocation of Plato and Greek philosophy we thus glimpse the momentary opening up of an epistemological space that would soon enough, and then not least because of Wilde's own tragic imprisonment as a sexual criminal, be reconquered in the name of new clinical or psychiatric languages of sexual pathology. This is the temporary space always implied, though never mentioned as such, in Foucault's influen-tial analysis of nineteenth-century sexuality, a space produced by the strain or rupture that occurs during the period when "homosexuality" as a psychiatric perversion is being dissociated from sodomy as a criminal act. The power and originality of Wilde's appeal to a Hellenic ideal lie in the way it exploits this space, outlining in irresistible terms an idea of male love as a mode of inward erotic orientation and sensibility wholly distinct from mere genital activity, and yet also a mode so far unreduced to the newer pathological models of medical and psychiatric science.

It is this originality that wins the spontaneous applause of the Old Bailey spectators. In all his previous successes, one of those spectators would later say, in all the acclaim earned during the unclouded years of his earlier career, Wilde had "never had so great a triumph."[2] Yet for all his strategic brilliance in seizing momentarily unoccupied ideological ground, Wilde's triumph must at a deeper level also be seen as the triumph of a Victorian Hellenism that had been gradually developing throughout the nineteenth century, ancient Greek life and thought as

2. This is Max Beerbohm writing to Reginald Turner: "Here was this man, who had been for a month in prison and loaded with insults and crushed and buffeted, perfectly self-possessed, dominating the Old Bailey with his fine presence and musical voice. He has never had so great a triumph, I am sure, as when the gallery burst into applause — I am sure it affected the jury" (Ellmann 463). Montgomery Hyde agrees that Wilde's speech almost surely staved off conviction in the first trial. Although Beerbohm, a younger Oxford friend of Wilde's, was in attendance, the spectators at the trials included few men of rank or fashion, as the newspapers noted at the time. See the excerpts in Goodman, *Wilde File*.

they had been reinterpreted by Victorian liberals seeking alternatives to older categories of civic discourse. This is Victorian Hellenism as so ably studied in recent years by such scholars as Richard Jenkyns and Frank Turner, in short; it both provides the context of Wilde's courtroom speech and then plays a central role in the modern emergence of homosexuality as a social identity.

To proclaim Wilde's apology for male love a modern discourse, however, is to do little more than invoke a now-familiar story of repression and freedom, outmoded and benighted prejudices giving way, at last and after much pain and turmoil, to progress and enlightened rationality. The great objection to this story is not, as is now sometimes said, that it too is merely ideological, a way of not seeing certain repressive impulses lurking in our own ideas of modernity and progress, but that it renders invisible as well the complex genealogy of Wilde's language of nobility and purity in male love. For Wilde's invocation of Plato and Greek philosophy signals not some unproblematic triumph of modernity over the dead past but, in just the way Foucault's work on sexuality so complexly insists, a moment in those ceaseless recombinations of cultural materials in which the new or contemporary or modern most often comes to birth through some transmutation, under the pressures of history and ideology, of the old or ancient or even the archaic.

This is why, for instance, the language of the Crown prosecutor in Wilde's trial signals, quite as much as does Wilde's own vocabulary of purity and noble aspiration, a crucial moment in the modern emergence of homosexuality as a positive social identity. For as Wilde's language belongs to a strategically revived idiom of Greek ideality, the prosecutor's belongs to an ancient tradition of classical republican thought which had come to dominate civic discourse in England through the seventeenth and eighteenth centuries, that language of "corruption" and "effeminacy" and "virtue" so richly elucidated in recent years by J. G. A. Pocock and those writing under his influence. It is only the dying echoes of classical republicanism, to be sure, which we hear in the prosecutor's dark warning that Wilde's sodomitical practices threaten the corruption of English society, but even in those echoes may be felt the presence of a discourse retaining a great measure of ideological potency. The applause greeting Wilde's impassioned defense of male love thus demands to be heard not merely as some unproblematic victory of modern views over outmoded prejudices, but as the victory of a new ideal of Greek civilization over an alternative vision of the ancient world which had governed public discourse in England for over two centuries.

❦

The great monument of classical republican anxiety over England's fate as a nation, a tract nearly forgotten for over two hundred years and only recently restored to its true significance by the work of Pocock and his school, is John Brown's *Estimate of the Manners and Principles of the Times* (1757), an angry and urgent warning that English society is being ruined by luxury and corruption, that like Athens and Sparta and Rome before her England has entered the last stage of an all but irreversible historical decline, that the English people are, as Brown vehemently puts it, "rolling to the brink of a precipice that must destroy us" (15).[3] One major achievement of Pocock's *Machiavellian Moment* has been to recover for students of European political thought the lost meanings of the two central terms in the classical republican vocabulary of civic alarm — "luxury" and "corruption" as these entail an entire theory of cyclical history and the possibility, the Machiavellian *ridurre ai principii*, of the last-minute moral regeneration of a society otherwise rolling to the brink of destruction.

The master terms in Brown's *Estimate*, as in Pocock's account of them, are indeed "luxury" and "corruption," but along with them there also occurs another term, "effeminacy," whose meaning in classical republican discourse we have only begun fully to grasp. For while the strangeness of "luxury" and "corruption" to modern ears is that they entail a theory of history in which no one any longer believes — indeed, which no one outside a small circle of intellectual historians even remembers to have existed — the strangeness of "effeminacy" is that it has nothing to do with maleness and femaleness in the modern sense, what Roland Barthes has called the "binary prison" of gender opposition

---

3. Here and in all subsequent quotations I have modernized earlier orthography and punctuation.

as it has emerged in the two centuries since Brown's *Estimate*. For when Brown inveighs, as he does throughout the *Estimate*, against "a vain, luxurious, and selfish EFFEMINACY" (67), he is not looking forward to modern gender categories but gazing backward to a vanished archaic past in which the survival of a community was sustained in an almost metaphysical as well as a wholly practical sense by the valor of its citizen soldiers.

The manner in which a metaphysics of community may always be seen to underlie the ancient ideal of martial valor is brilliantly caught by T. B. Macaulay, himself a lifelong and thoughtful student of ancient history, in an essay prompted by his rereading of Machiavelli's *Discourses*. No better epigraph could be chosen, perhaps, for Pocock's recent discussions of the neo-Harringtonian revival in Restoration England, or the militia question as it was endlessly debated in the eighteenth century by John Trenchard and Thomas Gordon and others in the "commonwealthman" tradition, or Brown as he thunders in the *Estimate* against an "effeminacy" ungraspable in modern terms, than Macaulay's depiction of the ancient Greek city-states:

> The state of society in the little commonwealths of Greece, the close connection and mutal dependence of the citizens, and the severity of the laws of war, tended to encourage an opinion which, under such circumstances, could hardly be called erroneous. The interests of every individual were inseparably bound up with those of the State. . . . When Pericles, in the Peloponnesian war, told the Athenians that, if their country triumphed, their private losses would speedily be repaired, but that, if their arms failed of success, every individual amongst them would probably be ruined, he spoke no more than the truth. . . . To be butchered on the smoking ruins of their city, to be dragged in chains to a slave-market, to see one child torn from them to dig in the quarries of Sicily, and another to guard the harems of Persepolis, these were the frequent and probable consequences of national calamities. ("Machiavelli" 311–12)

The language of corruption as it dominates English political discourse in the eighteenth century will always invoke at a general or abstract level the metaphysics of community implied in Macaulay's vision of ancient Greece, a view of citizenship in which the good of the citizen and that of the polity are always understood as wholly interdependent and reciprocal. The very meaning of "corruption" in such a context is the specter of genuine community dissolving into mere personal egoism or self-interest: "a neglect of all things that concern the public welfare," as Henry Neville would put it in 1681, speaking as one of the first important voices in English classical republicanism, "and a setting up our own private interest against it" (196). Against this specter such writers as Neville will always summon an ideal of the citizen drawn from Aristotle and Cicero and Machiavelli, a *zōon politikon* who fulfills his moral nature by subordinating his private desires to the public good, and in so doing creates a sphere in which his fellow citizens may in turn realize their own natures as human beings.

This metaphysics of community is underwritten at a deeper level, however, by a metaphysics of being and nonbeing or life and death already archaic at the time Aristotle was writing the *Politics*, a submerged collective memory of the warrior ethos in which the survival of the polity as a whole, its art and its thought and its ordinary life of field and village, is reducible in an absolutely literal sense to the willingness of a relatively small number of males to die on behalf of those too young or old or weak to go forth to battle. This underlying martial ethos too is something Macaulay's account of Greek antiquity brilliantly captures, the sense in which the life of the entire community is reduced in moments of dire extremity to the body of the single warrior as he is willing to have his throat cut by a sword or his chest pierced by a spear in the name of a community not present on the field of battle, and the manner in which certain rights of full citizenship derive directly from this willingness to die.

The enormous and now mystifying popularity of such eighteenth-century works as Joseph Addison's *Cato* (1713), Richard Glover's *Leonidas* (1737), and William Whitehead's *The Roman Father* (1750) has directly to do with the way classical republican discourse draws subliminally on the warrior ethos as the very measure of civic virtue. The etymology of *aretē*, the Greek word for "goodness" or "excellence," Bernard de Mandeville would remind his eighteenth-century readers, derives from Ares, the Greek god of war (iii). This is why, during the years of Country ideology and Opposition polemic, the years of Alexander Pope's anti-Walpole satires and Bolingbroke's *Craftsman*, the great symbol of virtue or civic selflessness, the mighty opposite of "corruption" as described by such writers as Neville, will be the republican hero dying or offering to die for Rome or Sparta. "How dreadful," says a character in *The Roman Father*, Whitehead's blank-verse tragedy on the Horatii and the Curii, "yet how lovely, is his virtue" (1:76).

On one level, such invocations of the warrior ethos serve to explain why a work like Brown's *Estimate* denounces, in its dire warnings about luxury and effeminacy, such apparent trivialities as the heated nurseries just coming into London fashion: children under five years, Aristotle had said in the *Politics*, "ought to be used to cold; to be thus habituated is most useful for future health and for the activities of warfare" (7:17). At a much more fundamental level, the metaphoric power of the warrior ideal, that willingness to die which could be taken as the symbolic essence of classical republican virtue, explains as well why "effeminacy" in such works as the *Estimate* has to do not with femaleness in any modern sense but with an absence or privation of value. The root of *virtus* in Latin is indeed *vir*, signifying "male" or "male person," but its meaning in classical republican discourse will then always be defined by the entire sphere of social existence populated by the nonwarrior or not-warrior: boys, girls, slaves, eunuchs, hermaphrodites, and all others perceived as unsuitable to or incapable of discharging the martial obligation to the polis.

The *effeminatus* in classical republican theory is thus always a composite or protean figure, the empty or negative symbol at once of civic enfeeblement and of the monstrous self-absorption that becomes visible in a society at just the moment at which, as we have heard Neville say, private interest has begun to prevail against those things that concern the public welfare. The protean nature of the *effeminatus* explains, for instance, the perplexity evident in recent gender criticism as it has attempted to deal with such figures as Sporus of Pope's *Epistle to Arbuthnot* as "homosexual" in the twentieth-century sense. For it is not simply that homosexual identity as we now understand it still lies far in the future when Pope composes his portrait of Sporus, but that all its monstrous mixture of social roles and sexual tendencies — that Sporus who is "now master up, now miss, / And he himself one vile antithesis"

(608, ll. 324–25) — has to do not with sexual but with civic incapacity, the dissolution of social categories which occurs when community itself has begun to dissolve into an aimless and self-regarding egoism.[4]

The *effeminatus* as represented in Pope's Sporus belongs to the same

4. To object, as an earlier mode of historicist criticism has been wont to do, that the Sporus of *Arbuthnot* is "really about" Pope's contemporary and enemy, John, Lord Hervey — and thus, presumably, about Pope's "homophobic" response to an effeminate man — is to fail to grasp the network of symbolic relations *already* constituting "Lord Hervey" within classical republican categories as a symbol and object of satire. For any attempt to reach behind Pope's Sporus to the "real" Hervey of, say, William Pulteney's *A Proper Reply* (1731), the pamphlet that supplied so many of the details for Pope's portrait, will merely encounter "Mr. Fainlove," a personage regarded by Pulteney as "a young beginner," a "boarding-school miss," "a delicate hermaphrodite," "a pretty, little master-miss" (4, 5, 6) — in short, a figure rendered visible precisely through the characters of civic incapacity — boy, girl, *effeminatus* — which the eighteenth-century revision of classical republican discourse had made so compelling.

This larger ideological context reabsorbs within its own symbolic system even the reference that has so frequently been assumed to represent a scandalous personal detail about Hervey — Pulteney's allusion to sodomy. Yet the crucial element in this reference to sodomy would have been, for contemporary readers, its function as a "parallel case" (Pulteney 27) to the political debauch or corruption of Hervey's master, Sir Robert Walpole. For when Pulteney declares that "the proof of the crime [of sodomy] hath been generally made by the pathic, but I believe that evidence will not be obtained quite so easily in the case of corruption, when a man enjoys every moment the fruits of his guilt" (27–28), he is attempting to dispose of a polemical difficulty that Hervey in an earlier pamphlet had raised for Walpole's opponents: how to provide *proof* of Walpole's "corruption" — the traffic in jobs, the misappropriation of pensions — which, as the Opposition believed, had converted the entire civic infrastructure from the office of Lord Privy Seal down to the lowliest tidesman's place into an infernal machinery for gratifying Walpole's own private ambitions.

In answering this demand for proof, Pulteney's response is first to compare Walpole's corruption to sodomy, because unlike common prostitution, "there must be two parties in this crime: the pathic and the agent, *both equally guilty*" (27; my emphasis). Pulteney then argues that Walpole's corruption is *worse* even than sodomy because it corrupts the only potential witness against it — the recipient — who, unlike the pathic or the recipient in sodomy, enjoys the criminal commerce too much to complain against it at law. Thus as the very distance of this passage in the text from Pulteney's personal characterizations of Hervey might ordinarily suggest, the allusion to sodomy here has only an incidental reference to Hervey's sexual conduct, its full polemical force being directed instead at "a certain, unnatural, reigning vice" the Opposition party knows to be far more pervasive and destructive than the individual genital transgressions involved in sodomy, namely, the rampant political debauch of England as a whole by Walpole.

classical republican menagerie as the eunuchs portrayed in Montesquieu's *Lettres persanes* (1721) or Bolingbroke's *Craftsman* essays (1726–
36), the pathics in *Cato's Letters* (1720–23), and the fops in David
Garrick's *Miss in Her Teens* (1747) or Nathaniel Lancaster's *Pretty Gentleman* (1747), all of them so physically enfeebled and morally emasculated as to unfit them for citizenship in the commonwealth of virtue as
Mandeville has it in mind when he insists that the true English translation of Latin *virtus* is "manliness" (iii). On the level of individual
behavior, the same concern with virtue translates directly into an emphasis on "manners" or "morals" as English equivalents to Aristotle's
nomos or Machiavelli's *buoni costumi*, and only against the background
of this assumed equivalence between manners and virtue does John
Brown's obsessive focus on what otherwise might appear to be the
minutiae of English social life — the music dwindled into "an eunuch's
effeminate trill" (46), the habit of traveling by "the effeminate covering
and conveyance of an easy chair" (36), that "fountain of weakness and
disease," a heated nursery (30) — stand revealed as what it really is, an
anguished meditation upon the causes of national survival or ruin.

The same classical republican vocabulary of effeminacy and weakness, always drawing in a subliminal way on the symbolism of the warrior
ideal, serves to explain why such works as *Satan's Harvest Home* (1749)
demand to be seen as popular or sensational versions of Brown's *Estimate*
rather than attacks on the sexual behavior of sodomites. "The effeminacy of our men's dress" (50), warns the author of *Satan's Harvest Home*,
their Italianate habit of "man-kissing" (54), the soft indulgence of "little
master . . . kept in the nursery till he is five or six years old" (47), all these
signal in the recognizable language of "luxury" and "effeminacy," of
pallid infants and overheated nurseries, that England is plunging toward
the precipice Brown too saw with such alarm: with Englishmen reckless
of a past more virtuous precisely as it was more martial or warlike, when
"our forefathers were trained up to arts and arms. . . and the fine
gentleman of former days, was equally fit for the council as the camp, the
boy (though perhaps a baronet's son) was taken early from the nursery"
(45).

This exploitation of classical republican civic alarm is visible as well
in the earlier cultural moment, the so-called reformation of morals
campaign of 1689–1709, which in an important sense prepared the way

for Brown's *Estimate* at midcentury. Thus, for instance, in Ned Ward's *History of the London Clubs* we come upon such gatherings as the No-Nose Club, an imaginary assembly of beakless sufferers of syphilis, and the Mollies' Club, where a "gang of wretches" who "fancy themselves women" are said to meet in a certain tavern (28). Though it is filled with the sort of circumstantial detail ("a woman's nightgown," "a high-crowned hat") associated with emergent fictional realism, Ward's account always operates by invoking the categories of classical republican civic anxiety and the warrior ethos. The problem of the "molly," who displays "all manner of effeminacy," is precisely that he is, as Ward puts it, "so far degenerated from all masculine deportment or manly exercises" (28). If Ward's *History* seems in some obvious sense to belong more to literary than to political discourse, it is simply because his eye, like that of his contemporary Mrs. Crackenthorpe, the Female Tatler, whose portraits of gushing shopmen and embroidering peers gave a new guise to the ancient figure of the *effeminatus*, would always be more fixed on new possibilities of readership, the audience addressed by *The Spectator* or Defoe's novels, than on the somberer sociopolitical responsibilities assumed by Pope or Bolingbroke or John Brown.

At the same time, recent gender criticism has not been altogether mistaken in seeing something resembling modern homosexuality here, for the great and important paradox is that such works as Ward's *History* and John Dunton's "The He-Strumpets" and Tobias Smollett's *Roderick Random*, operating all the while within the classical republican category of "effeminacy" in its symbolic relation to the warrior ideal, had nonetheless been helping to produce "homosexuality" in the twentieth-century sense as an unintended effect of their own discourse. For such imaginary characters as Garrick's Fribble or Pope's Sporus or Smollett's Captain Whiffle would supply a sudden mirror of social visibility to categories of male sexual behavior — "sodomite," "the crime not to be named among Christians" — always previously banished, as Alan Bray has cogently argued, to a dim region of nameless evil by English theological or religious discourse.[5] In this manner would eighteenth-century

---

5. Arguing that "the socially diffused homosexuality of the early seventeenth century" (92) remained invisible to most people *including its practitioners*, Bray joins such other recent historians of homosexuality as Randolph Trumbach, Mary McIntosh, and

versions of the *effeminatus* — foppish, fribbling, strutting as a lord — come to supply a social depth and specificity to hitherto nameless and unnoticeable men. This social embodiment in turn would become the inheritance, at the same time constricting and enabling, of the Victorian homosexual apologists.

In early 1872, provoked by Robert Buchanan's notorious attack on the Pre-Raphaelites as a Fleshly School of poetry, those fulminations he himself would impatiently label "the Fleshly polemic" (*Letters* 2:210), John Addington Symonds began the career for which he has become best known in our own day, as a leading Victorian homosexual apologist and advocate of reform in the British laws and attitudes governing homosexuality. In the years before 1872 Symonds had been struggling to come to grips with his own tormented feelings about male love by writing a series of poems cautiously circulated within a small group of intimate friends. Now, emboldened by the collapse of Buchanan's attack on the Fleshly School of poetry, Symonds shifted to prose and began to write the essays on Greek *paiderastia* which would later be published as part of *Studies of the Greek Poets* (1873) and *A Problem in Greek Ethics* (1883). With this writing Symonds for the first time begins conceiving in public terms his hopes for male erotic "comradeship," as well as

---

David Greenberg in identifying the sudden appearance of and the alarm over "effeminate" men, occurring around the turn of the eighteenth century, with the actual historical emergence of modern homosexuals.

The present book argues, by contrast, that fops and "mollies" constitute in the first instance discursive forms thrown off during the intense debate over "corruption" and "effeminacy" which gripped Britain from the time of the Glorious Revolution to that of the Seven Years' War. Subsequently colonized by actual men — whose behaviors may have corresponded to these discursive forms through, as Foucault says of the effeminatus, "a complex play of inductions and attitudes of defiance" (2:18) — these forms then become saturated with their new content, making it socially visible, so that by the end of the nineteenth century Wilde, for instance, could use "Sporus" as a synonym for "male sexual partner": "I want the Italians to realise that there has been more in my life than a love for Narcissus, or a passion for Sporus: fascinating though both may be" (*Letters* 695). For an account of the early eighteenth-century English fop, which valuably stresses the independence of this figure from modern notions of male homosexuality, see Staves.

directing those hopes toward a broader public sphere of debate and exchange, a realm of sympathetic comprehension he imagined as filled with "modern jurists, psychiatrists, writers on forensic medicine" (*Greek Ethics* 1).

The opportunity so unexpectedly opened up by Buchanan's denunciations of the Fleshly School derived from Buchanan's own gigantic miscalculation in imagining that he could mobilize the forces of Victorian moral propriety against Dante Gabriel Rossetti and the Pre-Raphaelites in just the same way as, earlier in the century, *Blackwood's Magazine* had mobilized public opinion against Keats and Leigh Hunt as a Cockney School of poetry. For in the collapse of Buchanan's enterprise, Symonds and other writers would perceive nothing less than the sudden possibility of vastly expanding the claims of sensuous pleasure, of widening the range of erotic fulfillment, and of advancing new modes of social identity. These goals, Symonds could now see, might under modern conditions be pursued in the name of a larger Victorian middle-class project already well under way — the aim of realizing a richer and more various human life which would ultimately be given its fullest expression in Pater's great celebration of sensuous renewal, *Studies in the History of the Renaissance*.

The reasons for the signal failure of Buchanan's denunciation of fleshliness, the "sensualism" and "animalism" he saw surging through Rossetti's poetry, may be seen to lie therefore in the momentous ideological transformation that had occurred precisely in the period separating *Blackwood's* attack on the Cockney School of poetry from Buchanan's similar attempt to wreak havoc on the Fleshly School. This transformation is that triumph of nineteenth-century liberalism associated at the political level with the great Reform Bill of 1832 and subsequent legislation, at the intellectual level with the voices of such writers as J. S. Mill and George Eliot and T. H. Greene. For the *Blackwood's* writers had taken up their pens against William Hazlitt and Keats and Leigh Hunt in a Britain still traumatized by the French Revolution, convinced that these English writers were the agents of a dangerous and unappeasable social modernity, the mindless partisans of that revolutionary dissoluteness and "profligacy" that in France had severed the bonds between parent and child, husband and wife, just as implacably as they had severed the tie between king and people. There is a deadly seriousness in *Blackwood's* attack on the Cockney School as the very heirs of Danton and Robespierre, "a crew of Jacobins and incendiaries" who would, if left unmolested, "sap the foundations of civil society and of social life" (*Blackwood's*, May 1818, 3:198).

By the time Buchanan takes up his pen to attack the Fleshly School in 1871, however, all such radical sympathies and tendencies as *Blackwood's* once identified with and so feared in the Cockney School will long since have been silently absorbed into the mainstream of Victorian liberalism. Against the broadening background of prosperity and social peace traditionally symbolized by the Crystal Palace exhibition of 1851, the militant demands for radical change once so dismayingly expressed in the post-Waterloo and pre–Reform Bill periods had through repetition and accommodation — and as Trygve Tholfsen has argued, through their assimilation to a familiar language of Romantic aspiration — been seemingly brought to a benign and cooperative resolution. By the end of the third quarter of the nineteenth century, the desperate shouts of Chartists and the Captain Swing rioters had modulated into audible but no longer alarming calls for improvement, inclusion, and shared responsibility. This is the mid-Victorian historical juncture within which Tom Paine's age of revolutions seemed to have given way silently before that "Mother-Age," as the speaker of Alfred Tennyson's "Locksley Hall" calls it in a moment of visionary confidence, which would serenely preside, or at least so it seemed possible for many Victorians to hope, over the progressive and peaceful evolution by which "the thoughts of men are widened with the process of the suns" (*Tennyson* 190).

With the disappearance of Jacobin incendiarism and its lurid flames of social revolution, it was Buchanan's own vehemence which seemed out of place, excessive, crude, violently illiberal, and therefore unworthy of the support of any self-respecting Victorian liberal. Meeting G. H. Lewes and George Eliot one day in Regent's Park, Buchanan was stunned to find himself reproached by the one and cut by the other (Cassidy 78). For Buchanan himself, the attack on the Fleshly School would prove a costly mistake; his literary fortunes and reputation immediately declined, never to recover. Yet the intuition that moved Buchanan to attack the Pre-Raphaelites in the same terms with which

Blackwood's had attacked the Cockney School points, for all that, to an otherwise hidden truth about the ideological antagonism between the *Blackwood's* reviewers and such writers as Hazlitt and Hunt. For what Buchanan had correctly seen in the *Blackwood's* attack was an older classical republican discourse being turned to new uses, modern English writers attempting to bring the ancient wisdom of Aristotle and Cicero and Machiavelli somehow to bear on the irrational and ungraspable new threats to English life thrown up by the French Revolution. It was his sense that the *Blackwood's* writers had been classical republicans trying to come to terms with a wholly and terrifyingly modern moment of class antagonism, urban aggrandizement, and the ceaseless proliferation of mindless, masterless bodies which permitted Buchanan, ultimately, to imagine his own discourse as the legitimate continuation of theirs.

The notion of the *Blackwood's* attack as classical republican discourse serves immediately to explain why certain familiar tropes of civic debil-ity — boy, girl, effeminatus — so powerfully control its comparison of Leigh Hunt to "a tea-sipping milliner girl," or its declaration that both Hunt and Keats indulge "a species of emasculated pruriency," a mode of writing which "looks as if it were the product of some imaginative eunuch's muse." In Hunt's *Story of Rimini*, says *Blackwood's*, looking back to Pope's immortal portrait of the classical republican effeminatus, there is "something effeminate," something "Sporus-like." It is at such mo-ments that we grasp the importance to *Blackwood's* of an Edinburgh worldview originating in the closeness of Scots intellectuals to an older world of gentry politics and agrarian values, the comparative ideological remoteness of Edinburgh from a more rapidly modernizing south Britain. The Edinburgh of *Blackwood's Edinburgh Magazine* is the metropolis so scathingly recalled later in the nineteenth century by Henry Cockburn, himself a Whig and a progressive; in this intellectual community, a quarter century after the French Revolution, "Jacobinism was a term denoting everything alarming and hateful, and every political objector was a Jacobin" (75).

Even as *Blackwood's* vocabulary of eunuchs and emasculation is oper-ating to keep an older, agrarian, Country-party world of civic compe-tence and civic debility steadily in its readers' view, however, there is emerging within it another system of metaphor summoned up by those

forces of Jacobinism which Scots Tory Edinburgh had undertaken to
hold at bay, a newer language of rampant, uncontrollable, and animalis-
tic sexuality. Giving voice to *Blackwood's* sense that beneath the Cockney poets' literary experiments there surged the darker energies of a
revolutionary or anarchic modernity, this language of subhuman or
bestial sexuality may be heard in the very epithet "Cockney." For
"Cockney," deriving from Middle English *cocken-ei* or "cock's egg," the
ostensibly impossible female product of a male fowl, registers at an
archaic level of etymological association precisely the sense of brutish
and unnatural powers, of uncontrollable appetites — and the monstrous
outcomes released by those appetites — which *Blackwood's* is trying to
suggest in, for instance, calling Leigh Hunt "the most contemptible
little capon of the bantam breed, that ever vainly dropped a wing, or
sidled up to a partlet" (December 1822, 12:775).[6]

The pressure on *Blackwood's* to undertake the attack on Leigh Hunt
and Keats in terms different from those Pope and Pulteney had used on
Hervey arose from the massive dislocation of civic discourse which had
occurred when the ideologues of the French Revolution had themselves
thundered forth their doctrines in the pure vocabulary of classical
republicanism. All the familiar civic categories and expressive language,
British writers antagonistic to the French Revolution were to find, had
been hideously usurped and contaminated by the Jacobins. The sum-
mary judicial executions of June–July 1794 had been so bloody, John
Wilson Croker would remind readers in nineteenth-century England,
that new "sanguiducts" were built at the guillotine site to carry off the
overflow. To hear Robespierre, the moving spirit of the Terror, vindicat-
ing such scenes in the language of "virtue" and "corruption," declaring
that "the security of conspirators lies in forgetfulness of principle and in
corruption, while that of the defenders of liberty resides entirely in the
public conscience" (436),[7] is to realize that the language of classical

6. For the role of cocks' eggs in both animal husbandry and the early study of human
sexuality, see Epstein 137 n.60.

7. See also "What is virtue? . . . . profound horror of tyranny, this compassionate zeal
for the oppressed, this sacred love of country, this most sublime and holy love of
humanity, without which a great revolution is only a brilliant [*éclatant*] crime that
destroys another crime" (Robespierre 434).

republicanism would never again be available to English writers on precisely the same terms as it had been to Pope and Bolingbroke, Pulteney and Brown. More than seventy years after Robespierre's terrifying attempt at a "Republic of Virtue," Leslie Stephen wryly noted, the word "republican" still suggested to educated Englishmen stark visions of "Marat and Robespierre, or at least an expulsion of the Queen by force of arms" (287).

Yet the problem the *Blackwood's* writers faced was not simply that an essential category of English civic discourse had been perverted by the French spokesmen of a gruesome revolutionary modernity. The problem was that the Parisian crowds sweeping Robespierre and the other Jacobins to their bloody pinnacle of power represented in themselves a force forever divorcing the old classical republican or Country-party world from the new world of anarchic urban change. For the ideal of civic virtue lying at the heart of English classical republican discourse had been from the beginning indissolubly linked to agrarian values and the ownership of land, to a belief in the martial power of the yeoman farmer and the disinterested leadership of the landed gentleman. It was precisely this agrarian world of organic social relations, of small communities and immemorial custom, which was to be denied and excluded, as the genocidal fury of the Jacobins against the farmers of the Vendée had already made so appallingly clear, in the emergent urban ethos of the cash nexus, the vast metropolis, and the rootless, unpredictable crowd.

In this context we are able to see taking shape in the minds of the *Blackwood's* reviewers an alternative political history of eighteenth-century England, a story in which every episode of urban violence or unrest is now in retrospect seen to harbor unwholesome premonitions of the French Revolution, and in which the older vocabulary of "virtue" and "corruption" actually used by eighteenth-century Englishmen appears hopelessly inadequate to an immensely more complex modern reality. For even observers at the time had sometimes seen that there was something new or unprecedented in the gradual emergence of a new urban entity lying outside the ancient categories of rank and status, a faceless, classless mass that had shown its true nature in episodes of increasing duration and violence, from the Excise Crisis of 1733 to the Wilkes and Liberty disturbances of 1763–74, culminating in the Gordon Riots of 1780. During what Dr. Johnson called the "universal panic" of the Gordon riots (430), a hundred houses were pulled down and plundered, the London prisons were broken open and their prisoners freed — even the fortress on Threadneedle Street, the Bank of England, was assaulted. "Such a time of terror," Johnson wrote Mrs. Thrale, "you have been happy in not seeing" (429). As the Gordon crowds surged out of the confines of the City to sack Lord Mansfield's house in Bloomsbury Square, looting and burning his invaluable law library, observers understood that some more significant boundary had been crossed, that the Gordon rioters represented something unfamiliar, something no longer belonging to the recognizable English world. "Mercy on us!" exclaimed Horace Walpole. "We seem to be plunging into the horrors of France in the reigns of Charles VI and VII!" (11:205).

To come to terms with such potentially revolutionary urban energies, classical republican theory possessed only the Aristotelian notion of the *demos* or "populace" as the irrational part of the body politic, what John Dryden had in mind in *Absalom and Achitophel* when he refers to the London crowd as "the dregs of a democracy," and what Pope and Jonathan Swift and John Gay portrayed in the satiric image of the urban mob. Yet that older notion of "populace" now wholly failed to encompass the unfathomable new forces being released by the invisible energies of a new credit economy, by social mobility, urban impersonality, and ideological abstraction. The Paris crowds who returned day after day to sate their eyes on the reeking guillotine, John Wilson Croker realized, could no longer be explained in terms of the Aristotelian *demos*, for this mob included men of various social ranks, and even women of a relatively prosperous class. "We wish we could safely say the *populace*," he told his readers, but the old idea failed to comprehend the appalling new reality of such a crowd as this, made up as it was of "*women*, in a station of life to be able to pay for that amusement," who "used to hire seats, and sit, and chat, and work" (565).

Nothing more clearly demonstrates the powerlessness of classical republican discourse to deal with this new world of Robespierre and the Parisian mob, perhaps, than the issue of sterility, which had always been central to the symbolism of "effeminacy" and the *effeminatus*. For the whole point of such figures as Pope's Sporus or the chief eunuch of

Montesquieu's *Lettres persanes* had been to represent a world running down into impotence, depopulation, and decline, the sparsely populated world we encounter as the Italy of John Dyer's *Ruins of Rome* or the Turkey of *Cato's Letters*, where in a landscape emptied by despotism only a few scattered peasants and wandering herdsmen live on among the ruined monuments of a once-teeming and energetic civilization:

> Mausoleums, Cirques,
> Naumachias, Forums: Trajan's column tall,
> From whose low base the sculptures wind aloft,
> And lead through various toils, up the rough steep,
> Its hero to the skies . . .
>   . . . and Phoebus' lettered dome,
> And the rough reliques of Carinae's street,
> Where now the shepherd to his nibbling sheep
> Sits piping with his oaten reed.
>   (Dyer ll.317–27)

The problem posed by Robespierre and the revolutionary crowds of Paris is that in this context they represent a threat of civic collapse utterly beyond the grasp of older theories of depopulation and decline, involving as in some very obvious sense they do the power of a teeming urban populace to reproduce itself at a rate that threatens to spill out and overwhelm the agrarian world yet lying outside the limits of the city, to erupt into the countryside and transform even farmland and manor house, the irreplaceable nursery of civic virtue in Country-party theory, into a scene of uncontrolled violence and clamorous disorder. The new term of social alarm in the English anxiety about civic collapse thus becomes not sterility but generativity, a new and irrational power of social transformation remaining to be grasped within the categories of an as-yet-uninvented language.

Looking back on the *Blackwood's* episode, as we now do, from a perspective determined by a century of Marxist analysis pronouncing class antagonism the engine of history, we are prone to hear in the attack on the Cockney School little more than echoes of nineteenth-century class warfare as Marx himself memorialized it. Yet the *Blackwood's* episode in reality represents something a great deal more complex, the spokesmen for an older discourse trying to bring its categories to bear on a threat of civic dissolution to which nothing in previous classical or European history corresponds. The significance of the term "Cockney" is not that it identifies some inferior social class but that it is an attempt to name something perceived to exist unnervingly outside all known categories of order, rank, or status, something the dark threat of which arises out of its very unfathomability. In this context "Cockney," as Marjorie Levinson has somewhere remarked, would become a name for experience that had not been permitted to assume determinate social form.

The most urgent need of the *Blackwood's* writers was for a symbol of the new energies represented in the revolutionary urban mob, with its horrifying power of multiplying its own numbers; the symbol that most compellingly suggested itself was the unclothed female, the lurid whore-mother out of whose "burning womb," in Jules Michelet's phrase, would burst forth the new sociopolitical order. Such sociopolitical fears explain why the appearance of the half-clad revolutionary woman, in a shriek-ing crowd or in a Jacobin pageant, so struck the imagination of English observers. A single image came to dominate: the notorious representa-tion of the goddess of Liberty during the Feast of Reason on 10 Novem-ber 1793. For in the moment that Mlle Aubry, the Opéra actress playing the part of Liberty, bared her breasts before the onlooking crowd, En-glish writers perceived symbolic sanction for the revolutionary decrees permitting sexual promiscuity and equalizing bastard children which would follow a few months later. The dress *à la grecque, à la sauvage, à l'amazonne* taken up by Mlle Aubry and so many others as *la mode révolutionnaire* signaled, in the view of such commentators as John Robison, nothing less than the Jacobins' determination to inflame sex-ual desire and incite profligacy in order to propagate more citizens for the Revolution. To the revolutionary leaders, Robison indignantly de-clared, a woman was only a "she-animal, the breeder of sans culottes" (438).

The image of the bare-breasted woman would in the years after Mlle Aubry become part of the iconography of revolution, attaining classic visual expression in Eugène Delacroix's famous allegorical painting *Lib-erty Leading the People at the Barricades of Paris* (1831). At the same time, however, the figure of the bare-breasted woman would always represent something more than maddened revolutionary maenads, something lying beyond the outlines set by the official history or iconography of the first French revolution or any of its successors. For the image of the half-clothed female would eventually come to symbolize, like those representations of revolutionary female frenzy so illuminatingly discussed by Catherine Gallagher in a related context, an emergent realm of irrational and unknowable forces, "the odd mobility and irrational intransigence of an expanding money economy," and "the possible independence of urban life and its forms of wealth from the more traditionally organized countryside" (195). Whenever they appear in the nineteenth century, such images will retain their power of evoking the possibility of "completely chaotic reproduction" — of bodies, of goods, of money, of value (195).

In this context *Blackwood's* otherwise anomalous shifts between symbolic or metaphoric registers become immediately intelligible. For as its writers move from the eunuchs and effeminati of classical republican discourse to an alternative language deploring heterosexual promiscuity, they are moving as well from a symbolic vocabulary of impotence and effeminacy to an idiom of that blind generativity — of bodies, of money, of value — threatening to overwhelm a middle-class world of controlled desire and legal marriage and the orderly transmission of property within society. The origins of the *Blackwood's* episode lie here, giving us, among other things, the underlying reason why a single literary work, Leigh Hunt's *Story of Rimini*, had been at the outset able to provoke *Blackwood's* whole series of attacks on the Cockney School.

The *Blackwood's* writers had persuaded themselves, in short, that the point of Hunt's narrative was to bestow literary sanction on precisely the legitimation of promiscuous sexual experience the Jacobins had sought to bring about as a matter of social policy. For though *The Story of Rimini* is Hunt's version of the famous story of Paolo and Francesca, Hunt's Francesca, unlike Dante's heroine, does not speak as an adulteress among the damned in hell, her passion for her husband's brother instead becoming for the *Blackwood's* reviewer nothing more than "a lewd tale" in which forbidden love is "wept over, palliated, justified, and held up to imitation, and the violators themselves worshipped as holy martyrs"

(*Blackwood's*, July 1818, 3:453), while the sacred sphere of English domestic life is polluted by salaciously detailed scenes of voluptuousness and profligacy. "A brother," *Blackwood's* angrily said of the book, "would tear it indignantly from a sister's hand, and the husband who saw his wife's eyes resting on it with any other expression than of contempt or disgust, would have reason to look with perplexing agony on the countenances of his children" (*Blackwood's*, May 1818, 3:200).

The *Blackwood's* writers here are mobilizing a moral vocabulary going back to classical antiquity, as in Horace's praise of Augustus as the great restorer of republican virtue after the nightmare of civil war: "laudantur simili prole puerperae" (mothers giving birth are praised for offspring resembling their fathers) (*Odes* 4.5.23). Yet a shriller, more desperate note is being sounded as well, for *Blackwood's* impassioned denunciation of Hunt arises from an obsessive conviction that in *Rimini* Hunt is somehow celebrating "incest." Only when we realize that the sexual union of Francesca with Paolo in fact involves no such transgression against the blood relation as that between Lot and his daughters or Oedipus and his mother — Paolo being Francesca's "brother" only by marriage, and Hunt having altered even this detail — do we see that "incest" here is functioning as a trope of abomination for the otherwise unnameable forces of an anarchic, ceaselessly proliferating modernity that *Blackwood's* sees rising up in this English "crew of Jacobins and incendiaries."

The *Blackwood's* episode remains notorious in literary history largely because of its reviewers' violent and seemingly uncontrolled response to Keats's poetry; it is the attack on Keats, the outspoken contempt of the *Blackwood's* writers for his bad taste in shirt collars and hair styles, the vulgarity of his poetic rhymes and grossly sensuous imagery, which has seemed so overwhelmingly to invite interpretation in terms of class antagonism. Yet beneath any transient idiom of class hostility, every such element in the *Blackwood's* attack has to do with the same dark threat of unrestained Jacobinism and anarchic modernity. Thus, for instance, *Blackwood's* obsessively attacks Keats's "Cockney" rhymes not because they involve lower-class pronunciation but because English verse constitutes for the *Blackwood's* writers an invisible but cherished literary institution, its forms and accents those given expression by poets from Chaucer and Milton to Pope and Wordsworth. It is within this context that the *Blackwood's* writers hear in Keats's rhyming of "thorns" with "fawns" (August 1818, 3:521) the sound of alien, unassimilable forces which are not simply ignorant of English intellectual and cultural tradition but actively antagonistic to it.

In just the same way, *Blackwood's* always reads in Keats's poetic language an underlying sympathy with French revolutionary voluptuousness and sexual profligacy. Thus, for instance, *Blackwood's* homes in unerringly on an early poem in which Keats imagines a woman as she might have appeared in an older world of fable and romance, transported back to a time when the gods spoke to men and female nakedness was the revelation of an entirely innocent beauty:

> With those beauties, scarce discern'd,
> Kept with such sweet privacy,
> That they seldom meet the eye
> Of the little loves that fly
> Round about with eager pry.
> Saving when, with freshening lave,
> Thou dipp'st them in the taintless wave;
> Like twin water lilies, born
> In the coolness of the morn.
> (*Blackwood's*, August 1818, 3:521)

In the twin water lilies of the bathing girl's exposed breasts, the *Blackwood's* writers are able only to recognize the revolutionary iconography of bared breasts and burning wombs. To say that Keats's imagery is "prurient and vulgar," as the *Blackwood's* reviewer of this poem did not hesitate to do, is thus simply to announce that it shares in the same Jacobinical incitement to "licentiousness" (*Blackwood's*, October 1819, 6:71) and "voluptuousness" (*Blackwood's*, December 1822, 12:766) that *Blackwood's* had sometime since identified in such Cockney writers as Leigh Hunt.

The same perspective explains why the *Blackwood's* attack on Hunt himself, always assailed in its pages as a "demoralizing incendiary" (*Blackwood's*, July 1818, 3:453), is carried out in a language in which politics and sexuality are interchangeable. For Hunt's mere mention in

Rimini of such fleshly details as a woman's waist and bosom demands
ultimately to be seen as "panderism to the vilest passions of that mob of
which he is himself a firebrand" (*Blackwood's*, July 1818, 3:453), a
literary exercise in sensualism whose theory is the Jacobinical tenet that
"every woman is useful only as a breeding machine" (*Blackwood's*,
October 1817, 2:40). It is this, the "extreme moral depravity of the
Cockney School" (*Blackwood's*, October 1817, 2:40) working on the
level of poetic language to dissolve away the intimate bonds between
husband and wife, father and child, annihilated by the Jacobins in favor
of such freezing abstractions as "fraternity," that leads *Blackwood's* to see
in Keats's bashful euphemism — "twin water lilies" — just what other
English observers had seen in the undraped breasts of Mlle Aubry's
Goddess of Liberty: the emblem of a much more violent liberty of
bodies, of arms, of appetites, and of energies more unnameable still.

The explanation of Robert Buchanan's attack on the Fleshly School
lies here. For in the Scottish Highlands where Buchanan had been
dwelling, while England and even Edinburgh had long since begun to
feel the transforming influence of a more general European liberalism,
the antirevolutionary Toryism of the *Blackwood's* writers had remained a
living reality, an intellectual and moral response to modernity that
seemed to have lost none of its validity in the intervening years.
Buchanan thus arrives in London in the 1870s almost as a visitor from
an otherwise vanished ideological world, and what he sees is precisely
the vision of a metropolis overwhelmed and transformed by the forces of
sensualism and animalism which *Blackwood's* had so detested and feared
in Jacobin Paris. "The streets are full of it," raged Buchanan: "Photo-
graphs of nude, indecent, and hideous harlots, in every possible attitude
that vice can devise, flaunt from the shopwindows, gloated over by the
fatuous glint of the libertine and the greedy open-mouthed stare of the
day-labourer" (3). When Buchanan reads Rossetti's descriptions of sexual love against this disturbing urban background of cancan dancers and
pornographic *cartes-de-visite* and the shameless public display of "Bosom
and Back" (4), he instantly imagines himself to have located the source
of all this "fleshliness" in a school of Fleshly poets who must be seen as
"public offenders, because they are diligently spreading the seeds of
disease broadcast wherever they are read and understood" (33).

In Buchanan, as we might expect, it is the image of the bared female breast which triggers the deepest ideological response. "Breast to breast we clung, even she and I," Rossetti says in *House of Life*; "each twin breast is an apple sweet," says the speaker of *Troy Town*. When Pre-Raphaelite poetry indulges such imagery in the name of a generalized sexual attraction, it is thus part of a familiar story, the horror of that Jacobin sexual "profligacy" and "animalism" in which the bared breast has become the emblem of the revolutionary and anarchic forces of social modernity and blind generativity. Yet even poetry portraying sexuality as a normal part of married love draws much the same response. At such moments, declares Buchanan, Rossetti is "wheeling his nuptial couch out into the public streets" (ix), and in his words we hear the earlier horror of the *Blackwood's* writers at the dissolution of the bonds of private domestic life in favor of that revolutionary "public virtue" proclaimed by Robespierre and his party.

By the time Buchanan mounted his attack on the Fleshly School, however, he would speak as a lonely, isolated, no longer entirely intelligible voice. For in a Victorian world utterly transformed by the invisible process so compellingly described by Foucault, the deployment of sexuality by the middle class as a means of its own self-affirmation, the sensuous emphasis on physical beauty and pleasure denounced by Buchanan in the language of *Blackwood's* and the Bible as "fleshliness" had come to represent a legitimate dimension to metropolitan middle-class life, part of an allowable domain of "aesthetic" values and domestic comforts within which many Victorians hoped, as David DeLaura has so well said, to "gain the spiritual benefits of the older culture simply by *participating* in the heady activity of the new acquisitive and sensate culture" ("Context" 380). Thus it will be possible for the narrator of one of Coventry Patmore's 1877 poems, for instance, to express his voluptuous delight in his young wife's body by recalling "The Rosy Bosom'd Hours" of their seaside idyll together, and thus Elizabeth Browning in *Aurora Leigh* will celebrate bared breasts as richly maternal — "luminous and harmonious like pure spheres" — and hail even a revolutionary bosom — "'Behold, — behold the paps we all have sucked! / This bosom seems to beat still, or at least / It sets ours beating'" (bk. 5, ll. 18, 219–21) — with a calm assurance that this bared breast has become the emblem, no longer of militant and bloody-minded revolution, but of the milder, millenarian revolution of regenerated hearts which will take place sometime in the distant, perfected future.[8]

At this moment the collapse of Buchanan's attack on fleshly poetry brings into view, for such writers as Oscar Wilde, Lord Alfred Douglas, and Theodore Wratislaw, the sudden possibility of a new counter-discourse of homosexual legitimacy, a language of expanded erotic and sensual experience drawing, at an only slightly further remove than Rossetti and the Pre-Raphaelite poets, on the ideological resources of an emergent European liberalism. For what Wilde and others were able to see is that, in the long years since Pope had attacked Sporus or the *Blackwood's* writers Keats and Leigh Hunt, the discourse of fleshliness had in a manner of speaking taken on a separate or autonomous exis-tence, being available not only to represent that intensification of the body associated by Foucault with an expanding sphere of middle-class existence but, at a more subliminal level, to summon up its earlier association with radical energies of social transformation. The pos-sibility of a homosexual counterdiscourse lies precisely here: if the established social order had once been threatened by a poetry of bared breasts, as Buchanan and the *Blackwood's* writers so drastically insisted, then a poetry of bared breasts might now be deliberately deployed to pose a threat to the established social order.

In general terms, the body of homoerotic poetry which develops in the wake of Buchanan's attack on the Fleshly School will exploit every resource of the discourse of fleshliness as it is transformed into a counter-discourse of male love. In these poems, beginning with such works as J. A. Symonds's privately circulated poems of the later 1860s and culmi-nating with Lord Alfred Douglas's *Poems* (1896), published in Paris in the aftermath of the Wilde scandal, we see that vocabulary of erotic sensuality so deplored by Buchanan being deliberately inverted in ways that are able now to give a name to previously unnameable masculine desire. Nowhere is the specific relation between discourse and counter-

---

8. Browning's image derives as well from the consoling breasts of Jerusalem cele-brated by the Psalmist. For a fuller development of the theme of the female breast in Victorian poetry, see Stone.

discourse so visible, perhaps, as in those poems which, like Symonds's "Lotus-Garland of Antinous" or Wratislaw's "To a Sicilian Boy," name the object of desire through an imagery of bared or naked breasts:

> Love, I adore the contours of thy shape,
> Thine exquisite breasts and arms adorable;
>
> . . . . .
>
> I love thee, sweet! Kiss me, again, again!
> Thy kisses soothe me, as tired earth the rain;
> Between thine arms I find my only bliss;
> Ah let me in thy bosom still enjoy
> Oblivion of the past, divinest boy,
> And the dull ennui of a woman's kiss!
>
> (Quoted in Reade 306)

Published in *The Artist, and Journal of Home Culture* in 1893, Wratislaw's poem marks the moment when the world of Oxford undergraduate passions and evanescent magazines converges upon the larger metropolitan world of culture, society, and politics. For *The Artist* was an Aestheticist magazine that in 1888 had been transformed by its editor, Charles Kains-Jackson, into a covert vehicle for homosexualist writing. Opening its pages not only to such Oxford undergraduates as Wratislaw and Douglas but to such older advocates of masculine love as Symonds, Kains-Jackson's journal daringly extended into the public sphere a previously private network of sexual and social relations. Although it would be abruptly brought to an end as a cultural era, in 1895 by the catastrophe of Wilde's trial and imprisonment, the 1890s represented a cultural space within which may be glimpsed the major themes of a subsequent twentieth-century struggle for homosexual tolerance and civil rights, a fully developed language of moral legitimacy, of physical wholesomeness, of the psychic richness, beauty, and creativity of male love.

It is precisely here, in the vision of diverse and enriching powers to be released through masculine love, that the important legacy of Oxford Hellenism to modern homosexual identity becomes distinctly visible. For beneath the familiar fin de siècle idiom of a newly liberated sensuality is a language of mind and spirit, of the "spiritual procreancy" needed to reenergize culture, deriving in unmistakable terms from Oxford Greek studies. "Had I the good fortune to live in Athens in the time of Pericles," Lord Alfred Douglas would declare after Wilde's conviction, "the very conduct which at present has led to my disgrace would then have resulted in my glory" (Hyde, *Lord* 97). Here is the language of moral legitimacy which would lead so many late-Victorians to see in Douglas and Wilde and Symonds the spokesmen of what would come to be called the "Greek movement."[9]

On one level of cultural politics, it is clear enough why the homosexual apologists should invoke ancient Greece: the prestige of Greece among educated middle-class Victorians, as Richard Jenkyns and Frank Turner have demonstrated in such compelling detail, was so massive that invocations of Hellenism could cast a veil of respectability over even a hitherto unmentionable vice or crime. The "love that dare not speak its name" could be spoken of, to those who knew their ancient history, as *paiderastia*, Greek love. The workings of this legitimating move may be glimpsed even in Wratislaw's poem, where the Sicilianness of the Sicilian boy, as Jenkyns suggests, is made to bear a sanctioning trace of Theocritus and the utopian world of the *Idylls* (290). Yet there is a far deeper level of cultural implication at which such poems as Wratislaw's "To a Sicilian Boy" or Douglas's "A Port in the Aegean" are expressing through invocations of the legitimating parallel of Hellas the larger legacy of Oxford Greek studies.

Wratislaw's homoerotic imagery of "exquisite breasts" or Douglas's Persian imagery of "sugar lips" involves not simply a reversal but a repudiation of the categories of heterosexual love. For in Wratislaw's notion of the female kiss as something lifeless or banal, as in the unmoved indifference of Douglas's speaker to the "wanton charms of

---

9. The phrase is used by Robert Sherard (206) as he describes his successful efforts to suppress Douglas's essay on the Wilde case which was to have been published in *Mercure de France* in the autumn of 1895. In the essay Douglas had declared that his friendship with Wilde "was love, real love, — love, it is true, completely pure but extremely passionate. Its origin was, in Mr Wilde, a purely physical admiration for beauty and grace (my beauty and my grace); it matters little whether they are real or whether they exist only in the imagination of my friend; what must be remarked is that it was a perfect love, more spiritual than sensual, a purely Platonic love, the love of an artist for a beautiful mind and a beautiful body" (Ellmann 488–89).

girls" (311), we encounter the language of a grander reversal, a symbolic renunciation of the blind generativity that the *Blackwood's* writers had once obsessively identified with the half-naked women of French revolutionary iconography, and thus the claim of a higher male eroticism that is more spiritual precisely as it has been freed from the baser imperatives of merely instinctual or animal reproductivity. This is why even amid these poetic speakers' sensuous dwelling upon the boys' breasts and lips there is nonetheless a clear reminiscence of the Socratic doctrine of the philosophic eros found in Plato's *Symposium*.

Wratislaw's proud indifference to "a woman's kiss" is meant to announce nothing other than his allegiance to the "heavenly" or Uranian Eros, and therefore to the ideal of a higher generativity, "procreancy," as Socrates calls it in *Symposium* 209a, "of the spirit rather than of the flesh" (Hamilton and Cairns ed. 560). Here is that higher principle of masculine desire whose language such writers as Pater and Symonds and Wilde had found was darkly legible in Greek literature and philosophy, the discourse of noble and ennobling male love hidden away in the hieroglyphic markings of Plato's *Symposium* and *Phaedrus* and then, only after having been unexpectedly named anew in a crisis of English civic anxiety over a now darkening future, given triumphant public expression once again by Wilde to the spontaneous applause of those attending his trial in the Old Bailey.

The moment of symbolic reversal signaled by spiritual procreancy as a late-Victorian cultural ideal serves to explain, for instance, why such a work as Kains-Jackson's *The New Chivalry* (1894), ostensibly a straightforward exercise in homosexual apologetics, is so concerned with the unlikely subject of English population growth. For *The New Chivalry* is among other things an attack, in the language of modern demographics, on the classical republican fear of a nation running down into depopulation and decline, a nation left defenseless due to a lack of warriors or fighting men. Ever since the battle of Crécy in 1356, Kains-Jackson reminds his readers, Englishmen have been feeling the acute "necessity for increasing the population, a necessity on which the national existence depended" (314). Even so recently as a hundred years ago, either France or Germany would have "conquered England twice over if valour were merely equal" (315), so much smaller were the numbers of England's fighting men. Today, however, with Britain's population approaching that of its military rivals, the ancient civic imperative to increase and multiply the number of England's soldiers by generating them through sexual procreation has been robbed of its force. At this moment a merely carnal generativity might thus be abandoned by men like himself and his fellow partisans, men whose powers of spiritual generativity existed far above the plane of "phallic filthiness" (314).

The dismissal of classical republicanism as a value system irrelevant to the modern age occurs in *The New Chivalry* as, specifically, a dismissal of Oliver Goldsmith's famous image in *The Deserted Village* of England as a nation in which "wealth accumlates and men decay." At the time Goldsmith wrote his poem, this concern with depopulation had been the very voice of classical republican anxiety over luxury and corruption, effeminacy and civic debility. A hundred years later, says Kains-Jackson, amid the growth and bustle of late-Victorian England, it stands exposed as the "trite and irritating commonsense of the Eighteenth Century" (313). For in this new age of material progress and growing population, Britain has visibly "emerged into conditions favourable to a real civilization and a high moral code," an "adult and perfect civilization" whose fullest flower, as all will surely recognize, "will be found in the New Chivalry or the exaltation of the youthful masculine ideal" (315).

The alternative vision of male love and spiritual procreancy then expressed in *The New Chivalry*, the new system of values summed up in Kains-Jackson's notions of "civilization" and "the ideal," is the direct legacy not simply of Victorian liberal Hellenism but of the revolution in modern historiography lying at the heart of Oxford Greek studies. For the older civic order within which "effeminate" men were deemed incapable of martial citizenship has now come to seem, to such men as Kains-Jackson, trite and outmoded not least because contemporary historians of ancient Greece have unexpectedly brought into view a Greece in which *paiderastia* and the warrior ideal, far from being incompatible, had been ritually related. In this context Greek love is able in the late-Victorian moment to be represented by such writers as Kains-Jackson as the animating spirit of a new chivalry, a warfare to be fought out not amid the blood and clamor of actual battlefields but on a higher plane of ideas. In this realm a strategically revived idiom of Greek ideality stands to reinvigorate English civilization far more effectually than any martial force of arms.

The role of Victorian Hellenism in legitimating "homosexuality" as an identity thus derives ultimately from its promise, so powerfully expressed by such advocates as Mill, Arnold, Gladstone, and Jowett, to restore and reinvigorate a nation fractured by the effects of laissez-faire capitalism and enervated by the approach of mass democracy. The specific consequence would be to give Hellenism, in the late-Victorian warfare of ideas and ideologies, precisely the same central structural place occupied by "virtue" in classical republican discourse more than a century before. As works such as *The New Chivalry* make clear, this struggle between competing discourses gives us the moment at which a lingering Victorian dread of "effeminacy" may be seen to have yielded to a newer and more urgent fear of cultural stagnation. In precisely this moment, filled with hope that the Hellenic gifts of self-development and diversity of talents might succeed in revitalizing Victorian culture, such writers as Symonds and Pater and Wilde would find the opening in which "homosexuality" might begin to be understood as itself a mode of self-development and diversity, no longer a sin or crime or disastrous civic debility but a social identity functioning within a fund of shared human potentialities, now recognized *as* shared, out of which the renewal or, as Pater would say, the renaissance of Victorian life might actually begin to rise.

VICTORIAN MANHOOD
AND THE WARRIOR IDEAL

Here is courage, mankind's finest possession, here is
the noblest prize that a young man can endeavor to win,
and it is a good thing his city and all the people share with him
when a man plants his feet and stands in the foremost spears
— Tyrtaeus, 7th century B.C.E.

The most memorable figure of J. A. Symonds's Oxford career, the man he met weekly for almost two years, and into whose beloved presence he never stepped without acute emotion, was Benjamin Jowett, Tutor of Balliol and Regius Professor of Greek. As Jowett supervised the younger man's preparation for the crucial final honors examination in classical philosophy and history, the course of study known at Oxford as *Literae humaniores* or Greats, Symonds found himself by turns crushed and uplifted by the intense experience of these tutorials, "feeling myself indescribably stupid, and utterly beneath my own high level," as he recalled, "but quitting the beloved presence with no diminution of an almost fanatical respect" (Brown 1:226). By the time such undergraduates as Symonds and Pater were coaching with him in the early 1860s, Jowett had become a celebrated tutor, whose students' brilliant successes in the examination schools so repeatedly foretold their subsequent achievements in the sphere of national and imperial affairs — in the Church, the Foreign Office, and Parliament — the worldly realm of power and duty which Jowett himself rated so high.

Yet it was not the worldly advantage unlocked by his teaching and sponsorship which Jowett's students would remember with such vividness, but instead the intensity of the tutorial itself, with its racking silences, penetrating queries, quenching utterances. Whatever were the pains inflicted by this experience, its pleasures seemed to the young men to be unexampled. Symonds, paralyzed by the conviction of his own complete inadequacy, nonetheless left the tutor's room feeling "obscurely yet vividly" that "my soul [had] grown by his contact, as it had never grown before" (1:226). This note is sounded repeatedly in the memoirs left by Jowett's pupils, of a moral counsel so capacious in its scope that it became a "pastoral supervision" (Campbell 203), of an intellectual stimulus that seemingly produced the requisite abilities in the very men from whom they were so harrowingly demanded, Jowett's labors as tutor always implying, as one Balliol student remembered, "a belief in powers hereafter to be developed, and the belief seemed to create the thing believed in" (200).

It was this intense Oxford "tutor worship," centering in Jowett especially but involving other dons as well, that contemporary Cambridge men regarded as so peculiarly Oxonian, a species of devotion, as one graduate insisted, which "does not flourish on the banks of the Cam" (Tollemache 181). Such modern commentators as Geoffrey Faber would seek to account for the peculiar intensity of Jowett's tutorial relationships by projecting upon it the categories of Freudian psychology, positing in Jowett a homosexual "sublimation" which early became for him "not only possible but necessary" (84). Yet it is only when we attend to the specific Victorian context of these Oxford tutorials, to their historical enmeshment in a series of urgent questions and fears about Britain's national survival, that the larger meaning of Oxford tutor worship, as well as its complex relationship to the emergence of homosexuality in the twentieth-century sense, becomes genuinely clear. For when we view it against its original mid-nineteenth-century background of deep and conflicting sociopolitical anxieties, Jowett's tutorial becomes visible as an instrument of profound ideological change, as a traditional structure now deployed to new purpose, effectively channeling a saving new secular gospel of intellectual self-development and diversity into the souls of the civic elite who would guide Britain, as Jowett believed, through the darkening wilderness of the century's end.

College tutorials had been conducted in some form at Oxford during

JOHN ADDINGTON SYMONDS
in 1864. (Photo reproduced
by kind permission of the
Librarian of the University
of Bristol.)

BENJAMIN JOWETT,
photographed by
Julia Margaret Cameron.
(Photo reproduced by
permission of the National
Portrait Gallery, London.)

the preceding two centuries. Only in the years following 1825, however, would this generally dry and formulaic interchange between tutor and pupil begin to assume a larger significance in English cultural life. For with its reinvention as a tradition by J. H. Newman and Hurrell Froude during the Anglican religious insurgency to be known as Tractarianism, the college tutorial began to function at Oxford as a vehicle for the intensifying reciprocal bonds of masculine interest, affection, and obligation to which modern cultural theory has given the name "male homosociality." In the hands of a few Tractarian teachers conversing with a few responsive undergraduates, the Oxford tutorial would become part of an ethos in which intellectual growth was to merge with religious awakening, and instruction would verge on intimacy. When in turn Jowett's no less insurgent generation of liberal dons later sought a vehicle for their own very different reforms, the Tractarian tutorial lay ready to hand. Coming to power through the revolution of university reform in the 1850s and 1860s, Jowett and the university liberals were to commandeer the Oxford tutorial, recommissioning it in the name of "mental illumination," Greek studies, and more generally, Hellenism.

Immediately after Oscar Wilde's trial for sodomic indecency, of course, it would be difficult to pronounce the word "Hellenism" without an insinuating leer. Behind that semantic corruption, however, lies a larger and more significant story of cultural transformation and unintended consequences. For so great was the success of Victorian liberal Hellenism in coming to represent all the dimensions of human experience denied under the Calvinist dispensation of religious fundamentalism or starved under the materialist regime of industrial modernity that it would open — in a way wholly unanticipated by the liberals themselves — the possibility of legitimating male love. Liberal partisans of Greek studies had instead been intent upon deploying Hellenism as a discursive language of sociocultural renewal. For by the 1860s such liberals as Jowett and Arnold, Gladstone and Mill would come to sense that the older ideological structures of public life were no longer capable of sustaining Britain in the struggle among nations. Precisely as such structures as the warrior ideal underlying classical republicanism came to seem increasingly irrelevant to the actual conditions imposed upon Britain by industrial modernity did the alternative values Victorian liberals located in Hellenism seem to promise the hope of cultural transformation. The great irony would thus always be that the mid-Victorian liberals, struggling in the face of the apparent powerlessness of classical republican "manliness" to rescue Britain from stagnation and future decay, would so far succeed in their polemical work on behalf of Hellenism as quite unexpectedly to persuade the late-Victorian homosexual apologists that in Hellenism they themselves would find a no less powerful, no less liberal language, a legitimating counterdiscourse of social identity and erotic liberation.

To speak of Tractarianism by its other customary name as the Oxford Movement is to see the University of Oxford as a decisive battleground in the Victorian struggle over the sociopolitical order being brought forth by secular materialism and industrial modernity. As an episcopal seat and the leading school of the Anglican church, Oxford would inevitably experience any changes in the relationship between church and state with the sharpest immediacy. With the tumultuous onset of political reform in Britain during the 1820s and 1830s, however, constitutional change seemed to those resisting it to bear a frighteningly revolutionary, even "Jacobinical" face. "Three of the great embankments of our Constitution have recently been cut through," declared Sir Thomas Acland, referring to the repeal of the Test and Corporation Acts in 1828, the Catholic Emancipation of 1829, and the great Reform Bill of 1832. "The first broke down the long established qualification for office in our Christian state," he continued, "the second *let in, as legislators,* men implacably hostile to the great living principle of all our institutions; the third, as a natural consequence of the two former poured into the House of Commons . . . the turbid waters of sheer *mammonry,* democracy and republicanism" (Brendon xv).

Inside the space of four short years, the hegemony of the Church of England, theoretically intact since the seventeenth century, had thus been broken. For after 1828 the Parliament that was constitutionally permitted to intervene in church affairs was no longer exclusively Anglican in membership; after 1829, it was no longer exclusively Protestant; and in 1830 a bill was introduced to admit Jews, Macaulay arguing with incomparable brio that there was no argument against admitting Jews which did not hold at least as strongly against seating Christians.[1] The violent agitation of 1831–32 over the Reform Bill saw outbreaks of hostility against the Church for its role as traditional ally of Tory intransigence. After 1832 the unmistakable momentum of reform suggested that disestablishment itself was near, with matriculations at Oxford falling by 20 percent as young men doubted there would still be a Church of England into which to be ordained (*Report* 17). Then, in the culminating event of the series, the new Parliament that had been elected by the tradesmen and tenant farmers enfranchised through the Reform Bill voted in 1833 to abolish ten bishoprics in Ireland. What could be the future of the Church, many Anglicans asked themselves, if powers so alien and antagonistic to it were allowed so large a share in determining its future?

Against this background of constitutional revolution and "national apostasy," Oxford became the center of the impassioned counterrevolution known as Tractarianism. Hurrell Froude and John Henry Newman, electrified by John Keble's "national apostasy" sermon of July 1833, and stirred by the example of the French bishops persecuted during the July Revolution of 1830 in France, joined their voices to reassert the ancient powers and privilege of the Church. Together they raised the cry of "The Church in danger!" not hurled in such vehemence since the Sacheverell crisis of 1710. "Open your eyes to the fearful change which has been so noiselessly effected," as Froude now commanded, "and acknowledge that BY STANDING STILL YOU BECOME A PARTY TO REVOLUTION" (8).

Within the fiery Tractarian insistence on reasserting the supernatural authority and agency of the Church, in turn, there surged a darker apprehension, the fear that the hectically "commercial" statecraft employed to secure the passage of the recent reforms in Parliament (Mozley

---

1. As a practical matter, the political disabilities of non-Anglican protestants had for over one hundred years been relieved through a series of toleration and indemnity acts passed by Parliament. With the sharp reaction to French revolutionary secularism and atheism in the early years of the nineteenth century, however, there came a reassertion of the Anglican rhetoric of religious hegemony. This in its turn prompted the demands of the 1820s and 1830s for wider concessions to non-Establishment religious groups. See Matthew; Best; and Clark, chapter 6.

1:141) was but the sign of a larger bankruptcy. Looking on in anger as essential religious principle was crassly exchanged for profitable or peaceful relations with powerful interest groups, the Tractarians became convinced that these greasy machinations — for which Sir Robert Peel's stunning reversal on the Catholic Emancipation he had originally opposed had become the unforgettable, unforgivable symbol — would soon obliterate the way to a higher, purer life. We have always understood that what Samuel Taylor Coleridge refers to in his brilliant and influential *Lay Sermon* of 1817 as the "overbalance of the commercial system" (117–18) was nothing other than the consequences of nineteenth-century modernity itself: the complex socioeconomic formation that was daily remaking Britain through the secularizing, materializing, and alienating effects of the cash nexus and urbanization, swelling population, social mobility, and class competition, the centralization, democratization, and homogenization produced through widening literacy and the new systems of transport and communication. Yet such Victorian movements as Tractarianism become fully intelligible only when we also see that this moment was still one in which modernity could not yet be grasped in secular terms. This is why Coleridge's *Lay Sermon* had been, in some sense, intended as an actual homily or sermon, and it is why his argument had been so concerned to offer the Church, conceived in somewhat altered terms, as a counterpoise to the "Commercial System."

The earliest stirrings of Tractarianism may thus be glimpsed in the growing conviction that Coleridge's vision of the Church partaking "not merely of a better but of an *other* life," regenerating the English community as "not so properly better as *other* men" (126), had instead been itself reduced to a passive instrument of the "Commercial Spirit." In the same way, Peel's pursuit of compromise and accommodation in Parliament had seemed to reduce his followers to contemptible puppets, each knowing that "whoever bound themselves to him might any day be called on to unsay all they had been saying and undo all they had been doing" (Mozley 1:141). This picture convinced the Tractarians that both the Church of England and English society as a whole were becoming dangerously unmoored from the realm of the transcendental — the domain of honor and ideals where men were, as Coleridge had said, "weighed not counted" (140). It was in this critical moment that

Newman at Oxford would issue his thrilling call to arms in the first of the *Tracts for the Times*: "CHOOSE YOUR SIDE. To remain neuter much longer will be itself to take a part" ("Tract" 10).

Newman grasped from the first that the Oxford Movement involved far more than just the hopes of those young men specifically intending to take Anglican orders, his genius perceiving the hunger among so many other impressionable and idealistic Oxford undergraduates for some higher rule of life. Like its equivalents at Harvard, Heidelberg, and Salamanca, a significant portion of the rising Oxford generation had felt "the deeper seriousness," as Arthur Stanley was to call it, "breathed into the minds of men . . . by the great convulsion of the French Revolution" (158). During this time, the English youths' sense of the apocalyptic immediacy of change was repeatedly sharpened by fears of rebellion by radicals, by the Irish, and later by the Chartists, just as their sense of the living alternative reality of the medieval past was heightened by Robert Southey's *Colloquies* (1829), Kenelm Digby's *Broad Stone of Honour* (1822), and the novels of Walter Scott, to whom Newman, as he would say in later years, owed his very self.

Newman's keen sense of the ardor and sincerity alive within the younger men with whom he dealt as tutor of Oriel and rector of St. Mary's, was in turn heightened by his indignant awareness that their idealism went unanswered — worse, was throttled into conformity or condemned as fanaticism by the conventional society of the day. Driven by the widening prosperity spread through the railway and shipbuilding boom of the 1830s, the demand for social acceptance on the part of hitherto disdained or excluded social classes was, he saw, at once encouraging and calcifying a regime of respectability. It was "a narrow and shallow system, that Protestant philosophy," as Newman called it, and it "forbids all the higher and more noble impulses of the mind, and forces men to eat, drink, and be merry, whether they will or no" ("Antony" 93).

What indeed, asked Newman, would have been the fate of a Saint Antony or any of the early church fathers had he to live instead according to the cramping formulas of present-day English existence? "Longing for some higher rule of life than any which the ordinary forms of society admit, and finding our present lines too rigidly drawn to include any character of mind that is much out of the way, any rule that is not 'gentlemanlike,' 'comfortable' and 'established'" (95), as Newman declared, such a man would have become a renegade to the craven society of "*sensible* Protestants" who will "not let a man do anything out of the way without stamping him with the name of fanatic" (93).

Profoundly, even contemptuously aware of the ignobly deforming powers exerted by social and commercial modernity, Newman perceived in the same moment that a single counterpoise to that modernity lay all about him, in the visible spires and invisible traditions of Oxford. Looking out upon his alma mater through the imaginative historical vision he had gained from Scott, he saw that "her present life is but the continuation of the life of past ages, and that her constituent members are, after all, in a new form and with new names, the Benedictines and Augustinians of a former day ("Oxford" 331). This monastic principle, execrated and defamed in the tradition of anti-Catholicism which had flourished in England ever since the expropriation of the monasteries under Henry VIII, was lingering still at Oxford and Cambridge. Absorbed everywhere else in the nation into "the frivolous or selfish tempers and opinions of an advanced civilization" (331), the monastic principle constituted nothing less than a vital principle of opposition to modernity, and Newman now called upon the ancient universities, "as being out of the world, to measure and expose the world, and, as being in the heart of the Church, to strengthen the Church to resist it" (331).

The specific staging ground for Newman's campaign to recover the ancient religious power lying latent within Oxford was the college rather than the university, for colleges constituted better, other "homes," as Newman said ("Rise" 189), and could function as intimate moral communities for each resident, "where his better thoughts will find countenance, and his good resolutions support" (189–90). Newman began by working to restore his own college, Oriel, to its medieval condition under the founding statutes as a body of resident fellows devoted to both educating younger students and pursuing their own studies. To recover the genuine educational function of the college was to strip structures such as the college tutorial of all their old accreted crust of condescension, impersonality and sloth, that eighteenth-century tradition of donnish coldness and indolence immortalized in Gibbon's *Autobiography* as the "almost incredible neglect" of pupils by tutors and the utterly "impassable gulf" lying between them (82).

Newman's idea of the tutorial connection, by contrast, insisted on its nature as a pastoral relationship, a cure of souls. Because by collegiate statute every tutor was a fellow, and every fellow was either in Anglican orders or preparing for them, Newman could insist that "a Tutor's profession was of a religious nature" (Culler 72) and could defend his claim by appealing to the statutes through which flowed the transcendental authority of the visible Church. In this way his reform in college teaching could be accomplished, not by proposing any new change, but simply by recalling the tutorial to its original religious purpose.

The pastoral relationship in turn supplied the metaphysical basis for what Newman himself recognized were the extraordinary new relations "not only of intimacy, and friendship, and almost of equality" (Faber, *Apostles* 166) arising between the Oriel tutors and their pupils, for Newman and Froude had come to stand "in the place of a father, or an elder and affectionate brother" to the younger men (Mozley 1:181). In Newman's hands the reformed tutorial represented the institutionalization of his doctrine of "personality" or personal influence, that "sovereign compulsory sway" which a "single individual, trained to practise what he teaches" may in a spirit of unconscious holiness exercise over "the weak, the timid, the wavering, and the inquiring" ("Personal" 94–95). Sustained and purified by the ideal disinterestedness of the pastoral bond, the tutorial relationship became a channel through which the presence and personality of the teacher — "the living voice, the breathing form, the expressive countenance" — could perform the "living and bodily communication of knowledge" ("Rise" 14, 13). Frustrated and short-lived as this tutorial experiment at Oriel proved to be, it yet became the core of a compelling pedagogical ideal, of teaching as a mode of intercourse comprehending the student in the full range of his humanity and potentiality, that would in the years to come remain at the heart of Oxford's institutional identity.

The tutorial revolution itself, however, comprised only one-half of Newman's effort to reconstitute Oriel on the lines of the medieval statutes. The other half was to recover the old monastic principle as a living motive for the tutors and fellows themselves. Newman's celebrated gift for friendship, coupled with the conditions of political threat outside Oxford as well as institutional persecution within, combined to generate around the Tractarians an exhilarating ethos of struggle, danger, sacrifice, and vital common purpose. Deeply moved by the ascetic example of the early fathers, Newman regarded monachism as a mode of life consisting "not in solitariness, but in austerities" ("Antony" 94), and perceived that such austerities as the celibacy requirement traditionally imposed on holders of college fellowships could contribute to their sense of community and solidarity, fellows wordlessly being encouraged to remain not only unmarried but resident in the college.[2]

If to shrink from celibacy, as R. W. Church would later say, was considered within Tractarian circles "a mark of want of strength or intelligence, of an unmanly preference for English home life, of insensibility to the generous devotion and purity of the saints" (321), celibacy itself gleamed outside those circles as the pattern for a high and noble sacrifice realizable within the limits of actual English life. This belief that an unseen, transcendent world just as utterly real and immediately present as the visible one could be approached through simple gestures of self-restraint is why the Tractarian practices of fasting and chastisement or the Tractarian desire "to live a virgin life, and to die a virgin," as one of Newman's younger colleagues, F. W. Faber, expressed the celibate ideal (Bowden 79), would move so many non-Tractarians to admiration. Tennyson, for example, otherwise so indifferent to theological controversy, would embody the celibate ideal in his 1834 poem "Sir Galahad," where the virgin knight's ecstatic vision of lilies and angels is shown to possess exactly the same degree of phenomenological reality as the driving hail that "crackles on the leads."

In this context an intense language of religious inwardness and confession would begin to operate as the idiom of daily life, first among the Tractarian partisans, and later among other disaffected and sensitive young men who were not of the Tractarian party. For the momentous questions concerning the survival of the Church in a hostile age were

2. The Aristotelian ideal of rational male friendship as a spiritual intimacy involving mutual ethical formation powerfully influenced, through the mediation of Cicero's *De Amicitia*, the early church fathers and, through them, the English Tractarians. See Richards.

paralleled on the personal level among the more serious Oxford undergraduates by no less momentous questions concerning each man's belief
and vocation, every commitment and every renunciation demanding an
examination of conscience which was pitiless in its scrutiny and all but
limitless in its scope. In these exigencies of conscience, a religious man
would turn to the confidential society of his friends, because his heart, as
Faber explained, "is teeming with a thousand high themes; and utterance brings the same kind of relief to him that tears do to the stupified
heart-bursting mourner" (Bowden 12–13). Here the traditional religious vocabulary of bitter self-reproach and headlong emotional
avowal, of "seaméd souls" and "filthy imaginings" and "love," becomes
detached from its wholly inward bearing on the soul or God. Merging
with a Wordsworthian idiom of emotional crisis and expressive relief,
this religious language is now made to incorporate an outward orientation toward the friend, as when Faber, for instance, addresses a trusted
companion:

> Now thou hast seen my heart. Was it too near?
> Didst thou recoil from the o'erpowering sight;
> That vision of a scarred and seaméd soul?
> Ah! yes: thy gentle eyes were filled with fear
> . . . . .
> Well, be it so, dear friend! it was but right
> That thou shouldst learn where blossoms yet may bless,
> . . . . .
> Thou saw'st my heart: and didst not love me less.
> (Faber 68)

At any such moment as this we hear expressed the Tractarian ideal of
friendship as spiritual communion which would so deeply color Oxford
sociality in later years, prompting both A. H. Clough and G. M. Hopkins to fill their Oxford diaries with brief but impassioned notations of
the ebb and flow in friendships. Even men at several removes of age or
religious allegiance from the Tractarians would feel the power of its ideal
of religious friendship — Jowett, for example, apologizing in an 1842
letter for not having written more about religion because "it seems so
cold and prosy to write to an intimate friend about anything else"

(Campbell 109–10). The same impulse would prompt R. L. Nettleship in 1869 to remind Henry Scott Holland of their Oxford years together, with their "memories of God approached together" in the "communion of souls" (Paget 37). As its original religious matrix receded, the Tractarian ideal of a friendship sealed in religion was to become instead simply an intense but secular religion of friendship at Oxford, while its defining assumption — that in the communion of souls one friend could show another the truth of his own "scarred and seaméd soul" — would become simply a plot device in Wilde's *Picture of Dorian Gray*. All these later developments would belong, however, to the interior history of Oxford. The great consequence of Tractarianism for the world outside Oxford, by contrast, lay upon a more immediate horizon.

With the dismaying conversion of Newman and other Tractarians to Roman Catholicism in the years around 1845, his enemies' darkest predictions of apostasy and betrayal were confirmed. Newman's "perversion" to Rome compelled the nation to accept as a fact, the *Oxford Protestant Magazine* insisted, "that for years the Universities have been the seat of a dangerous, and too successful conspiracy against the faith of which they were supposed to be the bulwarks" (Engel 23). The violently anti-Tractarian reaction that followed found its classic literary expression in the "muscular Christianity" of Charles Kingsley and J. A. Froude. This reaction arose, it is usually said, out of specifically religious and sexual anxieties, the sort of embittered panic that, for example, Kingsley underwent when he feared that his fiancée might be lost first to Tractarian "fanaticism" and then to Rome, or that Froude suffered when his early zeal for his elder brother Hurrell's Tractarianism wavered and reversed field at Newman's desertion, leading him into skepticism and heresy.[3]

In this view, the ten years following 1845 witnessed virtual hysteria

---

3. The most thorough-going attempt to interpret Kingsley's response to Newman and Tractarianism as a species of sexual hysteria is Susan Chitty's. R. B. Martin has suggested that Kingsley's extreme reaction to Tractarian "effeminacy" arose in part because of his fears over his brother Henry's sexual indeterminacy.

over the growing power of the Roman church. The Tractarian "perverts" were succeeded by the inrush of Catholic immigrants fleeing the potato famine in Ireland. And the savage "anti-Maynooth campaign" against increasing a parliamentary grant to an Irish Catholic seminary was followed by volcanic indignation at the "papal aggression" of 1850–51, when Pius IX, appropriating ancient English names for modern Roman purposes, presumed to create an "archbishop of Westminster." In that moment, "No Popery" frenzy reached its highest pitch since the Gordon Riots of 1780 (Wolffe 2).

Yet virulent and widespread as this anti-Catholic feeling undeniably was, especially among Dissenting and Evangelical Protestants, the response among such Victorians as Kingsley and Froude involved far more than religious prejudice alone. If Kingsley could contemptuously dismiss the vulgar fear that "Popery will in a few years become the popular religion of these realms" ("Fear" 467), he could not regard with the same equanimity the cultural transformations being wrought by Tractarianism—in particular, its legions of "sleek passionless men, who are too refined to be manly, and measure their grace by their effeminacy" (*Tragedy* 82). Intense, remote, ostentatiously pious, and most of all, flagrantly, inhumanly celibate, the new masculine ideal encouraged first by Tractarianism and then by the Roman Catholic converts had become the *beau idéal*, as Kingsley insisted, of a "mesmerizing, table-turning, spirit-rapping, Spiritualizing, Romanizing generation" ("Thoughts" 571). Everything he read, everywhere he looked, from the diseased poetic preference for Shelley over Byron, to the inexplicable success of the Spasmodic poets—convinced Kingsley that "the age is an effeminate one" (571).

Such fears, as David Newsome and Norman Vance have so well described, were to leap into apocalyptic vividness when viewed against the fiery backdrop of war and war scares which the decade of the 1850s was to supply—the French invasion scare of 1852, the Crimean War of 1854–56, the Indian Mutiny of 1857, and the renewed fright over French invasion in 1859–60. In the face of these dangers, Kingsley declared, the nation required "Tyrtaean strains" from its poets ("Alexander" 459), not the flaccid introspection of the Spasmodics or the "denationalized" maunderings of "those who have lately joined, or are inclined to join, the Church of Rome" ("Froude" 224). Such Tractarians as Frederick Faber had already hailed the decline in martial fervor among young men as a sign of spiritual growth; he declared, "I joy for the young that they lay not [England's] honour . . . in that which mere blood of her sons hath won her, / Her world-wide name of glory. / I joy for the loss of the noisy gladness / That hath made late ages dull" (293). To Kingsley and Froude, however, that noisy gladness was nothing less than the war cries of England's victorious sailors and soldiers at the Armada and at Waterloo. In the immensely popular works each man wrote during this time — Kingsley's *Westward Ho!* (1855) and Froude's *History of England from the Fall of Wolsey to the Defeat of the Spanish Armada* (1856–70) — they sought to reawaken English patriotism and make it noisier still.

It is precisely here, as Kingsley and Froude glory in the blood sacrifice of England's armies and navies, that the "muscularity" of "muscular Christianity" demands to be seen as a specifically civic response. For when Kingsley protests that the age is "an effeminate one" or warns that in Spasmodic poetry "the manhood, the 'virtus' is small" ("Thoughts" 576), we instantly recognize the old language of classical republicanism, invoked as it had been by John Brown a hundred years before when effeminate manners and heated nurseries appeared to be pushing England toward defeat in war. In the same way, we understand that Kingsley's indignation at the "sleek passionless men" brought forth from Anglo- and Roman Catholicism is nothing other than the ancient voice of civic alarm as it confronts the approach of dangers threatening the nation at its most fundamental level as a polity. For garbed in a Tractarian cassock, the effeminatus has reappeared upon the national stage, taking up from the fop, the eunuch, and the molly its traditional role within classical republican discourse as the invariable sign of onrushing civic debility and ruin.

The primordial anxiety underlying this language of civic alarm expresses itself, as we have seen in Chapter 1, in a sustained tendency among Western nations of the republican tradition to identify the very safety and stability of a human community with the warrior ideal. Almost as though it belonged to an archaic level of consciousness capable under the right conditions of generating seismic tremors of sociocultural dismay, this anxiety reads any signs of "effeminacy" as evidence that the deepest mental or spiritual foundations of the polity — the willingness and ability of its citizens to defend it even unto death — are threatened with collapse. This is why civic dread can be focused, even so late as the mid-nineteenth century, upon the figure of the warrior, and specifically on the citizen-soldier who embodies the political collectivity, both in war, when "the nation inscribes itself in the body . . . in the wound" (Scarry 112), and in peace, when the nation repays its obligation to the soldier's sacrifice by bestowing upon him the civic powers most completely defining citizenship in the polity.

The earliest and most memorable expression of this symbolic relation between citizen-soldier and polity is made in the Western political tradition by the seventh-century B.C.E Spartan poet Tyrtaeus:

> Here is courage [*aretē*], mankind's finest possession, here is
> the noblest prize that a young man can endeavor to win,
> and it is a good thing [*xūnon esthlon*] his city and all the people share
> with him
> when a man plants his feet and stands in the foremost spears
> (Lattimore 14)

Thus does Tyrtaeus capture in a single image the symbolic or synecdochic relation between the collectivity and the hoplite warrior — the *xūnon esthlon* or common good—which had come to birth in the historical moment when the older Homeric mode of warfare, consisting mainly of the berserk martial frenzy of a relatively small number of individual heroes engaged in single combat, was giving way to that new coordination of large numbers of soldiers, weaponry, and collective strategy called by historians of ancient Greece the "hoplite reform."

As the more expensive weapons and more difficult martial skills demanded in Homeric combat were replaced by the simpler panoply and skills of hoplite warfare, more men were enabled to fight. With the shift in tactics dictated by this increase in numbers, everything could now be seen to depend on the coordination and the self-discipline or restraint (*sōphrosynē*) of the Greek citizen-soldier acting as a part of a larger group or phalanx. For every hoplite was armed with a large round shield and spear, and, joining in the long, closely massed lines of his fellow hoplites, each man bore his shield overlapped to the left so as to protect his neighbor's unshielded right side. Mustered into battle by cadenced music, the entire phalanx thus moved as a single body, and the experience of this physical and tactical solidarity in combat generated, as Marcel Detienne has so brilliantly described, the very experience of collectivity and the common good which was to constitute the new Greek idea of political community.

Writing in the first moment when the experience of the phalanx and the polis began to coalesce as a sense of political communality, Tyrtaeus celebrates excellence or virtue (*aretē*) as a complex of specifically martial qualities. Emphasizing not only the physical courage required in hand-to-hand combat, when the hoplites had to stand and stab at their opponents, fighting "toe to toe and shield against shield hard driven, / crest against crest and helmet on helmet, chest against chest" (16), Tyrtaeus insists as well upon the psychic firmness and solidarity needed to sustain the phalanx in the bloody throes of battle: "All thought of foul flight completely forgotten, / [the hoplite] has well trained his heart to be steadfast and to endure, / and with words encourages the man who is stationed beside him" (14).

When Aristotle relocates this *aretē* within the ethical system of the *Politics*, the martial dimension to "virtue," even as it is subsumed within a larger morality of citizenship, will never be forgotten: the fighting qualities required by the hoplite phalanx remain the general or symbolic type of excellence to be aspired to by every citizen (3:7). In Aristotelian theory, the stark physical need of the polis for defense thus comes to be completed by the ethical need of the citizen to fulfill his telos as a man (*zōon politikon*) through the pursuit of civic excellence. In the republican tradition of succeeding centuries, this archaic warrior core will always retain something of its original potency. For Machiavelli, for Harrington, for John Brown, it is as crucial as for Aristotle, a psychocultural substrate that when disturbed never fails to respond with shattering force.

This is the buried level of martial consciousness stirred so powerfully in Kingsley and Tennyson during the war and invasion-scare years of the 1850s. It imparts in turn to such furiously topical anti-French poems of 1852 as Tennyson's "Form, Riflemen, Form" a deeper resonance with

John Brown's dire warnings about the unmanned English coasts, and endows Tennyson's famous "Charge of the Light Brigade" of 1854 with its preeminent symbolic status as a poem of war. With its dactylic rhythms summoning up the rigorously controlled canter of the British cavalrymen as they rode directly into the murderous cannon fire at the battle of Balaclava, Tennyson's "Charge of the Light Brigade" re-creates the primal scene of republican polity — soldiers' lives volunteered in blood sacrifice for the common good — and portrays that sacrifice under its Tyrtaean conditions.

The extraordinary compression in Tennyson's description of the actual fighting at Balaclava has helped obscure this point in much modern commentary on the poem (see, for example, McGann), so it may be well to emphasize it here. For the description,

> Flashed all their sabres bare,
> Flashed as they turned in air
> Sabring the gunners there
> *(Tennyson* 510)

is precise in its detail and specifically military in its reference, depicting not the static pose of some Romantic hussar out of Géricault, but instead the urgently mobile action of the cavalrymen's sabers as they execute the sword stroke known as the *moulinet*, that "almost ceaseless play . . . whirling round and round overhead" (Kinglake 4:169) which helps riders desperately beset on all sides keep their attackers at bay. "Sabring the gunners there" — the enemy whose bodies are "Shattered and sundered" — Tennyson's cavalrymen thus are fighting with all the relentless violence amid all the hideous visceral havoc of Tyrtaeus's hoplites fighting "toe to toe" so many centuries before.

This sudden and shocking reappearance, in the middle of the nineteenth century, of the Tyrtaean aspect of war is what would give the charge of the Light Brigade its enormous symbolic importance for Victorian civilization. It explains in turn why Kingsley would first have to struggle with disbelief and amazement ("I tell you the whole thing stuns me") before he could recognize that his own earlier call for "Tyrtaean strains" in poetry had in fact been answered by Tennyson, who, as

Kingsley now said upon reading "Charge of the Light Brigade," "has a glimpse of what Tyrtaeus ought to be" (F. Kingsley 180–81). Through an extraordinary chance of war, topography, and human "blunder," the conditions of ancient warfare had resurfaced in a valley of the Crimea, tragically entrapping in anachronistic hand-to-hand combat a modern brigade of British cavalrymen whose normal military function was to harry the enemy, not attack fixed-gun emplacements.

The self-discipline — the *sōphrosynē* — and solidarity of these cavalrymen as they preserved the set pace and order of their lines down the long valley under deadly crossfire were breathtaking. Continuously closing up their ranks each time a rider fell so that "to distant observers, the alternate distension and contraction of the line seemed to have the precision and sameness which belong to mechanic contrivance," the measured advance of the Light Brigade under the hellish fire moved the French general Pierre Bosquet to protest in admiration, "C'est magnifique; mais ce n'est pas la guerre" (quoted in Kinglake 4:265–66 n.369). Yet it was precisely because it was war, war thrown so far back upon its ancient political premise as no longer to resemble any enterprise of modern military science, that the charge of the Light Brigade transfixed Tennyson, Kingsley, and the breathless Victorian public.

This in turn is why Tennyson's speaker, in recounting the approach, attack, and retreat of the brigade, is able to accomplish the complex illocutionary act Christopher Ricks and Edgar Shannon have noted as one of the great achievements of the poem, his "combining the immediacy of an eyewitness with the respectful distance of the acknowledged non-combatant" (18). For the speaker understands and keenly feels his own direct civic involvement in the distant battle, and does so according to the ancient terms of republican discourse: these young men have represented *him*, just as they have represented or taken the place of all the others too young or old or weak to go to war. The young men have suffered and died on behalf of the polity and the common good, and so the speaker concludes by calling on the polity to complete the circuit of civic excellence: to acknowledge the greatness of the young men's sacrifice, and the corresponding magnitude of its own debt: "Honour the charge they made! / Honour the Light Brigade" (*Tennyson* 511).

Yet "Charge of the Light Brigade" also contains a disquieting sign that all this courage and glory are mere illusion. For the display of archaic *aretē* and *sōphrosynē* embodied in the famous six hundred cavalrymen comes to light on this occasion only as the result of a grotesque series of errors — "Some one had blundered." The textual history of this famous line underscores its problematic relationship to the "glory" — the *aretē* — the poet wishes to celebrate, for Tennyson originally included, then excluded, then restored it, as if detesting the fact of the appalling "blunder" yet aware that it finally could not be separated from the extraordinary act of courage which was its outcome and very antithesis. Taking over "blunder" from a lead story in the *Times*, Tennyson makes use of a word rich in connotations of heavy clumsiness, and gross blindness, to convey the heedlessly unseeing, namelessly bureaucratic mentality that originated the fatal order. This fumbling stupidity he then contrasts to the brilliant grace and poise of the Light Brigade — smaller-made men, lightly armed, mounted on lighter-weight horses — who had with such a fearsomely clear-eyed devotion looked into the eyes of their own individual deaths and nonetheless carried the order out.

In fact, as such episodes as Florence Nightingale's struggle to establish a barrack hospital at Scutari made clear, the Crimean War itself belonged not to the world of Tyrtaeus at all but to the incomparably more complicated, bureaucratic world of modern war. This sphere was filled with professionalized cadres of officers and enlisted men, geopolitical strategic considerations, impersonal deployment of forces, complex logistical, support and resupply problems, tactical theories, inter-ally diplomacy, inter-service rivalry, press and public relations — to name merely those aspects playing a role at Balaclava. It is this bureaucratized world in all its baffling and unmartial complexity which first presses into view behind the line "Some one had blundered," only to resurface again in Tennyson's uneasy awareness that he could keep this world neither out of his poem nor from enmeshing its brilliant Tyrtaean moment in an enormously complex web of material relations and civilian considerations wholly removed from the clear and noble imperatives of the ancient martial ideal.

The crucial poem for understanding the paradox of an archaic warrior ideal surfacing in the midst of a bewilderingly complex modernity thus becomes Tennyson's *Maud* (1855). In that work the Crimean War both is and is not the solution to the maddened narrator's misery. For it restores him to relative mental stability and function in the world as he goes off to fight at the end of the poem, yet it is at the same time clearly powerless to sweep the world clean of all the evils of modernity which have combined with the narrator's morbid temperament and his personal losses — his father's suicide, his mother's death, the duel with Maud's brother, Maud's death — to push him to, and then over, the brink of madness. The massive disparity between the speaker's belief that the war will bring beneficial change to the world and the likelihood of any genuine amelioration actually coming from war is one Tennyson's critics have from the first been keenly attentive to, in recent years arguing that the speaker's faith in war is proof of his continuing madness or of some obscurer satiric purpose or of a lobotomized jingoism, in Herbert Tucker's pungent phrase, so massive as to constitute a complete moral abdication (429).

The great virtue of this critical response has been that it underscores the degree of disjunction and tension between two competing sociocultural systems, whether these are termed realist versus romantic, or middle class versus aristocratic, or modern versus traditional. Its limitation, however, has been to identify the speaker's martial commitment at the end of *Maud* with an aristocratic or medieval-chivalric ideal of war. Instead, the martial ideal voiced in Maud's song — and hence in the speaker's decision to go to war which is shown to flow directly from her song — demands to be understood within the context of civic republicanism. For when the song tells of men who "March with banner and bugle and fife / To the death, for their native land,"[4] it refers not to any medieval campaigns or chivalric crusades but to a mode of combat in defense of the *patria* arising out of the Renaissance effort, so closely identified with Machiavelli's *Discourses* and *Art of War*, to revive the citizen militias of the classical republics. Here lies the great significance of so seemingly minor a detail as the fife music the soldiers march to in Maud's song. For the fife had first been adopted as a military instrument

---

4. *Tennyson* 531, pt. I, ll. 171–72. Subsequent references are to part and line numbers of *Maud*.

in England at the initiative of Henry VIII (Schlesinger 331), and thereafter became quite literally the instrument of the revived citizen militia ideal.

"Gallant and gay," Maud's song thus belongs to the frank, daylight world of such broadside ballads as "Duke William" (1746) or "Brave Wolfe" (1759) with their vivid retelling of the English victories at Culloden and Quebec[5] rather than to the eerie, mournful realm summoned up by a Border ballad such as "Sir Patrick Spens." In the same way, it is only within the ideological universe of classical republicanism that the "readiness" of the soldiers ("Ready in heart and ready in hand" [I:170]) can ever be a matter of genuine praise, for only citizen-soldiers are free to choose to fight — medieval fighting men, by contrast, having been stripped of such voluntary agency either by their oaths of fealty or by their pay as mercenaries.

Viewed against the background of classical republican assumptions, Maud's song thus becomes the voice ("Not her, not her, but a voice" [I:189]) of the archaic martial ethos that undergirds, as we have seen, the reciprocity and interdependence of polity and citizen at the deepest level of Western political experience. Taking Maud as its mouthpiece,

---

5. Cf. the second stanza of "Duke William":

> Our Soldiers so brave,
> With rage being fired,
> Had what they desired,
> With the rebels to fight;
> For they never would flinch,
> Nor give back an inch,
> Till they made them fly,
> For noble Duke William,
> For noble Duke William,
> They'll conquer or die.
>
> (Palmer 52)

The third son of George II, William Augustus, duke of Cumberland, destroyed the Highlander forces of the Jacobite pretender to the throne, Charles Stuart ("Bonnie Prince Charlie"), at Culloden on 16 April 1746, thereby ending the threat to Hanoverian rule. Cumberland had taken pains to train the English troops to withstand the extraordinary ferocity of the Highlanders' onslaught, which had been the key to their earlier victories in England. His own savage reprisals at Culloden would earn him the nickname "the Butcher."

this ancient ethos speaks to the narrator "an air that is known to me," and this responsive substrate of martial consciousness within him, once touched, continues to reverberate throughout the rest of the poem. At first paining him with the contrast between its "glory" (I:183) and his own languor and baseness (I:179), then rousing him to less self-centered and self-exculpatory thoughts (I:382–97), this ancient martial mentality finally moves the young man to the selflessness of enlisting to fight for the *patria* ("I have felt with my native land, I am one with my kind" [III:58]).

In this context, the speaker's concluding hope that, with the onset of war, the "glory of manhood" will "stand on his ancient height" (III:21) must be identified, not merely with some local anxiety about sex or gender in the twentieth-century sense, but with *virtus* or *aretē*. For that complex of martial and civic excellences will now be restored to a site that is "ancient" in the sense of "former" as well as in the sense of "extremely old," at least as old as Tennyson's source for this image in the early fifth-century B.C.E. Greek poet Simonides:

> There is one story
> that Virtue [*aretē*, feminine noun] has her dwelling place above
>   rock walls hard to climb
>
>   . . . . .
>
> and she is not to be looked upon by the eyes of every mortal,
> only by one who with sweat, with clenched concentration
> and courage, climbs to the peak [*akron* = the highest point or
>   height]
>
> (Lattimore 55)

—lines Tennyson himself had copied into a volume in 1851 as the motto for his laureateship (Francis 123).

Even to glance through Tennyson's *Maud* is to see how deeply the categories of classical republican or Country-party ideology supply at each crucial juncture of the poem materials for the speaker's impassioned critique of commercial modernity. For such famous party rallying cries as the "paper credit" of Davenant and Pope, the "oriental despotism" of Trenchard and Gordon, the "master-miss" and "effeminacy" of Pulteney and Brown still may be heard resounding within Tennyson's poem, from the "vast speculation" that drives the speaker's ruined father to suicide, to Maud's "Sultan" brother who would marry her to a rich suitor, to the monied suitor himself, a "wanton, dissolute" and, in an earlier version of the poem, "effeminate" boy (I:387). The speaker himself, so shrunken by isolation, poverty, and misanthropy as to have become a bitterly inarticulate monad of Mandevillian egoism and Ricardian self-interest ("A wounded thing with a rancorous cry" [I:363]), can find a vocabulary with which to arraign the age for its monstrous selfishness only because he can still recall the classical republican language of commonality with its ideal of the *xūnon esthlon*, here called "the public good" (II:283).

At the same time, however, a fundamental tension persists throughout the poem between this ancient "voice" of martial citizenship and its modern incarnation in Maud, the beautiful young girl who opens to the speaker a private world of intimacy, sympathy, and erotic bliss so much more genuine and intensely real to him ("I have led her home, my love, my only friend. / There is none like her, none" [I:599–600]), as we are likely to believe, than any counterworld of the res publica summoned up by bugle and fife. The symptoms of an underlying tension or instability of values in both *Maud* and "Charge of the Light Brigade" thus reveal the degree to which the classical republican ideal of martial and civic "virtue" by the middle of the nineteenth century belonged to a discourse no longer answering to any lived historical reality.

Thus, as the equation of martial and civic competence at its core proved ever less relevant to the emergent modernity signaled by Coleridge's "Commercial System," the language of classical republicanism becomes so obviously reduced, as in *Maud*, to the status of a merely critical language, useful in sounding a certain sort of civic alarm but now only residually or intermittently capable of enunciating a positive ideal. For though such isolated and anomalous moments as "Charge of the Light Brigade" might for an instant restore its urgency, its power to comprehend the historical process had long since been negated by that "spirit which the ancients did not recognize," as Coleridge had long ago called it, "namely the Spirit of Commerce" (149). In this sense Macaulay's brilliant insight into the martial reality underlying and shaping Greek political ideals ("to be butchered on the smoking ruins of their city, to be dragged in chains") achieves its superb clarity precisely because it comes at the *end* of the historical stage of which it speaks, and hence can see it whole.

❦

Yet the sense of civic danger or crisis so evident in Tennyson's Crimean War poems would remain at the center of Victorian intellectual consciousness, giving us the corresponding sense in which Victorian liberalism would arise as the project of mastering the crisis through an alternative system of thought or discourse adequate to the bewilderments of modernity in its unending social transformations. The great representative figure in this enterprise is, as we have always recognized, John Stuart Mill. Deeply responsive to the critique of commercial society developed by Adam Smith and Adam Ferguson in the Scottish Enlightenment, and powerfully influenced as well by Alexis de Tocqueville's analysis of democratic polities, Mill's writings give us, as John Burrow and Stefan Collini have so suggestively conveyed, something like the precise moment when English cultural analysis would turn away from an ethical perspective and toward a sociological one. For an account of Hellenism and homosexuality in Victorian Oxford, the crucial point lies in the way Mill's liberalism takes over the insight of such theorists as Smith and Ferguson into the dialectical nature of historical progress — that civilization must produce, as the very price of its advance, uncivilizing effects that in their turn retard or undermine the very civilization that had produced the progress.

The great difficulty Mill confronted was thus to reassert the genuine progressiveness of human progress, in the face of its regressive consequences in the nineteenth century, by recovering some compensatory power to offset or overcome those regressive effects. To find Mill in this posture regarding progress and social modernity is to see him once again as what he acknowledged he was — Coleridge's intellectual heir as much as Jeremy Bentham's. For by the 1850s as Mill prepared to write *On Liberty*, his enormously influential analysis of social and industrial modernity, he found himself in the position Coleridge had earlier occupied in the *Lay Sermon* of 1817 — searching for a "counterpoise", indeed, Mill will borrow the very word, to the excesses of the "Commercial System."

At the same time, the situation of such Victorian liberal intellectuals as Mill had become much more difficult by the 1850s, because now there could be no more appeal to the counterpoise of the Church or religious belief of the sort Newman and the Tractarians had once raised. For by the 1850s it had become clear that at a deep and unsuspected level of cultural formation, religion itself was contributing to the problem of commercial modernity, not to its solution. From the Ritualist movement that was succeeding to the place of Tractarianism within the Anglican church to the Dissenting sects outside the Church so mindlessly agitated by the battle against "popery," the apparent resurgence of Victorian religious belief was providing a convenient screen for the demigod of respectability and the goddess of getting-on, whose worship was resulting, as Mill warned in *On Liberty*, in "a low, abject, servile type of character" (256). This character was, for Mill, precisely the reverse of the psychic and intellectual qualities now so urgently needed: that ideal of a rich individuality, as John Burrow has described it, "nurtured by free exposure to 'variety of experience' and diverse modes of life, issuing in an independence of mind and spirit which Mill presents both as the goal of individual human self-development and the guarantee of future social progress" (*Whigs* 81).

By contrast, the most regressive of the Victorian religious groups — the growing body of fundamentalist believers newly empowered by prosperity and political privilege — were able to impart energy to their money-making activities alone. Everywhere else — in science, in art, in society — the pinched and hidebound Calvinist character Matthew Arnold was to call Philistinism, and Dickens would depict under a myriad of fictional guises as the deadliest enemy to joy, sought to inhibit and constrain energy, wherever it could not utterly crush it as the irrefutable evidence of evil human self-will.

The stultifying effect of this narrow religious character, in turn, was being intensified and extended by other consequences of industrial modernity. From the civil servant's craven self-effacement within a torpid bureaucracy, to the silent assimilation of "different ranks, different neighbourhoods, different trades and professions" (274) into the stupefying homogeneities of mass society, to the invasive psychosocial regimentation imposed by the burgeoning movements intent on the improvement of morals, the new conditions bred of industrial modernity were generating forces, as Mill believed, that would eventually crush out the independence and free creative powers of the gifted individual. It was precisely these qualities which were so necessary, in his view, to the further development of society as a whole. In an economic order increasingly determined by ideas rather than material resources or physical power, any deficit or stagnation in intellectual force must inevitably assume a great and ominous significance for Britain's future. Presided over by men and women too fearful "of doing 'what nobody does,' or of not doing 'what everybody does'" (270), the nation would lose its way, as Mill warned, unless individuals "of another stamp" arose to prevent its decline (272).

At this point in Mill's cultural analysis of modernity he resorts to a vocabulary of "Chinese stationariness" and "stagnation" to express his anxious sense of sociocultural crisis. For with the massive change in underlying historiographical paradigms which had begun to gather force in the later eighteenth century came a shift away from the cyclical model of history so central to classical republican thought, with its recurrent rise and fall of polities as each in its turn plays out the four-act Polybian drama of virtue, luxury, corruption, and ruin — and toward the model of progressive linearism, with its story of a single, cumulative ascent from barbarism to enlightenment. With this paradigm shift, in turn, must come a correlative shift away from the old explanatory categories of classical republican discourse — "virtue" "effeminacy" "corruption" — toward a conceptual idiom that is, as Burrow has so persuasively described in *Whigs and Liberals*, only residually civic humanist if indeed it is at all — the idiom of "stagnation" and "stationariness" and "uniformity."

Mill thus grasped with a clairvoyance born of genius and reading Tocqueville what Kingsley was constitutionally unable to see — that in an age when Britain's gravest danger lay in the weakness of its ideas rather than its defenses, the nation's central excellence — its *aretē* — could no longer be vested in any simply martial or muscular notion of "manliness." In the same way, Mill grasped through the medium of rational discourse what Tennyson was able to intuit only through the incomparably sensitive instrument of his poetry — that the old conceptual categories made available through classical republicanism were emptying and thinning out, slipping away from the new formations being raised throughout mid-Victorian culture by the forces of commercial and industrial modernity.

As soon as the crisis Mill identified in mid-Victorian Britain was perceived by his contemporaries as centering in the spread of social and intellectual "stagnation" and "uniformity," and no longer in civic "corruption," the compensatory excellence needed to oppose it could no longer be located in simple "manliness" but must be looked for in something like "energy" and "individuality" and "diversity." As soon as the residually Calvinist religious fundamentalism — what Mill now termed "this narrow theory of life" (256) and Newman had earlier called the "shallow and narrow system, that Protestant philosophy" — could no longer be restored to civic usefulness as a counterpoise to modernity by a simple resurgence of religious faith, there must be found elsewhere an alternative, secular ideal, and a conceptual language through which to express it. This positive ideal and conceptual language Mill and other Victorian liberals discovered in Hellenism.

A fierce struggle of antagonistic or competing discourses thus underlies the emergence of Hellenism as a major element in Victorian culture. For the burden assumed by Victorian liberalism was not merely that of inventing some alternative discourse adequate to the complexities of the modern age, but also of demonstrating, through the very form of its own discourse, why the great heritage of classical republican thought was no longer relevant to the modern world. The solution of Mill, Grote, Arnold, and other liberals would be precisely to counterpose to the Graeco-Roman model of classical republicanism its own image of a far different Greece, to challenge the authority of the classical republican model of the recurrent rise and fall of polities by insisting on Attic or Athenian Greece as the earliest embodiment of an enlightened rational progressiveness, the very engine of all subsequent Western advance. Without the momentous 150-year interval of high Athenian civilization, declared Mill as he reviewed Grote's *History of Greece*, the work that so massively transformed the Victorians' view of Athens, there would have been no other source "from which freedom and intellectual cultivation could have come, any other means by which the light never since extinguished might have been kindled" ("Grote II" 313).

Yet as the epigraph Mill chose for *On Liberty* — "the absolute and

essential importance of human development in its richest diversity"
(215) — would always suggest, Mill's Hellenic ideal represented no direct recovery of an ancient model so much as the powerfully mediated
version of Greece produced by eighteenth-century German Hellenism.
Behind this epigraph to *On Liberty*, which Mill is borrowing from
Wilhelm von Humboldt's essay on the powers of government, lies the
enormously rich idea of *Bildung* — of autonomous self-cultivation directed toward the end of a fully rounded and harmonious development
of individual human potentiality — as it had been elucidated and en-
larged for over fifty years by J. J. Winckelmann, J. G. Herder, Goethe,
Schiller, Humboldt, and a score of others. Thus what Stefan Collini has
called the distinctively Millian note of "variety, not uniformity" ("Introduction" lii) will always be heard to ring most immediately with echoes
of a German *Kultur*, *Bildung*, and *Vielseitigkeit* (many-sidedness).

This German reinterpretation of Greece is in turn why the words of
Pericles' Funeral Oration, to which Grote and Mill were both wont to
appeal as the authorizing text for their ideal of Hellenism, would come
to assume this particular aspect of "variety not uniformity" only during
the later nineteenth century, after the influence of Germano-Hellenism
had been diffused throughout Victorian literary culture. For the knotty
Greek shorthand of Thucydides' account of the Periclean oration admits
of many interpretative readings, and the word *eutrapelōs* (2.41.1), which
such Victorian translators as Benjamin Jowett and Henry Dale, working
by the light of liberal Hellenism, would render as "with versatility" or
"versatile," had earlier been translated in a far less positive sense. When
Samuel Bloomfield had translated the passage in 1828, for instance, his
version clearly suggested that the flexibility or suppleness of character
which Pericles so praised in the Athenians as *eutrapelōs* might to an
Englishman writing thirteen years after Waterloo in fact resemble
nothing so much as the volatility and perfidy of the French (Bloomfield
1:383n).

Only now, looking back on the founding moment of Victorian liberalism and Victorian Hellenism from a historical standpoint well beyond
them, can we grasp the justice of Isaiah Berlin's observation that "variety as a positive value is a new idea. . . . Some think that Pericles said
something of this kind in his famous Funeral Speech. He came close to it

but does not reach it" (53). For the Hellenic ideal Mill and Grote found in fifth-century Athens, that "picture of generous tolerance towards social dissent, and spontaneity of individual taste, which we read in the speech of the Athenian statesman" ("Grote II" 320), and all Mill meant by "variety not uniformity" and "human development in its richest diversity" belong preeminently to the midcentury moment of the Victorian sociocultural crisis. Only then, during the anxious transition when culture, as Pocock has noted, finally replaced property as the qualifying characteristic of the civic elite, did the Funeral Oration of Pericles come to be ranked among the sacred writings of Western civilization (500).

Within Mill's call for a new ideal of individuality and diversity, for a modern-day Hellenism encompassing such elements as "pagan self-assertion," "nonconformity," "freedom," and "variety of situations," there may already be glimpsed the outlines of a late-Victorian counter-discourse of sensuous diversity and homosexual dissent. Yet a more immediate question arises: on what basis could the new discourse of liberal Hellenism, unmartial, aesthetic, and inward-turning as it seemed to be, engage the allegiance of a Victorian civic elite whose instinctive psychosocial responses had been, as we have seen, so deeply molded by the martial, arms-bearing traditions of classical republicanism and Country-party ideology?

The answer in turn is that Victorian Hellenism could supplement, and in time come so largely to supplant, the older republican ideal of martial and civic *virtus* because at the deepest level of its own discursive genealogy it encompassed a position understood to be no less martial and essential to the polity: civic diversity. The doctrine of civic diversity, brought to something like classic formulation by Machiavelli during the "nightmare of degradation and imminent ruin" (de Grazia 16) imposed on Florence in 1494 by Charles VIII's invading mercenary armies, referred to two crucial centers of concern: first, to the variety of citizens inhabiting a polity. For it was only this "diversità de' cittadini," as Machiavelli said (*Discorsi* 3:9), which would allow the polity to adapt to the changing circumstances imposed by fortune — producing a bold general like Scipio or a temporizing one like Fabius as the occasion might require. Second, there needed to be a variety of talents within the individual citizen, for only this "anima ad omnia versatilia," as the character was described in Leonardo Bruni's *De Militia* (Bayley 199), could so easily shift from civilian to military roles and back again as to preserve the polity not only from its external enemies but also from subjection at the hands of the mercenary army it would otherwise have to employ for its own defense.

When the notion of civic diversity is relocated within German and later Victorian liberal Hellenism, this underlying martial dimension to diversity and versatility, even as they both are being deployed in a larger campaign against the psychic fragmentation and cultural stagnation produced by social and industrial modernity, continues on a buried level of psychocultural implication to impart a public and civic orientation to a Hellenism that might otherwise seem to be entirely private and aesthetic. Seamlessly meshing with the native emphasis on diversity within both the English tradition of religious Dissent and the newer discourse of biological or Darwinistic evolution, the diversity ideal within Victorian Hellenism thus allows Hellenism silently to fulfill one of the central sociopolitical functions of the fading older discourse of classical republicanism. At the same time, Hellenism is explicitly embraced by such liberals as Mill and Matthew Arnold as the solution to the problems raised by industrial modernity, which classical republicanism can now no longer grasp.[6]

Viewed against this background of the Victorian liberals' argument for Hellenism as the means of rescuing England from the uniformity and stagnation of industrial modernity, the Oxford university-reform movement of the 1850s and 1860s thus becomes visible as the translation of that abstract or theoretical argument into specific curricular or institutional terms. For the whole effort of the reformers was to reintegrate Oxford into the national life, "opening the University to the nation and

---

6. The classic account of Arnold's Hellenism is DeLaura, *Hebrew and Hellene*, which gives a particularly full and nuanced account of Arnold's debt to Humboldt and German Hellenism generally (see esp. 181–91). For Arnold's rigorous suppression of Mill's deep influence upon him, see Super's edition of Arnold, *Culture and Anarchy*, in *Prose Works*.

to the world," as Mark Pattison was to declare in an influential statement of the reformers' goal, "allowing the full and entire play of free
competition in instruction" which would, as he said, "increase our
power and elasticity" (*Report* 44). Critics outside Oxford called for the
admission of more poor students and, for the first time, of non-Anglicans
as the best ways of breaking up the intellectually desolating regime of
snobbery and extravagance encouraged by the traditional predominance within Oxford's undergraduate body of orthodox and aristocratic
elements.

In the same way, critics inside Oxford urged toughening undergraduate curricular requirements, and opening the competition for college
fellowships to all candidates, rather than just the descendants of the
founder's kin or residents of a specific county or graduates of a certain
school or whatever else might be specified by the college statutes. Such
changes as these, the liberal reformers declared, were the way to spread
throughout the institutionally crucial echelon of college fellows the
intellectual vibrancy and comprehensiveness of mind which had hitherto prevailed at scarcely more than two colleges: Oriel and Balliol. So
pervasive did the liberal vocabulary of energy versus stagnation become
that one Victorian, surveying the long struggle for Oxford reform in
1869, was to use Mill's language without any sense of its ideological
innovativeness as he recounted the story of "a stagnant and aimless
University [that] has been shaken out of its torpor and inspired with new
hopes and a new life" (Fyffe 187).

By contrast, the Tractarian movement of the 1830s and 1840s now
seemed to the academic liberals like a temporary and incomprehensible
episode, a passage verging on institutional nightmare in the larger life of
Oxford. "It seemed incredible," as Pattison was to recall in mock amazement, "that we had been spending years in debating any matter so flimsy
as whether England was in a state of schism or no" (*Memoirs* 123). Once
the hurricane of Tractarianism had blown itself out and the all-absorb-
ing vortex of its exclusively theological concerns had dispersed, broader,
fresher intellectual currents flooded in from the Continent and especially from Germany: B. G. Niebuhr, Hegel, Comte, Ferdinand Baur.
Much of the new and invigorating intellectual atmosphere at Oxford, as
one graduate remarked, was due to Thomas Arnold and his Rugby

pupils, much of it to the introduction of new books and the general advance of knowledge. But no less influential than these, he noted, were "the genius and energy of a living professor, and the interest in German literature which he has awakened" (Fyffe 185). This man was Benjamin Jowett.

Jowett's role as an agent of revolutionary change at Oxford, especially as that change was to flow through the Greats curriculum, can scarcely be overestimated. First exerting a politic but insistent pressure during the lull after the Tractarian storm, he was able to shift the curricular bias of Greats both away from Latin and toward Greek, and away from the narrowly grammatical emphasis in reading ancient texts and toward a powerfully engaged mode of reading which insisted on the vivid contemporaneity and philosophical depth of these works. At Jowett's initiative, Francis Bacon's *Novum Organon* and Plato's *Republic* were incorporated into the Greats curriculum. More important, he contributed, perhaps more than anyone else at Oxford, to that larger intellectual movement within Victorian Hellenism that Frank Turner has analyzed so extensively, by which Greek studies became a vehicle for channeling modern progressive thought into the Victorian civic elite. For Jowett's own study and teaching of Hegel would open the way to the widely influential philosophical and civic idealism of T. H. Green among others later in the century.

The great danger posed by such studies would always be their excessively solvent, even destabilizing effects on the religious faith of Oxford men, as Jowett himself recognized from the first. "When I was an undergraduate," as he wrote an intimate friend, "almost all teaching leaned to the support of doctrines of authority." With university reform, however, had come a revolution in Oxford's teaching of metaphysics through the new reading list in Greats: Bacon, Locke, Mill's *Logic*, Plato, Aristotle, and the history of ancient philosophy. "See how impossible," Jowett declared, "this makes a return to the old doctrines of authority" (Campbell 412).

Convinced by the German critical and historicist movements that all such attempts as the Tractarians' to revive the old doctrines of clerical and theological authority ran futilely against the irresistible tide of modern thought, Jowett came to believe that "if religion is to be saved at all it must be through the laity and statesmen, &c., not through the clergy" (150). Long before his own persecution as a clergyman for heresy during the *Essays and Reviews* controversy of 1860–62, Jowett was to perceive that the center of institutional gravity at Oxford was shifting, in A. J. Engel's phrase, from clergyman to don. "One need [not] look upon one's occupation as gone" because the older, transcendental role of the clergy was being undermined by history, science, and the clergy's own failures, as Jowett told his friend: "It is in reality a higher work that opens, trying to make the laity act up to and feel their own religious principles" (Campbell 150). This higher work was Jowett's intellectual ministry to the civic elite at Oxford, his "pastoral supervision . . . of young thinkers" (203).

To guarantee that this work genuinely was "higher," Jowett and the other Oxford reformers half-unconsciously turned to a source of legitimation near to hand, the very attempt of the Tractarians to resacralize Oxford as the seminary of a spiritually renewed English clergy. The Tractarians were considered disloyal religious fanatics, discredited by their series of defections to Roman Catholicism. Yet the Tractarian vision of an Oxford able to provide an England demoralized by secular materialism and commercial modernity with a class of spiritual leaders — men whose very claim to leadership lay in their communication with a transcendental realm of spiritual purpose — had nonetheless survived. It lived on in the institutional forms developed at Oxford by the Tractarians themselves: the college tutorial, the college friendship as an intense "communion of souls," and the belief in "personality" as a force in the living and bodily communication of knowledge.

This appropriation of Tractarian forms is why Jowett and Pattison in their testimony to the Royal Commission investigating Oxford in 1850 both would so vigorously defend the college system as it centered in the tutorial: because its central emphasis on "the personal influence of mind upon mind," as Pattison would say, "the mind of the fully instructed upon the young mind it seeks to form" (*Memoirs* 133), translated to the level of "the practical ideal" (Campbell 142) the moral legitimacy of Newman's tutorial cure of souls. In turn, this process of appropriation is why Dean Church would so immediately perceive how directly the Oxford liberals had become the heirs of Newman and Hurrell Froude, succeeding "where the Tractarians had failed, in becoming the masters and reformers of Oxford" (337).

The great effect of the university liberals' move to reappropriate these institutional structures and attitudes, originally molded by Tractarianism to channel an intense male homosociality toward religious ends, would be to recenter them instead upon Greek studies, a secular, indeed "pagan," body of thought now regarded within Victorian liberalism as uniquely valuable because capable of regenerating an English society threatened by uniformity and stagnation. Yet in the very intensity of these male relationships coming into being in Jowett's Oxford, as we have seen, are felt the claims of a mode of feeling for which neither the older discourse of classical republicanism nor the newer discourse of Victorian liberalism has a vocabulary.

For though Victorian liberalism has begun to supplant such categories of the older discourse as "effeminacy" which had previously set rigid limits, albeit in an incidental or unintended way, on any positive cultural response to the notion of masculine love, the newer liberal discourse remains in itself silent on such issues. Yet both in the specific program of Greek studies shaped by Jowett and the Oxford reformers and in the diversity ideal more generally diffused by Victorian Hellenism there lies a possibility undreamt of by Victorian liberals: the legitimation of love between men. In this context such late-Victorian writers as Pater, Symonds, and Wilde, urged by Victorian liberalism to save the English polity by taking Greek history and philosophy seriously, will begin to glimpse in Plato's defense of transcendental, "Uranian" love a vocabulary adequate to their own inmost hopes, and to see in "Greek love" itself the promise of a Hellenic individuality and diversity with the most positive implications for Victorian civilization.

THE SOCRATIC EROS

Those whose procreancy is of the body turn to woman as the object of
their love, and raise a family, in the blessed hope that by doing so they
will keep their memory green. . . . But those whose procreancy is of the
spirit rather than of the flesh — and they are not unknown, Socrates —
conceive and bear the things of the spirit. And what are they? you ask.
Wisdom and all her sister virtues.

— Plato, *Symposium* 209a, 4th century B.C.E.

Preparing for a reading assignment in Plato's *Apology* during his final
year at Harrow, J. A. Symonds "stumbled upon" two other dialogues,
the *Phaedrus* and the *Symposium*. The accident transformed his life.
"Here in the *Phaedrus* and the *Symposium*," as he was to recall thirty
years later, "I discovered the true *liber amoris* at last, the revelation I had
been waiting for" (*Memoirs* 99). Symonds, who had earlier been both a
witness to appalling scenes of the rankest schoolboy sex as well as a
queasy recipient of unwelcome caresses from his headmaster, now realized that the erotic dream of ideal male love which he had cherished
since early boyhood remained untainted by the brutalities of contemporary Harrow: "It was just as though the voice of my own soul spoke to me
through Plato, as though in some antenatal experience I had lived the
life of [a] philosophical Greek lover" (99).

The full power of Plato's "book of love," however, would not become
clear until Symonds reached Oxford. For it was only there that the
Platonic works that solaced and inspired him as a private revelation
would stand forth as essential texts within the public, curricular heart of
Oxford — in *Literae humaniores* or Greats, the course of classical studies

which drew not only a majority of Oxford undergraduates but by universal admission the larger proportion of the ablest men as well.[1]

To grasp the full dimensions of the political and pedagogical change
that had thrust Plato's works into the center of Oxford teaching and
study we need only recall J. S. Mill's indignant remark of 1834 that "of
the young men who have obtained university honours during the last
ten years, we are much misinformed if there be six who had even looked
into his writings" ("*Protagoras*" 39–40). From this unpromising beginning among scattered and idiosyncratic students was to grow a broad
cadre of Platonic partisans, some of them like Mill operating outside
academic life, others such as F. D. Maurice at King's College, London,
and William Johnson at Eton working to spread Plato's thought from
within.[2]

At Oxford, as we have seen, it was Benjamin Jowett who set the stage
for the curricular predominance of Plato. As a young tutor in the late
1840s, he introduced lectures on the *Republic* at Balliol, where for earlier
tutors in Greek philosophy, as one student recalled, "the *Ethics* and the
Rhetoric of Aristotle had been all in all" (Campbell 132). Jowett's
innovation then became official policy within the university as a whole:
when the reformed Oxford examination system went into effect in 1853,
Plato's *Republic* joined Aristotle's *Ethics* as one of the set texts for
examination.

The great significance of Jowett's innovation, however, would always
have to do with the way Plato functioned within the machinery of the
improved curriculum as a metaphysical basis for the liberalism of the

1. Fyffe (188n) estimates that during the years 1865–68, some 55 percent of
undergraduates reading for an honors degree (roughly one-third of the total) were
enrolled in the Greats school, the other "schools" or courses of study and examination at
Oxford during this time consisting of Modern History, Mathematics, and Natural Science. In the 1880s one observer would characterize the Greats school as "the chief of the
Oxford Honour Schools. For a classical man, a first-class in it is still the crowning
distinction in his career, without which even the most brilliant series of scholarships and
prizes is incomplete; and although the University has now, for many years, granted its
honours in other than classical subjects, the fact remains that, by universal admission, the
larger proportion of the ablest men every year seek their honours in the old school"
(Wells 244).

2. Cf. Mill's remark in the early version of his *Autobiography*: "I have ever felt myself,
beyond any modern that I know of except my father and perhaps beyond even him, a

Oxford reformers. As Jowett and Pattison maneuvered against their conservative clerical opponents at Oxford, they held up a specifically Greek ideal — the belief "that the mind can become an end to itself," as Pattison would express this faith in a famous university sermon, "that it can propose to itself its own perfection as a work to be wrought out by its own effort, that mental illumination is an illumination within the soul" ("Sermon V" 125). It remains a minor irony of their search for legitimating authority that Jowett and the Oxford liberals were deploying a transcendental Plato which the clerical party had once mobilized in its own defense.

Yet when such Tractarian fellow-travelers as William Sewell had earlier invoked Platonic philosophy against the partisans, as Sewell had so derisively called them, "of sensualism in philosophy, of expediency in morals, of scepticism in reason, and of rationalism in religion" (Turner 375), they regarded Plato simply as a supplemental source of transcendental authority. To these conservative clerics Plato was useful in combating such enemies as the Utilitarians, who were roundly unimpressed by either Church or Scripture, but he was in no sense essential to their larger enterprise of Christian apologetics. To religious liberals such as Jowett, by contrast, Plato became central and indispensable.

For as Jowett surveyed the future of religious belief in the nineteenth century, he became convinced that the great danger to English faith would come not from rationalism or atheism per se, but from the quieter rejection by serious people of "the truth itself, when stated in grotesque and impossible forms" (Campbell 260). Reading widely in both contemporary German philosophy and biblical criticism, Jowett knew the German that J. H. Newman never learned, the German that would have vastly altered the fortunes of the Church of England, as A. P. Stanley once remarked to Pattison, had Newman only been able to read it.[3]

---

pupil of Plato, and cast in the mould of his dialectics" (24); and Maurice's in a letter of 5 March 1850: "I have never taken up any dialogue of Plato's without getting more from it than from any book not in the Bible" (152); and Johnson's in his Cambridge prize poem *Plato*: "Others are names — thou art a living friend" (9).

3. Pattison, *Memoirs*: "A. P. Stanley once said to me, 'How different the fortunes of the Church of England might have been if Newman had been able to read German.' That puts the matter in a nut-shell; Newman assumed and adorned the narrow basis on which Laud had stood 200 years before. All the grand development of human reason, from

With German learning and criticism beginning to penetrate beyond advanced intellectual circles into the wider middle-class elite, Jowett saw that it would soon make ridiculous and untenable all such Christian religious truths as had been framed in "grotesque and impossible forms," by which he meant the impossible evangelical literalism in interpreting Scripture and what seemed to him the pious frauds and grotesque dogmatic encrustations maintained by popular religious hysteria.

In this context Jowett's double career as Broad Church priest and theologian on the one hand, and professor of Greek and translator of Plato on the other, dramatically resolves, as Frank Turner has argued, into a single focus. For Plato on Jowett's terms was to serve as a surrogate to the Christianity that could be neither defended on the old dogmatic basis nor yet safely questioned in the light of modern thought, especially during the 1850s when even to be known as having read Hegel or Lessing or Schleiermacher could fatally compromise a clerical reputation at Oxford with the damning taint of "Germanism."[4]

Attacked and officially humiliated for his contribution to *Essays and Reviews* (1860), a controversial collection of "Germanizing" theological speculation, Jowett turned in the years after 1860 from theological to philosophical questions, leaving Saint Paul for Plato without ever abandoning the search for transcendental truth. As he told a crowded audience for his lectures on the *Republic* at this time, he wished "to examine what I may call *the greatest uninspired writing*" (Campbell 241). Out of these lectures, attended by men both inside and outside Balliol, would grow the famous translation of the *Dialogues* (1871, 1875, 1892) which would spread Plato's reputation as well as his translator's far beyond the precincts of Oxford.

Aristotle down to Hegel, was a sealed book to him. There lay a unity, a unity of all thought, which far transcended the mere mechanical association of the unthinking members of the Catholic Church; a great spiritual unity, by the side of which all sects and denominations shrink into vanity" (111–12).

4. Cf. Campbell: "That [Jowett] had read Lessing and Schleiermacher, and had studied Hegel, could not but be known to the younger men, and less than this was enough to compromise a clerical reputation in the early fifties" (211). Neither Jowett's actual pronouncements nor his practice as a historicist interpreter were ever as "Germanizing" — as skeptical and relativist — as his enemies maintained. See Matthew, and Hinchliff, chapter 6. Inevitably, however, in the contentious atmosphere of the 1860s Jowett was largely understood on his enemies' terms and not on his own.

To the intrinsic stress within Plato's works upon a transcendental realm of truth beyond the flux of mortal reality — what *Phaedrus* 247c calls the "colourless and formless and intangible essence and only reality . . . visible to the mind alone" (Jowett trans. 2:124) — Jowett would impart a decisive new emphasis. Both in his lectures and in the long interpretative introductions with which he prefaced the individual dialogues, he repeatedly sought to naturalize and make vitally relevant the unfamiliar or alien turns of Platonic thought by presenting them in terms of Christian and English parallels. Jowett summarized Diotima's famous speech about the philosophy of love [*ta erōtika*] in *Symposium* 202–12, for example, by offering a host of religious and literary analogues. So suggestive did Jowett's enhanced version of the philosophic eros become that Oscar Wilde would later copy this passage into his Oxford commonplace book:

> As the Christian might speak of hungering and thirsting after righteousness; or of divine loves under the figure of human (cp. Eph. v. 32: 'This is a great mystery, but I speak concerning Christ and the church'); as the mediaeval saint might speak of the 'fruitio Dei'; as Dante saw all things contained in his love of Beatrice, so Plato would have us absorb all other loves and desires in the love of knowledge. (Jowett trans. 2:18)

In the same way, Jowett was to write and rewrite his translations of the *Dialogues* until virtually all the various Platonic speakers, from Socrates to Aristophanes to Charmides, seem to be speaking in the recognizable accents — so reassuring to Victorian readers — of the Authorized Version of the Bible (Turner 415).

Once Plato's *Republic* had been established at the center of the Greats curriculum as the guarantee that the Oxford liberals had not turned aside from the pursuit of transcendental truth, Jowett could in turn appeal to this "*greatest uninspired writing*" as evidence that his plans for transforming Oxford into a school for national and imperial leaders were similarly disinterested. Assiduous in arranging for Indian and Home Civil Service candidates, as well as foreign students, to be educated at Balliol, Jowett in later years sought to bring army cadets to the college on similar terms. Many liberal reformers at Oxford had insisted on the urgent need to bring the university into the larger life of the nation — to free it, as Goldwin Smith declared in a representative polemic, from those "pestilential coils of party in which the University has lain for three disastrous centuries, choked, paralyzed, isolated from the nation" (20). It would be Jowett's distinction, however, to seek to bring the nation into the university — recruiting, reforming, and funneling ambitious plebeians and energetic peers alike into that civic elite of laity and statesmen whom he trusted, as we have seen, to take over the work of the English clergy.

Nor did Jowett's ambition for an Oxford-trained elite pause at the nation's boundaries. "I should like to govern the world through my pupils," he once jested to Florence Nightingale, (R. Symonds 24), and by the end of the century Jowett's sally was scarcely an exaggeration. From Cecil Rhodes (Oriel) and Alfred Milner (Balliol) of Africa to George Curzon (Balliol) of India and C. H. Pearson (Oriel) of Australia, men from Jowett's college and university had come to preponderate in decisive posts throughout the empire. If the classical parallel which rose most frequently in the minds of such imperial proconsuls was that of Rome, the alternative imperial model supplied by the Greek colonial experience in Sicily, as Richard Jenkyns has noted, was never remote, and the pervasive ethos of Oxford Hellenism returns in force whenever we encounter, for example, Cecil Rhodes confiding that he traversed the South African veldt in the company of both Marcus Aurelius and *Marius the Epicurean* (Ross, "Brand" 41).

Constituting a quasi-Platonic set of guardians at home and abroad, such men as Rhodes and Curzon were able to communicate through precisely the lingua franca of Literae humaniores which George Grote's brother John had earlier envisioned when he called classical study "a point of intellectual sympathy among men over a considerable surface of the world" and a "bond of intellectual communion among civilized men" (Turner 4). Oxford graduates prospered from the civil service connections first established at Balliol by Jowett, not least of all because Jowett managed to arrange that classical studies would count for more points on the civil service exam than other subjects.

The most immediate problem posed by the Greats school to Jowett was thus how to teach the Platonic and other classical texts in such a way as to make them genuinely bear upon "the practical ideal" and the larger sphere of British civic and imperial affairs. Such a goal demanded that Jowett break decisively with the venerable Oxford pedagogical tradition in lectures and tutorials that involved, as Pattison described his own dreary experience in the 1830s, "the class construing, in turns, some twenty lines of a classical text to the tutor, who corrected you when you were wrong." This exercise was not in itself wholly unintellectual, except that, as Pattison noted with dry contempt, "this one exercise was about the whole of what our teachers ever attempted to do for us" (Memoirs 44).

Such a remark provides the larger context for Sydney Smith's wry calculation that by the age of eighteen the average English youth matriculating at either ancient university had produced some ten thousand lines of Latin verse alone, the equivalent of the Aeneid in sheer volume though in nothing else (47). It was precisely the dead weight of this narrowly grammatical and rhetorical training which Jowett sought to dislodge at Oxford by opening up to his pupils the full range of philosophical and historical implication within the Greats texts, and allowing the best Continental thought and scholarship to play upon them. "In the place of the bare interpretation of the letter," as one of these students was to recall, "it seemed as if every aspiration of the new world" filled the matter of ancient Greece and Rome with "the life-giving breath of Continental thought" (Fyffe 189, 188).

To see Jowett at work channeling the reanimating streams of Continental thought upon the honors school of Literae humaniores in the interest of English civil life, however, is to recognize that his educational project involved two quite different approaches to the past which would have great and unanticipated consequences for Oxford Hellenism. For the historical study of Greece which Jowett so massively influenced embraced both an ethically centered providentialism and an ethically relativizing historicism. With the first insisting on the extraordinary value and relevance of the Greek achievement for the English, while the second was minimizing the relevance of English moral categories for the Greeks, such students of Oxford Hellenism as Symonds and Pater and Wilde would find that Greek paiderastia was, through the agency of the Greats curriculum, brought vividly and compellingly to life even as English religious prohibitions on sodomy were simultaneously being made to recede.

Deriving in part from his reading of Hegel, Jowett's providentialist approach to the past drew at its deepest level upon the English tradition Duncan Forbes has called Liberal Anglican historiography. Through this mode of idealist historical analysis, a recurrent historical pattern of national growth, maturity, and decline was shown to be exempt from its otherwise obvious determinism by being incorporated on a higher level as the unfolding, providential plan of a benignant deity (65–66). Within this Liberal Anglican analysis, a series of discontinuous Viconian cycles operated to align certain parallel phases of human history — here Victorian liberals pointed to fifth-century Athens and nineteenth-century England — revealing them in their exact and vital similitude. This living historical identity between a specific past and a specific present in turn gave to certain ancient writers — usually Thucydides and Plato were named — their extraordinary power to speak as truly living contemporaries to the English, offering them, as Thomas Arnold said of Thucydides, "a wisdom more applicable to us politically than the wisdom even of our own countrymen who lived in the middle ages" ("Social" 325–26).

Dr. Arnold's thrilling lectures as professor of modern history — "no other races remain behind to perform what we have neglected or to restore what we have ruined" ("Inaugural" 31) — first opened this providentialist view of history to the great mass of Oxford undergraduates in the early 1840s. Jowett's lectures and more especially his introductions to the *Dialogues* may in turn be said to conclude it. Throughout both, Jowett's deep sense of Plato's undying philosophical power — "he is fresh and blooming, and is always begetting new ideas in the minds of men" (Abbott 406) — would express in compelling terms the present significance of the Greek past to the Victorians, doing so even at the occasional cost of misrepresenting that past. Of this cost the salient example for any account of late-Victorian homosexuality would always be Jowett's imperturbable transposition of Plato's remarks about the Greek love of boys to Victorian men's love of women: "We may raise the same question in another form," as Jowett said of the specifically homoerotic questions raised in the *Phaedrus*, "Is marriage preferable with or without love?" (Jowett trans. 2:89).

Against this ethical and present-oriented thrust in Jowett's teaching of Plato, however, there strained the powerfully relativizing force of a largely German scientific historicism. Jowett's enthusiasm for the Tübingen school of Ferdinand Baur and Eduard Zeller and the work of such German students of Greece as K. O. Müller, Ludwig Preller, and Ernst Curtius prompted him to introduce these writers to his Balliol pupils as they read for Greats. With the sharpening of academic competition which followed the reforms of the 1850 Oxford University commission, Jowett's extraordinary success in guiding his pupils both to the highest honors in the Greats examination and to such other glittering prizes as Oxford college fellowships meant that his methods and reading materials became widely influential. German historicist scholarship on Greece became in this way current among the most intellectually ambitious Oxford undergraduates and their tutors, for whom the Balliol model continuously operated as a standard.

Intent on recovering a sense of the past as it actually was — Ranke's famous ideal of *wie es eigentlich gewesen ist*—the German historicist approach insisted on viewing the past in its own terms and in its own widest context — encompassing art, mythology, religion, race, archaeology — while declining to hold past stages of history accountable to the moral assumptions of a later day. With regard to ancient Greece, the great example of this ethically detached historicist view was K. O. Müller's account in *Die Dorier* (*The History and Antiquities of the Doric Race*, 1830) of Greek *paiderastia* which began with Müller's announcement that he would include no ethical censure of it — "eine ethische Kritik scheint gar nicht hieher zu gehören" (3:290). Müller's calmly neutral view of paiderastia would then reappear in Jowett's introductions to the *Phaedrus* and the *Symposium*, where the hitherto obligatory phrases of English moral condemnation — "the most degrading passion," "the greatest evil of Greek life" (Jowett trans. 2:20) — arise only to be tempered by Jowett's incomparable suavity and disinterested views.

The attitude of objective detachment encouraged by the German historiographical revolution was powerfully reinforced, in turn, by the deliberate "Socraticism" encouraged by Jowett, in which Plato's dialogues supplied not simply the object of study but the inspiration for the spirit in which such study was to be conducted. This is the famous Socratic or skeptical Plato first put forward in George Grote's *History of Greece* (1846–6) and in J. S. Mill's various discussions of Greece. If as Turner has argued, Jowett strongly resisted the Utilitarian strain in

Grote's account, there can be no question but that Jowett's own essentially Hegelian view of Plato as "always moving onwards" because
convinced "that truth is greater than consistency" (Abbott 406) was
regarded by many conservative Victorians as approving skepticism in no
lesser degree than did the radical Grote himself. Even Jowett's liberal
partisans felt the solvent effect of his evasive subtlety of thought —
Symonds, for example, admitting that Jowett "gave a sceptical and
sophistical direction to those pupils who accepted his ways of dealing
with problems" (*Memoirs* 226).

Plato's method of dialectic — "that of close discussion between two
persons, one of whom interrogates, and the other answers" (Mill, "*Protagoras*" 44) — was for Grote and Mill the best mode of teaching, an ideal
contrivance, as Mill calls it in *On Liberty*, "for making the difficulties of
the question as present to the learner's consciousness, as if they were
pressed upon him by a dissentient champion, eager for his conversion"
(251). At Oxford the college tutorial system Jowett and Pattison had
appropriated from the Tractarians and reoriented toward the transcendental secular end of "mental illumination" became, as Pattison told the
Royal commissioners, "the nearest approach we make to the Socratic
principle of education" (*Report* 48). Jowett's conduct as tutor was uni-
versally regarded as "Socratic" in some degree, ranging from Symonds's
affectionate memory of a specific occasion when Jowett, pouring tea,
had exclaimed, "like Socrates — 'Now I will give you some tea, O my
good friend'" (*Letters* 1:274) to G. C. Brodrick's far more comprehensive
estimate that Jowett's "greatest skill consisted, like that of Socrates, in
helping us to learn and think for ourselves" (Faber, *Jowett* 167).

Yet the darker, subversive dimension to Jowett's and, more generally,
to all tutorial Socraticism would always be the fatal character of Socrates
as a "corrupter of youth." In the aftermath of the conservative clerical
challenge to Jowett's religious orthodoxy which made him such a hero to
undergraduates during 1860–63, this darker Socratic character was
never to be far from the foreboding imaginations of many at Oxford.
Even Brodrick himself, a political ally of Jowett's, did not absolutely
reject the notion that Jowett may have deliberately instilled theological
doubt into his pupils, while the judgment of Richard St. John Tyrwhitt,
as voiced by a character in his novelistic memoir *Hugh Heron, Christ*

Church (1880), would express a deep mistrust of all such tutors who "take pleasure in unsettling lads' minds, and think they were like Socrates whenever they succeeded in that" (166).

This sense that wholly secular, even pagan standards were coming to substitute at Oxford for Christian religious assumptions, and that Jowett, "like Socrates," was centrally responsible for the change, angered and oppressed many religiously minded undergraduates. "Jowler preached yesterday in Chapel . . . the most lovely little practical sermon," reported one of them, adding, "It was just Platonism flavoured with a little Christian charity: Christianity is gutted by him," and concluding, "I admire the Symposium with all my heart and soul; but I must have something more to have brought God down to death to procure for me" (Paget 33, 34). For such other undergraduates as Symonds and Pater, however, Jowett and the Greats curriculum he had reformed by introducing Plato's *Republic*, and reading it in its full context with the *Symposium*, the *Phaedrus*, and the other dialogues, brought an extraordinary intellectual and emotional liberation, for it made available to them a revolutionarily new Plato, and a Plato, moreover, now enshrined at the institutional heart of elite Victorian values.

Symonds and Pater came into possession of this liberating new Plato at a time during the 1860s when the transcendental and providential claims made for the Hellenic world were being widely urged within the larger Victorian culture. This was the moment when Socrates, as Jenkyns has reminded us, was becoming for Matthew Arnold in *Culture and Anarchy* a kind of Holy Spirit ("in his own breast does not every man carry . . . a possible Socrates?") and serving for J. S. Mill in *On Liberty* as a kind of Christ (Jenkyns 230, 231). When W. E. Gladstone addressed the students of Edinburgh University in his rectorial address of 1865, he proposed to them that "the solid and fruitful materials of the Greek civilisation came in aid, by a wise Providence, of the restorative principles, precepts, and powers of the Gospel, to take part in securing a well-balanced development of the powers of the Christian system" (86). Gladstone was particularly devoted to Homer; he prized the purity and nobility of the Homeric world precisely because it had escaped "those shameless lusts, which formed the incredible and indelible disgrace of Greece," by which he meant the paiderastic eros of Plato and Pausanias (62).

At the same time, Gladstone's own insistence that Greek philosophy had quite properly asserted "the place of the Body in human education" and "the right of the body to be cared for, and to be reared in its various organs up to the highest excellence it is capable of attaining" as being, "like the soul, an integral part of man himself" (74–75), was boldly valorizing bodily beauty and power under the aegis of Christian theories of the Incarnation. This emphasis on the place and the right of the body would help to prepare Victorian readers for Pater's later meditations on the "beauty of the *palaestra*" and the "worship of the body" in *The Renaissance* (166, 4). In the same way, Gladstone's theory of a double revelation — Hellenic *and* Hebraic — by which Hellenism had rescued early Christianity from its one-sidedness and ascetic repressions was simultaneously working to validate the liberal argument of Mill and Matthew Arnold: that Hebraism without Hellenism was insufficient; that other ethics, as Mill urged, "must exist side by side with Christian ethics to produce the moral regeneration of mankind" (*Liberty* 257).

In this context, the specific effect of the continuous translation of Christian into Hellenic terms at Oxford was to bypass the ancient religious objections to homosexual behavior — now seen as a matter of faith or taboo fading along with the older and insufficient notions of Christian orthodoxy and ethics — and to situate the problem of masculine love on grounds as secular as the aims of the Oxford reformers themselves. Jowett's "practical ideal" of a civic elite serving the nation and empire, and Pattison's transcendent ideal of the "culture of the intellect for its own sake" both substituted for Christian theology a Platonic ideality as a ground of transcendence, a displacement that would simultaneously relocate masculine love within the realm of secular questions or values, out of the reach of religious objections and taboos.

At the same time as it puts the love of men beyond the reach of religious objections as such, Oxford Hellenism gives to writers like Symonds and Pater a powerful means of answering what had always been the most telling secular objections to masculine love: that classical republican language of debility and "effeminacy" we have examined in earlier chapters. For the German-inspired revolution in the historiography of ancient Greece reveals that paiderastia was martial in origin, closely related to that inspiring warrior ideal with which the classical republican tradition had always identified the health or survival of the polity.

Müller's *Dorians* now allows its Victorian readers to see that "Greek love was," as Symonds was repeatedly to proclaim in *A Problem in Greek Ethics* and *Studies of the Greek Poets*, "in its origin and essence, military. . . . nor had *Malachia*, effeminacy, a place in its vocabulary" (*Greek Ethics* 8). Suddenly the whole idiom of "effeminacy" can be turned on its head, and male love triumphantly proclaimed the very fountain of civic health in a polity that has been urged to take as its cultural model the ancient city-state of Athens. Symonds's "manly" Greek lovers with their erotic "chivalry" and martial "comrade-love" were constantly to reappear in the homosexual apologist writings of the years to come.[5]

At one level, then, Oxford Hellenism provides the means of undermining the whole vast accretion of negative associations with male love which had remained strong through the beginning of the nineteenth century. On another level, the revisionary Greek ideal lying at the center of Oxford Hellenism could be presented as the purest model of Victorian liberalism itself. For the liberalism of the Oxford reformers, as we have seen, and of their allies at the national level, had proposed in urgent terms that England could be saved from the stagnation and uniformity born of democratizing and industrial modernity only through

5. Symonds's characteristic themes, for instance, are taken up and disseminated in the works of Edward Carpenter (1844–1929), as when Carpenter quotes from *A Problem in Greek Ethics* in the Manchester lecture he later published as "Homogenic Love" (1894). Matriculating at Cambridge, Carpenter developed into a homosexual apologist along the earnest, enthusiastic, and activist lines characteristic of that university, although he was no less dependent on the ideal of the Socratic eros so central to the Oxford writers treated here. Compare, for example, "Homogenic Love": "just as the ordinary sex-love should have its special function in the propagation of the race, so the other love should have its special function in social and heroic work, and in the generation — not of bodily children — but of those children of the mind, the philosophical conceptions and ideals which transform our lives and those of society" (343). For Carpenter's work as a homosexual activist, see Weeks, and Lauritsen and Thorstad.

new ideas. Only through the "play of thought" and "spontaneity of consciousness" Matthew Arnold was calling Hellenism, or through the "pagan self-assertion" John Sterling had described in an 1838 essay that deeply influenced both Mill and Arnold, could the English learn in time "how we may come to understand the faculties we are to work with, and the rules to which their operation ought to be subjected" (Sterling 100).

Pointing to the Renaissance, the Enlightenment, and the Goethe-zeit — the three periods in the European past of the widest intellectual freedom and the most intense productive activity, epochs to which "every single improvement which has taken place either in the human mind or in institutions may be traced" — Mill warned that the stimulative impulses from these three periods had ebbed away and by the middle of the nineteenth century were all but exhausted in Britain. Without some new liberating impulse, without some new source of intellectual energy through which Victorians could "again assert our mental freedom," as Mill declared, "we can expect no fresh start" (*Liberty* 243).

This is precisely the context in which such writers as Symonds and Pater would come to assert, in all seriousness, that the Socratic eros was essential to the survival of liberal England. For this erotic bond represented to them a pure form of intellectual procreancy and regeneration, the two men insisting on the truth and genuine Victorian relevance of Plato's famous teaching in *Symposium* 209 that at the highest level of masculine love, men who love men are procreating *ideas* — generating the creative arts, philosophy, "wisdom and all her sister virtues," especially that kind of wisdom "which governs the ordering of society" (Hamilton and Cairns ed. 560).

Yet the notion of a masculine "procreancy . . . of the spirit" — "en tais psychais kuousin" — (560), as Symonds and Pater both realized, did not merely derive from the writings of Plato. It had already assumed a living reality, as they saw, in the pedagogic institutions of a reformed Oxford. For whenever an Oxford pupil speaks, as we have heard Symonds and others say of Jowett, of the growth of his "soul" or of the powers "created" in him by a tutor's teaching, the Platonic vocabulary of "souls" and "creation" declares how fully Plato and the ancient and modern philosophy of the Greats curriculum have already come to shape the terms in which Oxford life is understood by those living it in the 1860s.

At the same time, it is precisely here that the reformed institutions of Oxford homosociality — that reciprocal network or system of bonds facilitating the interchange of masculine affection, interest, advantage, and obligation — will become in the same moment available to such apologists of male love as Symonds and Pater. For the philosophic or intellectual transcendentalism that the Oxford reformers had located in Plato, and substituted for the transcendental religious truth once defining the Tractarian tutorial, could be extended, as Pater and Symonds both immediately saw, to the ideal education of the Platonic or Socratic doctrine of eros. This model of love — by which an older man, moved to love by the visible beauty of a younger man, and desirous of winning immortality through that love, undertakes the younger man's education in virtue and wisdom (*Symposium* 209–11) — could be recaptured within the existing structures of Oxford homosociality: the intense friendship, the tutorial, the essay society.

Giving us something like the first textual exploration of this new scope for masculine love opened within Oxford institutional forms by liberal Hellenism is the early essay by Pater known as "Diaphaneitè" (1864). Written for the Oxford essay society Old Mortality, to which Pater and Symonds both belonged, the essay at once describes and addresses another member of the society, Charles Lancelot Shadwell (Monsman, "Old" 386). Shadwell, to whom Pater would later dedicate *The Renaissance*, was the younger man by a year, and had first been Pater's private pupil before becoming his most intimate Oxford friend (Seiler 223). As a matriculant of Christ Church, the most aristocratic of the Oxford colleges, Shadwell inhabited a social sphere widely different from that of Pater, a slum doctor's son who had won an exhibition or scholarship to a much less brilliant college, Queen's. Meeting Shadwell many years after this time, A. C. Benson would find him "a clever, handsome, *disagreeable* man" and conclude that Shadwell was "vain, I think, demanding homage" (Seiler 255). "Diaphaneitè" is an instance of that homage, an almost classical paean to a beautiful youth by an older admirer. It was Shadwell who preserved the paper, transcribing it in his own hand (Inman, *Reading-1* 74), and publishing it after Pater's death "with some hesitation" (Shadwell 1), so relatively crude and unnuanced is Pater's writing there.

It is, however, precisely this stylistic baldness which lays bare the central emphasis of "Diaphaneitè." So far as the paper is, in Richard Dellamora's useful suggestion, a response to a set topic or question (62), the essay undertakes to describe the kind of human character which will accomplish the "regeneration" or revolution of society ("Diaphaneitè" 254): this figure is the crystalline or diaphanous, one so naturally perfected that its simple being in the world accomplishes more for the world than all the hectic activity of such other, more usual revolutionaries as the artist and the saint.

Yet the paper, read aloud at a specific meeting of Old Mortality in July 1864, pursues its description with an acute sense of the concrete existence and virtual presence of the character being described — "this nature," "the character before us," "the nature here indicated" — and does so with a dazzled awareness that the outward bodily appearance of the crystalline character, corresponding to its inward nature, is one of great beauty. The comparisons Pater resorts to in describing the figure are those of the painter Raphael, statues of Greek gods, and Charlotte Corday as described by Thomas Carlyle ("cruel-lovely, with half-angelic, half-daemonic splendour" [253]).[6]

6. This theme of high beauty endowing its possessor with an overweening sense of personal worth, authorizing in turn a demand for erotic servility from others, was to persist with Pater even to his unfinished novel *Gaston de Latour* (1888–94). In that work, especially in chapter 10 ("Anteros"), Gaston, a "trim, discreet, almost priestly scholar," becomes conscious of "the question (of a kind seductive for the thoughtful) in what exact proportions a cool, grave, self-possessed intelligence might coexist with the physical throb of youth" (Monsman, "Unpublished Chapters" 287). Here Gaston finds himself at the court of Marguerite of Valois, surrounded by the flower of virginal youth summoned from all corners of the nation: "They swarmed here, those luscious heavy-petalled blossoms, those momentarily beautiful faces, lips, eyes, with your own eyes on which you might forget, or desire to forget, all beside" (285). The parallel with the charged atmosphere and pulse of youth in Pater's Oxford, with its thrice-yearly flux and reflux of poignant young faces, is striking: "You seemed to expect, to have known something of them before they came; after a few minutes' intercourse, to have known them always. They filled a place made ready for them by the books, the pictures, the very fashions of the day — nay more than filled it, they superseded all this daringly. And might this be perhaps the fulfilment of Gaston's early boyish dreams [of some great passion] awaiting him here — somewhere among these faces, pathetic, appealing, in spite of their pride, passing so constantly about him by day, and at night fixed steadily upon the dark wall of the brain?" (286).

Changing at times abruptly, the tone of the paper shifts with a sort of *odi et amo* alternation between praise for the radiant transparency of the diaphanous character and a countervailing desire that its brilliant beauty might somehow be hidden or sacrificed, as when Pater says that in a "crisis, where it must needs be that some human victim be sent down into the grave," the crystalline man would be the one "whom in its profound emotion humanity might choose to send" (253). Half-enthralled, half-resistant, Pater veils his ambivalence in the Greek word he uses to define the crystal man's sense of his own worth — *khlidē* — a word he translates as "pride of life" (252) but which in Plato carries darker connotations of "delicacy," "luxury," and "effeminacy."

In the same way, the raw materials of Pater's essay — the Platonic vocabulary of *khlidē* and *philosophēsas pote met' erōtos*, the allusions and references to such contemporary Victorian writers as Mill and Carlyle — imperfectly subordinated to a larger design as they are, reveal Pater's effort to carry out the mission of Jowett's Greats curriculum or, indeed, even surpass it. For Pater wants to bring the ancient world and the modern world fruitfully to bear on one another by confronting modern "professors" who "often strive in vain to form" the culture and the character of young men (251) — as, in 1864, Professors Jowett and Matthew Arnold were both striving to do at Oxford — face to face with that "forgotten culture that once adorned the mind" (250). This is the culture of someone who is "philosophēsas pote met' erōtos" — or "lover and philosopher at once," as Pater would translate the phrase (*Renaissance* 155) — by definition, then, the ancient Greek culture of Plato and paiderastia.

To see Pater's "Diaphaneitè" in the paiderastic tradition of Greece is to recognize that the very occasion of his essay — read aloud to a listener who is its subject within a symposiumlike scene of all-male sociability, refreshment, and philosophic discourse — allows Pater not simply to invoke the forgotten culture of the *Symposium* but to enact it as well. For Pater is here taking up the Platonic lover's pedagogical role, the role which, among the Dorians, as he knew from K. O. Müller, was that of the *eispnēlās* or "inspirer" who addresses his *aitās* or "hearer" — "the elder inspiring the younger," as Pater would describe the relation years later in *Plato and Platonism*, "with his own strength and noble taste in things" (232).

Seen in the context of such other politically liberal undergraduate essay societies as the Cambridge Apostles of Tennyson and A. H. Hallam or the Decade of Matthew Arnold and A. H. Clough, the Old Mortality society of Pater and Symonds, T. H. Green and James Bryce thus stands forth as a two-handed engine of cultural transformation by which liberal influences are to be introjected into the larger society, as Christopher Harvie has so illuminatingly described, as well as into Tory Oxford itself. The language of this transforming influence would always be that of the Oxford intellectual elite: the discursive vocabulary of the Greats course with its intermixture of Plato, Hegel, and J. S. Mill, that procreant combination Pater's essay adopts when it joins the "forgotten culture" of philosophic love to the cultural anxieties of *On Liberty*. Pater thus allows his "hearer" to understand that precisely the answer to Millian fears about the "regeneration of the world" or about "our collective life" sinking "to the level of a colourless uninteresting existence" ("Diaphaneitè" 252) may indeed mean returning to the Platonic eros, as to "a relic from the classical age, laid open by accident to our alien modern atmosphere" (251)—Pater's central image for cultural renaissance to which he would constantly recur.

Sharing in Pater's sense of a dawning moment of extraordinary cultural expansion and possibility, Symonds, writing in an 1863 prize essay, had already read enough Michelet and Burckhardt to be able to declare that the Renaissance itself began when the Aristotle of the medieval schoolmen yielded his place to Plato, whose "sublime guesses and far-reaching speculations suited the spirit of the awakening age" (*Renaissance* 47). On the most obvious level, one readily apprehensible to themselves, Pater and Symonds are both participating in the moment when the full mission of the reformed Greats curriculum was being carried out in the spirit of Mill's ringing dictum in *On Liberty*—that one's first duty as a thinker is "to follow his intellect to whatever conclusions it may lead" (242). Pater and Symonds are quietly determined to do nothing less than follow Mill's notion of a culturally reinvigorating liberty of opinion and experience to its boldest conclusion: a "liberty of the heart," as Pater was to call it in *The Renaissance* (3), so free as to encompass even male love.[7] If Mill himself, as John

7. Pater knew Mill's work well, as is revealed by his remark to a pupil preparing for

Burrow has noted, "seems scarcely aware" of the threat to moral rigor contained in such extrapolations of his ideas by his disciples (*Whigs* 95), he is yet fully cognizant that such liberal young thinkers as those in Old Mortality were already making a difference in the nation's intellectual life: "free enquiry and speculation on the deepest and highest questions, instead of being crushed or deadened," as Mill declared in a letter of 1863, "are now more rife there [at Oxford and Cambridge] than almost anywhere else in England" (Collini, "Introduction" lii).

On a less obvious level, however, one that would become clear only years later, after the moment itself had passed, Pater and Symonds and the other members of Old Mortality were taking part in the unique moment of Oxford masculine comradeship, a window or halcyon interval of particularly intense male homosociality which flourished between the first two waves of university reform: beginning after the 1854 reforms threw open the competition for college fellowships and expanded the number of nonclerical fellowships — so that graduates like Pater could stay on to teach at Oxford without taking Anglican orders — and concluding with the reforms of the 1877 Oxford commission, taking effect in 1884, which, in abolishing the celibacy requirement for fellows, ended the ethos of a wholly male residential society.[8]

This period in the communal life of Oxford would in later years be recalled with great tenderness by the men who had experienced it either as undergraduates or as dons. The marriage of fellows, as E. A. Freeman was to declare in 1887, had effectively destroyed the older notion of college life as "a society, a brotherhood, of men living a common life,

---

the Greats examination: "the great thing is to read authors *whole*; read Plato *whole*; read Kant *whole*; read Mill *whole*" (A. C. Benson 194). Mill's *System of Logic* (1843) became a set text in the Greats curriculum after the collapse of Tractarianism in 1845 and reigned there into the 1880s. Pater gained a second class in Greats in 1862, when Symonds won the best First of the year.

8. Lady Margaret and Somerville were founded in 1879 as residential halls for women who were auditing Oxford lectures. Like the equivalent institutions founded for poorer men, such halls were held to be disablingly remote from the authentic life of the university, which, according to the conventional view, took place exclusively within its colleges. The permission to marry which was made available en masse to college fellows in 1884 (for some individual permissions had been granted earlier) began the process of weakening the male homosocial college bond which would be continued by the gradual admission of women to the lectures, schools, degrees, and colleges of Oxford.

and having many things in common" (615). Even the liberal reformer Goldwin Smith would recognize on his return to Oxford in 1886 that with the reform of celibacy "something had been lost," the "old, close, corporate feeling, the old, intimate comradeship of men and boys . . . weakened" (Mallet 3:348n). So indelibly distinct did the Oxford ethos of the 1860s and earlier 1870s come to seem in retrospect that George Saintsbury, meditating upon a biography of Pater written by the Cambridge don A. C. Benson, would conclude that not only could no Cambridge man understand Pater in his formative moment, but no Oxford man could either who had not been bred of the same moment — the decisive "interval between the first and second University Commissions," as Saintsbury said, "when the absolute partition wall between the [undergraduate and the don] was being much broken down" (Seiler 263, 265).

It was precisely within this historical window of intense Oxford homosociality that Symonds, as we have earlier seen, could begin to hope for the eventual legitimation of male love. First coming up to Oxford after having "devoured Greek literature and fed upon the reproductions of Greek plastic art" during his revelatory last term at Harrow (*Memoirs* 106), Symonds found himself at Balliol in the autumn of 1858 in a world where perfervid friendships between undergraduates, and to a lesser extent between undergraduates and dons, were commonplace if not quite unremarkable. Taken up by John Conington, Corpus Professor of Latin, Symonds came to full intellectual consciousness in a circumambient atmosphere, as he said, compounded in almost equal parts of boy-love and Literae humaniores (119). Conington, with the gesture that was to become a central literary trope for imaginative initiation among late-Victorian Decadent writers, gave the younger man a book — William Johnson's *Ionica* (1858) — a volume of verse which, as Symonds was to remember, "went straight to my heart and inflamed my imagination" (109).

To read the poems of *Ionica* today is to glimpse the divergent streams of Victorian liberal idealism — patriotic, republican, Hellenic, humanitarian — as they were rising toward convergence in the great Liberal electoral victory of 1868 which would sweep Gladstone into office for the first time as prime minister. To these forces, Johnson, a vigorous intellect, classicist, and master at Eton, had fused a romantic belief in Platonic paiderastia, filling his verses with "the faith," as he had once declared in a private letter, "that my best Fourth-Form are most noble, most generous, most kind — as virtuous as men, without men's pride and knowingness, as interesting as women, without women's timorousness and artifice" (*Letters* 41). Symonds was utterly beguiled by the Arcadian world of friendship and chaste affection which Johnson had so eloquently shaped from brilliant translations of Greek poetry ("I wept, as I remembered, how often you and I / Had tired the sun with talking and sent him down the sky" [*Ionica* 7]) and poignant experiences as a schoolmaster:

> The wonder flushing in the cheek,
>   The questions many a score,
> When I grow eloquent, and speak
>   Of England, and of war —
>   (*Ionica* 27)

He wrote to Johnson at Eton, receiving in reply "a long epistle on paiderastia in modern times, defending it and laying down the principle that affection between people of the same sex is no less natural and rational than the ordinary passionate relations" (*Memoirs* 109).[9]

Yet even as Symonds's own hopes for a wholly spiritual male romance expanded in response to the encouragement of *Ionica* and later of Walt Whitman's "Calamus" poems, he underwent the first countermovements of external repression and inward self-betrayal which would finally so afflict his psychic life that he would at last seek a sexual release from the Platonic imprisonment of a purely intellectual love. Incautiously vesting his confidences, first in Conington, and then in an unscrupulous undergraduate friend named C.G.H. Shorting, Symonds

---

9. Johnson was to leave Eton abruptly in 1872 after what appears to have been a parent's complaint about his overly intimate relationship with a pupil. Upon adopting the family name of Cory, by which he is better known today, Johnson would marry, have a son, and end his days teaching Greek to young women.

became implicated in two extraordinarily painful scandals, the first in 1859–60 involving his former headmaster at Harrow and the second in 1862–63 centering on himself as a probationary fellow at Magdalen. Emerging from them both vindicated only in a technical sense, Symonds was utterly exhausted and oppressed by his experience of the central contradiction within Oxford homosocial Hellenism — its willful denial of the paiderastia so crucial to the Greek culture it otherwise held up to emulation and praise. This desperate anomaly between "2 favourite prejudices that are apt cruelly to jar," as Jeremy Bentham had once described them in an unpublished paper of 1774, "the one in disfavour of this vice [of Greek love], the other in favour of antiquity, especially ancient Greece" (Crompton 290), was one that Symonds would in later years trace to Jowett's pedagogical influence at Oxford.

Yet even during the later 1860s Symonds clearly intuits Jowett's role in helping to construct the crushing contradiction between English law and English education which had already so nearly ruined his own young life in the Magdalen scandal: "My name is soiled with an unbearable suspicion; my usefulness in the college is destroyed, and Oxford is made an impossibility" (*Memoirs* 132). Falsely accused by Shorting of having corrupted Magdalen College choirboys, Symonds was actively and sympathetically succored by Jowett throughout the interminable year of accusation, investigation, and acquittal which ended only with Symonds's complete breakdown in health. Symonds remained grateful for Jowett's help in this crisis. Even to glance, however, at such a poem as *Gabriel* (composed ca. 1868) is to recognize how cruelly equivocal Jowett's Oxford Hellenism was already coming to seem to his former pupil.

Set, much like Pater's late prose tale "Apollo in Picardy" (1893), in a remote monastery whose quiet life is disrupted by the arrival of a handsome, pagan stranger, Symonds's long narrative poem *Gabriel* demands to be read as an allegory of Greek studies at Oxford under Jowett. For if the monks resemble Oxford inmates, in their studies and conversational walks together, the old hermit who restores order at the monastery by ridding it of the handsome interloper unmistakably resembles Jowett — with his "icy eyes" and "bushy penthouse brow / Where Will sat centred in supreme content" (*Gabriel* ll. 329, 335–36).

At the same time, what the poem suggests about the old man is his

own deep involvement with the aesthetic and erotic intoxication represented by the handsome youth, whom the monks name Gabriel but
"who no name in any tongue / Of Christians owned" (ll. 209–10). The
hermit denounces the youth as an "unexorcised demon" to the assem-
bled monks precisely because he himself had once fallen under Gabriel's
power many years before, saving himself only by listening to an inward
voice saying, " 'His life for thine: or thou shalt surely die' " (l. 369).
Having earlier "fought and conquered thee" by tearing away the green
jade belt Gabriel insists on wearing next to his skin, the old man now
strips it away again, killing the youth. As the monks carry the corpse out
of the chapel to an unconsecrated grave, they notice with astonishment
that the visage of this "strange sad youth untimely slain" (l. 404) is
exactly that of the image of the crucified Christ above them: "Like
brother's unto brother" (l. 402). The pagan interloper is not alien after
all.

Still raised only implicitly here, Symonds's reproach to Jowett for
condemning what he had himself loved and, more fatally, had taught
other men to love — the incomparably beautiful world of the Platonic
eros — would be made openly only much later in 1889, after Symonds
had suffered miserably for years trying to live up to the delusive regime of
idealist love demanded by the Socratic doctrine of eros. In the years
immediately following *Gabriel*, by contrast, Symonds would continue to
make the case for the idealized love of comrades, first privately in his
letters and poems and then, in the heady moment of cultural liberaliza-
tion we have glanced at in an earlier chapter, more expansively to a
general public in the two volumes of *Studies of the Greek Poets* (1873,
1876).

The origin of these books recapitulates with a self-conscious symme-
try exactly the claim for a spiritual procreancy between men made by the
Platonic Socrates, for they derive from a series of lectures Symonds
contrived to give at Clifton College in order to be near one of its sixth-
formers, Norman Moor. Moved by the boy's beauty, Symonds decided
"to educate Norman and to stimulate his intellect," and his pupil in turn
exerted a stimulating influence upon the tutor, helping, as Symonds was
to assert in his *Memoirs*, "to emancipate my intellect and will" (196,
194).

This stimulating effect is legible in the first volume of *Studies of the*

Greek Poets, where all the worthies of Oxford liberalism — Mill, Goethe, Hegel, Pericles — are found speaking in the accents of Pater and Swinburne, enunciating a cultural ideal of "variety not uniformity," as when, for example, Symonds declares that "the ideal of Greek life imposed no commonplace conformity to one fixed standard on individuals, but each man was encouraged to complete and realize the type of himself to the utmost" (415). To this cultural ideal of Victorian Hellenism Symonds gives a startlingly vivid incarnation flowing out of his own unstaunched sexual yearnings: "Like a young man newly come from the wrestling-ground, anointed, chapleted, and very calm, the Genius of the Greeks appears before us. Upon his soul there is no burden of the world's pain; the whole creation that groaneth and travaileth together, has touched him with no sense of anguish; nor has he yet felt sin" (399). Here Symonds attempts to make real to his "hearers" and readers the noble ideality of Hellenism with all the concreteness of Greek plastic art, and all the enchanting music of Pater's prose.[10] Precisely here, however, as Symonds's descriptions of Greek sculpture attempt to make visible the statues' shapely limbs, crisp curls, and flowerlike mouths, and as he calls on his audience so imperatively — "we must imitate the Greeks, not by trying to reproduce their modes of life and feeling, but by approximating to their free and fearless attitude of mind" (422n) — does Symonds draw down upon himself the scathing attack of the Oxford conservatives.

Symonds's effusions over Greek sculpture, together with his assertion that "Walt Whitman is more truly Greek than any other man of modern times" (422n), were in early March 1877 to become the focus of Richard St. John Tyrwhitt's attack on "The Greek Spirit in Modern Literature." Published in the *Contemporary Review*, Tyrwhitt's essay, as Richard

---

10. When he was an Oxford undergraduate, Oscar Wilde rated Symonds's prose equal to that of Pater and Ruskin and ("at times") Ouida. Even earlier at Trinity College, Dublin, as one of Wilde's classmates was to recall, Symonds's works "were perpetually in his hands" (Harris 23). In an unpublished MS review of Symonds's 1873 volume *Studies of the Greek Poets* (The Pierpont Morgan Library, New York. MA 3574) quoted here by permission, Wilde urged his readers to read "this eloquent Essay" in its entirety, declaring, "Mr. Gladstone has told us of [Helen's] sorrow and repentance. Mr. Symonds has shown us her beauty." Wilde's unpublished MS review of Symonds's second volume of *Greek Poets* is preserved in the William Andrews Clark Library in Los Angeles.

Dellamora has noted, maintains as its ulterior motive the destruction of Symonds's chances for election to the Oxford Professorship of Poetry. This heated contest, into which Pater as well as Francis Palgrave and W. J. Courthope would be drawn, was a struggle virtually national in scope because all Oxford M.A.'s, resident and nonresident alike, were entitled to vote in it. Although the professorship was a largely ceremonial office at Oxford, ever since Matthew Arnold had held it during 1857–67, and initiated the practice of lecturing in English, it had come to be considered one of great symbolic importance and influence.

Tyrwhitt, who was soon to assault the pretensions of Balliol Hellenism by glorifying forthright, fox-hunting, aristocratic passmen in *Hugh Heron, Christ Church,* now sought to pierce the idealist glamour of Jowett's Platonizing pedagogy with Ithuriel's spear. Like the celebrated cherub of *Paradise Lost,* he wanted to make falsehood assume its real shape so that "Anglo-Hellenism" could be recognized for what he believed it was — a screen for sodomy. "Mr. Symonds is probably the most innocent of men," Tyrwhitt blandly assured his readers, some of whom would know what Tyrwhitt must have known as rector of the Oxford university parish of St. Mary's — that the Magdalen scandal had soiled Symonds's name with an unbearable suspicion of sexual guilt. Advancing onto this "awkward ground," Tyrwhitt now made bold to declare in one of the great Victorian periodicals regularly entering upper-middle-class parlors that the "emotions of Socrates at sight of the beauty of young Charmides. . . . are not natural: and it is well known that Greek love of nature and beauty went frequently against nature" ("Greek" 557).

Tyrwhitt chose to end his attack on Symonds with a long quote from the account of Greek morals given in Jowett's commentary on the Epistles of Saint Paul (1859), where Jowett had declared "there is a great gulf fixed between us and them, which no willingness to make allowance for the difference of ages and countries would enable us to pass" (quoted in "Greek" 565). Yet if Tyrwhitt invokes Jowett here, it is hardly because he wanted, as Dellamora has ventured to suggest, somehow to force Jowett's hand and propel him from an earlier electoral neutrality into an active partisanship — a counterproductive stratagem at best. Instead, Tyrwhitt wished to confront the Reverend Mr. Jowett with the cultural consequences of his own abandonment of theological authority in favor of the merely intellectual mastery represented by Anglo-Hellenism, to force the Master of Balliol to recognize the probable moral consequences of a sophistical and fully "Socratic" pedagogy.

Looking back at such an episode from a perspective shaped by the late twentieth-century struggle over civil rights for homosexuals, it is difficult to realize the devastating force of such relatively innocuous words as Tyrwhitt's. Yet Symonds, though at first attempting to pass off the seriousness of the matter, felt it as a "fierce onslaught," recognized it as "a good party move in the matter of the Professorship" (*Letters* 2:462), and soon realized that his candidature had been dealt a mortal blow. After withdrawing from the contest for the professorship in late May just before the vote was to be taken, Symonds began to reconsider his larger strategy for urging the claims to legitimacy of male love.

With his physical withdrawal from England to Switzerland dictated by his seriously damaged health, and the slow repair of well-being which would be traceable, as he later came to believe, to the beginning of his sexual relations with men, Symonds shifted the focus of his hopes for homosexual legitimation from the broad public he had attempted to persuade in *Greek Poets* to a narrower, specialist public. This was the professional audience of jurists, medical doctors, and psychologists to whom he believed he could speak more openly through the neutral idiom of "science" in *A Problem in Greek Ethics* and *A Problem in Modern Ethics*. Within the circumscribed venue offered by such works, Symonds was to continue his attempt to make Victorian liberalism genuinely confront the radical hope for a wider emotional and erotic liberation — that "liberty of the heart" — so unintentionally yet unmistakably posited within its own advocacy of Hellenism.

The more momentous move toward a genuine radicalization of Victorian liberal assumptions would thus be made by Pater, and would be more momentous, paradoxically, to just the degree Pater chose to conduct his campaign from within the boundaries of Victorian liberal discourse, not posing any open challenge to liberal assumptions as such but devising a "coded" version of liberalism in which its more radical implications became visible to anyone who knew how to read. For Pater

WALTER PATER in 1872,
as drawn by Simeon Solomon.
(Photo used by permission of
the Gabinetto Disegni e
Stampe degli Uffizi, Florence.)

W. H. MALLOCK.
(Photo by permission
of Bettmann/Hulton.)

would throughout a long lifetime of writing demonstrate by his very neutrality and urbanity that he was writing from within the great tradition of humanist thought. Yet his writing would always consist of a daring texture of covert allusions working continuously and unmistakably to demonstrate that the reiterated liberal claims for liberty, individuality, self-development, and diversity as the qualities capable of rescuing England are unintelligible unless viewed within the context of a Socratic eros of men loving men in spiritual procreancy.

Pater's mode is never that of outright statement or even suggestion. It is one, rather, of a constantly beckoning and receding suggestiveness, as homoerotic themes — most often Platonic ones — are constantly either raised to visibility or veiled in their explicitness within the richly various materials of Pater's prose. Thus, for instance, the Platonic-sounding phrase we have already noticed from "Diaphaneitè" — "philosophēsas pote met' erōtos" ("lover and philosopher at once") — is coined by Pater to hold the place of such authentically Platonic but unspeakably explicit phrases as *Phaedrus* 249a: "him who . . . has been a *paiderastēs* with [= in conjunction with] philosophy" (as translated in Dover 165).[11]

Conversely, the curious phrase from Plato's *Symposium* (197d–e) which resurfaces in Pater's early essay on Coleridge as a description of the Greek spirit — Pater speaking of "its engaging naturalness, simple, chastened, debonair, *truphēs, habrotētos, khlidēs, kharitōn, himērou pothou patēr*" ("Coleridge's Writings" 132) — becomes a gesture to those who recognize the origin of the phrase in Plato's description of the paiderastic Eros. For this phrase, which speaks of "the father of delicacy, daintiness, elegance, and grace, of longing and desire" (Hamilton and Cairns ed. 550), signals that Pater, whose own name is veiled in the decent obscurity of the Greek script as *patēr*, also knows the longing and desire within Hellenism, experiencing that desire as the "Sangraal of an endless pilgrimage" ("Coleridge's Writings" 132).[12]

---

11. That Pater is coining rather than quoting from Plato here has been posited by William Shuter in his forthcoming edition of Pater's *Plato and Platonism*. For Pater's "seductive 'beckoning' to a well-disposed audience through a double suggestion," see DeLaura, "Reading Inman" 7–9.

12. It has become a convention in Pater criticism to note that Pater from schoolboy days considered the *Latin* meaning of his unusual name a valuable asset. See, for example, Wright 1:87 and 92–93 and Monsman, *Art, passim*.

To uncover the full homoerotic implicativeness of Pater's writing would thus be to comb the complex surfaces of his prose with an analytical patience and insight at least equivalent to his own deliberate brilliance in its composition. The larger significance of such an undertaking, however, would be to reveal the way in which Pater accepts the transcendent Plato of the Greats curriculum but does so on thoroughly "critical" or historicist terms, allowing his readers to see that the paiderastic dimension to Plato's thought is no mere figure of speech, as Jowett had been wont to maintain, but instead a constitutive element of that thought, and thus of the Western tradition itself. For to recontextualize Plato's work, as Pater would later say, "as far as possible in the group of conditions, intellectual, social, material, amid which it was produced" (*Plato* 9), is to locate it within the paiderastic ethos of ancient Greece, and thus to understand that many a phase of earlier historical experience or speculation which seems "at first sight abnormal" can yet possess "a reasonable meaning for us," much as a "strangely twisted pine-tree, which would be a freak of nature on an English lawn," becomes comprehensible when we imaginatively restore it to its native alpine environment of torrent and storm (10). At any such moment as this, Pater's unspoken but discernible premise will always be that to restore such ostensible anomalies as "abnormal" emotions between men to their native home in ancient Greece is to glimpse such figures no longer as strangely twisted freaks of nature but as natures undeformed.

The crucial text for any account of Pater's tacit recovery of the paiderastic dimension of Western culture thus becomes "Winckelmann," the masterly essay devoted to the eighteenth-century German art historian which concludes the historical sequence of *The Renaissance* with such a striking incongruity. First published in that zealous and influential advocate of the doctrines of the advanced liberal party, the *Westminster Review* in 1867, the essay draws on materials developed even earlier in the Old Mortality paper "Diaphaneitè." Yet its great significance for Pater's larger cultural project is not, as sometimes is said, that there more openly than elsewhere Pater reveals "a certain sympathy with a certain aspect of Greek life," as one Oxford friend constrainedly noted (Jackson 79), or even that there the "latently homosexual circumstances" of Winckelmann's life and death may express a parallel to Pater's own personal desires and fears (Monsman, *Art* 141).

Instead, Pater's "Winckelmann" undertakes to suggest how fully the proudest humanist tradition of Western civilization—that "freedom and intellectual cultivation," as Mill had called it, that "light never since extinguished"—not only had first been kindled at the altar of the paiderastic Eros, but could be reignited, much as Mill had called for, even now at the same ardent flame. This is why Pater shows Winckelmann as a student before all else of Plato. Pater is at pains to insist that Winckelmann's almost divinatory power over the sculpture of the ancient world—so famously enabling him to perceive through the turbid medium of later Roman copies the truer outlines of genuine Hellenic art—flowed directly out of his "enthusiasm . . . in the broad Platonic sense of the *Phaedrus*" (*Renaissance* 152). This is precisely the "enthusiasm" of *Phaedrus* 249d–e, understood in its full etymological force as *entheos*, possession by a god. In the Platonic context of the *Phaedrus* it is specifically possession by the god of love, the paiderastic Eros—"the best of all forms of divine possession," as Socrates says there, "both in itself and in its sources, both for him that has it and for him that shares therein—and when he that loves beauty is touched by such madness [*mania*] he is called a lover" (Hamilton and Cairns ed. 496).

Winckelmann, "the quick, susceptible enthusiast" (*Renaissance* 154), whose romantic, fervent friendships with young men called forth in him sympathies and affinities with Hellenism so receptive as to constitute nothing less than "a new organ for the human spirit" (141), thus emerges for Pater as the ideal representative of cultural renaissance. For on the most obvious level of the actual history of the Renaissance, Winckelmann, "penetrating into the antique world by his passion, his temperament" (176), and then opening out that richly intuited Hellenic world to Goethe as to so many others, reproduces in his own activity the fructifying commerce between past and present—specifically between past "paganism" and the desire for a "more liberal mode of life" (160, 146). This ceaseless recombination of cultural materials is exactly the process Pater has already shown in the earlier essays of the book to have been the underlying dynamic of the Renaissance itself.

On a much less obvious level of historical implication, however, Pater's ambitions in the essay are more radical still. For it is only when we read "Winckelmann" in its original, unrevised form as a contribution to the *Westminster Review* that his project of steadily insisting on Socratic "enthusiasm," on male spiritual procreancy as the hidden engine of cultural repair and regeneration, becomes genuinely clear. Precisely in the sections omitted from the book version of "Winckelmann" does Pater's larger concern for contemporary cultural rebirth — for nothing less than a *Victorian* renaissance — come into view. For as Pater meditates upon the requisite conditions for any "historical revival" ("Winckelmann" 49), and contrasts Winckelmann's authentic classicism with the "artificial classicism" that is the "false tradition of the era of Louis XIV" (49), he allows his *Westminster* readers to see that what is said about genuine and false classicisms is no less true of genuine and false Hellenisms.

On this view, Pater is suggesting to his liberal readers that if the saving Hellenism so eloquently and urgently recommended to them by Mill and Arnold is actually to regenerate Victorian civilization, it too must be divorced from its enfeebled contemporary equivalent. Victorians must reject the facile contemporary Hellenism that prefers the "substituted text to the original" and supposes "that there was some shorter way of reaching and commanding this manner than a knowledge of the vital laws" of Hellenic culture (49). In short, they must take their Hellenism in a truly Hellenic spirit, setting aside the craven modern version that so consistently bowdlerizes the paiderastic eros from the text of authentic Hellenism and transposes the vital intellectual procreancy of Plato's *Symposium*, as Jowett had so famously done, into the merely carnal fecundity of the Victorian marriage. Through an adroit redirection of syntax, Pater now says to his own age what Winckelmann had once declared to his: "In opposition to that classicism become a platitude, Winckelmann says, the Hellenic manner is the blossom of the Hellenic spirit and culture, that spirit and culture depend on certain conditions, and those conditions are peculiar to a certain age. Reproduce those conditions, attain the actual root, and blossoms may again be produced of a triumphant colour" (49).

"Reproduce those conditions": Pater points not to any exact imitation of the Greek past — an impossible task, in any case, and one habitually dismissed by him with the word "antiquarian" — but to the enlargement of already existing human capacities according to the

manner of the Greeks, the manner that Winckelmann himself had so
signally rediscovered with his swift and vivid "escape from abstract
theory to intuition, to the exercise of sight and touch" (*Renaissance*
147). In this context the project of sensuous intensification — of "gath-
ering all we are into one desperate effort to see and touch" — assumes its
electrifying force in Pater's famous "Conclusion" to *The Renaissance*
(189). There, in that most disturbing and invigorating passage of all his
prose, Pater urges the claims of the aesthetic dimension to life, not as an
abstract theory drained even of its intellectual interest by a pallid and
conventional philosophizing, but at its most fundamental level, as
aisthēsis — sensation in all its sharp immediacy and richest variety: "any
stirring of the senses, strange dyes, strange colours, and curious odours,
or work of the artist's hands, or the face of one's *friend*" (189; my
emphasis).

Pater's startling effacement here of the distinction between art and
life, between the artist's work and the face of one's friend, demands in
turn to be seen within the context of the Platonic pedagogy of the
Symposium. For it is there that Diotima declares, "it is only when he
discerns beauty itself through what makes it *visible* that a man will be
quickened with the true, and not the seeming, virtue," and there that
the heavenly ladder leading to universal beauty and virtue must always
start in the frank and shameless *aisthēsis* of falling "in love with the
beauty of one *individual* body" (Hamilton and Cairns ed., 563 and 561;
my emphases).[13]

This is why the "education" Pater implicitly advances throughout
The Renaissance (xx, 181) must begin in sensuous impressions: "What
we have to do," as Pater tells his readers, "is to be for ever curiously
testing new opinions and courting new impressions" (189). And this is
doubtless why he urges an aesthetic education upon these readers with
such a passionate sense that it represents precisely "our one chance" in
life. For Pater is reacting here less to the shortness of life per se than to

---

13. In this context, the remark of Pater's close friend F. W. Bussell in his funeral
eulogy of Pater assumes a larger significance: "His whole life seemed to me to be . . . an
almost literally exact advance through the stages of admiration in the *Symposium*" (Seiler
180).

the unbearable briefness of *youth*. He is responding to the loss of masculine beauty with a sharp Hellenic grief, later to be matched only by A. E. Housman's lament for that "garland briefer than a girl's" and Lord Henry Wotton's horrifying warning to Dorian Gray, "The pulse of joy that beats in us at twenty, becomes sluggish. Our limbs fail, our senses rot" (Wilde, *Dorian* 24).

If Pater concludes *The Renaissance* by saying that the love of art for its own sake will offer the young men he projects as his audience the most of wisdom and a quickened, multiplied consciousness, it is equally clear that "great passions," "ecstasy and sorrow of love," and "the various forms of enthusiastic activity, disinterested or otherwise" will offer them scarcely less (190). Passion, ecstasy, enthusiasm, love — here the erotic diversity, the spiritual procreancy, and now so provocatively, the sensuous pulsation itself of the paiderastic eros surge forward into view.

This is the moment in which Pater's publication of the "Conclusion" to *The Renaissance* under his own name in 1873 — for the essay had earlier appeared as part of an anonymous review — marks a turning point in the history of Oxford Hellenism and homosociality. For in pursuing his conclusions, in the Millian way, wherever they might lead, and in publishing them as an identifiable fellow and tutor of Brasenose College, Oxford, Pater forced into devastating collision, as was instantly apparent to friend and foe alike, two of the essential legitimating structures of Oxford liberalism: freedom of opinion and the tutorial system.

"I should be faithless to myself and to the beliefs which I hold," as John Wordsworth, a junior colleague at Brasenose, wrote to Pater immediately after publication, if "*as tutor* next in standing to yourself I were to let your book pass without a word." "If you had not reprinted it with your name," he declared, no one could reasonably object. But as Wordsworth and other Oxford conservatives now realized, Pater could safely "stand on your right under the University Tests Act *to teach* and publish whatever you please" (Pater, *Letters* 13–14; my emphases). For the Tests Act of 1871, shepherded by Gladstone after a long and bitter struggle through Commons and Lords, had at a stroke disestablished Anglican teaching (except in divinity) at Oxford and Cambridge by opening all such lay posts as tutorships to men of whatever creed. No longer could Jowett's political and theological enemies attempt to control his unorthodox views by the threat of degradation before the vice-chancellor. Now, however, the question must arise of what would be the consequences of such a vastly expanded pedagogical freedom for Oxford liberalism itself.

Already during the autumn immediately following publication of Pater's book, the Rev. Mr. W. W. Capes, Pater's own former tutor at Queen's, was warning dons and undergraduates that the Hellenizing men of the Renaissance had indeed trained "their many-sided powers, and varied fitfully their moods of passion" but that such *Vielseitigkeit* had only left their country "deeper sunk in the mire of national degradation" (Inman, *Reading-1* 329). By spring of 1875 the bishop of Oxford would urgently press his clergy, so many of whom were still directly involved in teaching at the university, to speak up for Christian beliefs because an abyss of skepticism and infidelity had opened at their feet. "Can you wonder," the bishop demanded after quoting from Pater's "Conclusion," that many Oxford fathers now "refuse to let their sons imbibe lessons so alien from the lore they themselves learned?" (Inman, *Reading-2* 154).

Ordinarily such conservative clerical reactions might be dismissed by liberal opponents as altogether predictable partisan rant. By early 1874, however, it had already become apparent to at least a handful of liberals at Balliol that the darker implications of Pater's call for sensuous intensification and a new "liberty of the heart" were being realized in fact. For at about this time, these Balliol men learned — probably by means of the informal "system of espionage," maintained in the interest of moral supervision by the university authorities, and conducted largely by college servants (*Report* 83) — that Pater was romantically involved with a nineteen-year-old Balliol undergraduate named William Money Hardinge.

The details of this long suppressed episode, recently recovered through the work of Richard Ellmann and B. A. Inman, remain obscure, but Hardinge appears to have been a young man who enjoyed shocking others not only with ideas and poems about, in the words of one undergraduate friend, "*unnatural* profligacy," but also with his actions. Hardinge, as this friend continued, "confesses to lying in another man's arms kissing him" and to "*having been found doing it, as there is the* strongest evidence to prove," as well as exchanging letters "in wh. they

address one another as 'darling' & sign themselves 'yours lovingly,' "
with verses "written from one man to another too vile to blot this
paper." If "Hardinge had not yet irretrievably committed himself with
Pater," his friend declared, this did not mean "that a criminal act, if not
committed already, may not be committed any day" (Inman, "Estrangement" 6–8).

Only the most fugitive rumors of this long-suppressed and still shad-
owy episode have survived until now to suggest that Pater may have
enacted as well as inculcated the Socratic eros.[14] Pater was Tutor of
Brasenose, with a set of college rooms painted primrose which he kept
for life. There he would conduct tutorials for the men of his own college
as well as for such extramural pupils as G. M. Hopkins of Balliol. For
Pater was known to be so knowledgeable about the German philosophy
necessary for success in the Greats exam that Jowett and other dons had
taken to referring pupils to him for private coaching. Now at the peak of
his literary celebrity, with a dangerous glamour of skepticism and "advanced views" hovering about him, Pater encouraged unorthodoxy in
the young — "Pater talking two hours against Xtianity," as Hopkins
noted in his journal (138) — for he was deeply sympathetic to them, and
all but worshiped their high spirits and bodily beauty. "They are like
playful young tigers, that have been fed," Edmund Gosse (270) would
report him as saying.

At the same time, Pater as tutor "had no sort of desire to be a master

14. This episode, it would appear, is the one Robert Ross was alluding to in a 1906
review of A. C. Benson's life of Pater. Ross, seducer of Wilde and keeper of many sexual
secrets, found it necessary to deny, without elaboration, an assertion made by Benson
concerning Pater's experience of passion: "Mr. Benson is careful to insist on the diver-
gence between Rossetti and Pater, and on page eighty-six says something which is
ludicrously untrue" ("Mr. Benson's 'Pater'" 133). This is what Benson had said in his
biography: "the innermost world of mystical passion in which Rossetti lived was as a
locked and darkened chamber to Pater. . . . the heated atmosphere of passion being
foreign and almost antipathetic . . . the physical ardours of love, the longing for enam-
oured passion, with this Pater had nothing in common" (86). Himself an adept in chaste
male affection, Benson found the task of writing Pater's biography difficult and at times
antipathetic. Recent research into Benson's diary now suggests, however, that Benson
had not been in complete possession of the available facts when he asserted that Pater was
a stranger to physical passion. For a fuller treatment of this matter, see Brake.

or a leader," as A. C. Benson (25) would declare in a phrase implicitly contrasting Pater to Jowett, the Master of Balliol.[15] The Balliol model of tutorial relations was even now beginning to calcify into a fixed pursuit of good "classes" in the "schools": "Come up to Balliol," Hardinge himself would report Jowett as saying to prospective and promising pupils, "and go in for a prize" (174). Pater, by contrast, seems to have been persuaded that an education conducted along the old lines of Greek paiderastia — of an older man "inspiring" a younger "hearer" with "his own strength and noble taste in things" — would genuinely fulfill the liberal ideal of education. Whether or not he tutored Hardinge, Pater's feeling for the "slender and willowy undergraduate" (Raffalovich, "Giles" 25) soon intensified into passionate relations. Yet as it did so, it inevitably imparted a wholly unanticipated and intolerable new meaning to the tutorial ideal established by J. H. Newman when he had described the college tutor as performing the "living and bodily communication of knowledge."

The great significance of the Pater-Hardinge affair for any account of Oxford Hellenism and homosexuality thus becomes on one level its threat to the institutional and political legitimacy established by the university liberals, and grounded by them in the transcendental authority of philosophical thought, especially the thought of Plato. Precisely this legitimacy would be utterly discredited if "Socratic" tutors were suddenly revealed as having been enabled through a Millian liberty of opinion to "corrupt" Oxford youth in mind or body or spirit. Thus Jowett, when he had by late February of 1874 learned "all about Pater — at any rate quite enough" (Inman, "Estrangement" 5), found himself compelled to assert that Pater had betrayed his trust as a university officer, and immediately intervened at Brasenose to block what would have otherwise been Pater's automatic election to the valuable post of university proctor.[16] Jowett's dramatic intervention in one form of in-

15. Deeply sympathetic to the Socratic eros in its ideal form, Benson would note in his diary concerning the relationship between a Cambridge undergraduate and a college fellow, "these romantic attachments may do great good both to the inspirer and the inspired" (Newsome, *Edge* 202). For the fullest account of Pater's work as an Oxford don, see Shuter, "Don" and "Academy's."

16. The proctorship, an office with extensive powers over undergraduate discipline and the awarding of degrees, was a two-year post that would have meant at least six

stitutional machinery — the proctorial election — was thus intended to save another form — the tutorial institution which lay at the heart of the liberal educational ideal. By sacrificing Pater, whose university career was to be deeply overshadowed for twenty years, Jowett would be able to preserve the system he had so largely helped to shape for the national and imperial ends in which he so steadfastly believed.

Yet Jowett's maneuver was not without significant consequences which would play out on quite another level of cultural implication. For the quarrel between Jowett and Pater was from the first to be recognized as a quarrel specifically within Oxford liberalism, a breach involving the claims to tolerance and candor as well as to the renegotiated settlement with modernity of liberalism itself. To disparage Pater, as Jowett famously did, as a "demoralizing moralizer," was to open up a space of equivocation between what was said and what was meant about the high freedoms of opinion and experience, and to flinch before the very consequences of the intellect which one had been urged to follow "wherever they might lead." It is precisely here in the perilously equivocal space between Platonic relations and spiritual procreancy on the one hand, and Greek love and the Socratic corruption of youth on the other that the counterdiscourse of a legitimated male love — for "homosexuality" in its emergently twentieth-century sense — would find its scope to grow.

---

hundred additional pounds to Pater, who had two unmarried sisters to support. By tradition, the post was rotated in succession from college to college, and within each college was awarded by election among the fellows traditionally on the basis of seniority.

THE HIGHER SODOMY

Some delicate dawning of a new desire,
   Distilling fragrant fire
On hearts of men prophetically fain
   To feel earth young again.
         —Lionel Johnson, "Walter Pater," 1894

"I rather look upon life as a chamber," says Mr. Rose in W. H. Mallock's *New Republic* (1877), his voice like a lonely flute, "which we decorate as we would decorate the chamber of the woman or the youth that we love" (21). Mr. Rose's utterance marks the moment when the sexual ambivalence within Oxford Hellenism, so plausibly depicted by Pater as the very engine of past and future cultural regeneration, is thrust into a scandalous visibility upon the national stage. For Mr. Rose, as contemporary readers were at once aware, is Pater, and if Pater and his notions of cultural renaissance had thus far not been much regarded outside the circles of advanced Victorian thought, *The New Republic* changed all that. Mallock's book transformed the Hellenizing Mr. Rose, with his interest in "artistic" fabrics and handsome young pages, into a national byword, the first in a procession of effeminate English aes-thetes — for George du Maurier's Postlethwaite and W. S. Gilbert's Bunthorne would soon follow — which would find its perfect epitome in Oscar Wilde.

To grasp the larger significance of this portrait of Pater, however, is to restore it to its full context in Oxford politics. For Mallock's satire arises in the most immediate terms from his embittered sense that Pater's Hellenism and Jowett's Hellenism were at a deeper level identical to each other and found their common basis in Balliol liberalism. It was, indeed, at Balliol, where Mallock was an undergraduate from 1869 to 1874, that he experienced the Greats machinery operated by Jowett as a harrowing of his early religious faith, a spiritual devastation from which nothing good or even remotely compensatory had come. In place of the incomparable reassurance that belief in the divinity and atonement of Jesus Christ and the immortality of the soul could bestow, Jowett held out to such undergraduates as Mallock nothing more than an intellectual temper. This mode of skeptical, analytical, inconclusive play with ideas was one by which they might obtain, or so Jowett's "practical ideal" seemed to propose, mere worldly advantage: college fellowships, posts in the Foreign Office, and other glittering prizes. A First in Greats, according to this view, represented the essential first step in any truly brilliant Oxford career. Yet the path of hard philosophical reading so sternly pointed out by Jowett now seemed to lead less inevitably to virtue or truth "on his ancient height" than simply to what one successful aspirant called "the chilly Caucasus of an atheistical First" (Wilde, *More Letters* 33).[1]

Satirized in *The New Republic* under the name of Dr. Jenkinson, Jowett thus becomes in Mallock's hands the up-to-date Anglican churchman who has liberalized Christianity out of all recognition — "Dr. Jenkinson's Christianity," as one disillusioned and cynical young man named Robert Leslie remarks, "is really a new firm trading under an old name, and trying to purchase the goodwill of the former establishment" (83). Having busily cobbled together this complacently expedient amalgam of religious beliefs, Jenkinson now must look on as it collapses before the desolating and purely secular systems projected by the other characters portrayed in *The New Republic* — Mr. Rose with his Paterian ethic of sensuous indulgence, Mr. Luke with his Arnoldian ideal of "culture," Mr.

1. The growing power of Jowett's Greats curriculum in conjunction with the reformed civil service to determine a young man's future after Oxford is suggested by Matthew Arnold's bleak assessment of his own son's chances in 1878 when Dicky Arnold was compelled by the Balliol tutors to leave Oxford without taking a degree: even a "fourth class [the lowest rank in the honor degrees] would not have qualified him for the [Education] Council Office — the best opening I could see for him [i.e., the very lowest clerkship]" (Honan 379).

Storks with his Huxleyan evolutionism, and Mr. Saunders whose atheistic materialism is that of W. K. Clifford. "Christianity," as Dr. Jenkinson is so famously and fatuously reduced to declaring, "really embraces all religions, even any honest denial of itself" (209).

Set beside the malicious brilliance of Mallock's portrayal of these variously liberal intellectual positions, the remarks of the two young men in the novel — the cynical Leslie and the melancholy Laurence — are scarcely noticeable. It is, however, precisely on behalf of these two friends that Mallock in fact conducts his satiric attack. For these two young men are quite simply Mallock himself and all other young graduates and undergraduates at Oxford and elsewhere who are being undone by liberalism, the weary cynicism of Leslie and the anguished doubt of Laurence thus standing for a whole spoiled, bewildered, and "corrupted" generation yearly brought forth out of Jowett's Socratic educational ideal.

Yet Mallock's satiric anger goes deeper even than this. For his sense that English youth was being corrupted by the new liberalism arose not least from his personal awareness of a single crucial episode involving a personal friend, the incident we have already glanced at in the preceding chapter under the rubric of the Pater-Hardinge affair. For as Mallock himself had observed, William Money Hardinge had been an ordinary young man who was transformed into a jaded and blasphemous trifler under the influence of such liberal teachers as Pater.[2] This is why Mallock's portrait of Pater as Mr. Rose — "which is made," as one reviewer noted uneasily, "the only dark one in the book, by certain traits and speeches" ("Essays" 1099) — is edged with a pointed hostility that did not materially vary over the first two versions of *The New Republic* he

2. Resident in Oxford during the time Hardinge matriculated at Balliol in February of 1873 to the outbreak of the Pater-Hardinge scandal in February of 1874, Mallock like others at Oxford looked on with growing mistrust as such undergraduates as Hardinge changed under the deforming pressures of Oxford liberalism: "Leslie is oddly changed," says his friend Laurence in *The New Republic*. "He never lets any melancholy subdue him. He can always laugh it down in a moment" (54), and it was just this vapid and jarring levity that so disturbed Hardinge's friends when they sought to extricate him from his entanglement with Pater. Hardinge did often use blasphemous expressions, said one friend, in his attempt to smooth over the matter with Jowett, but only as "the mere echoes of sharp things he had heard from other men" (Inman, "Estrangement" 7).

published.[3] And this is why the Oxford insiders identified the cynical Leslie with Hardinge so quickly that a contemporary key to *The New Republic* could publish the information immediately after the first version appeared in print.[4]

This *Belgravia* version, with its description of Mr. Rose as "the pale creature, with large moustache" ("New Republic" 29:521), reproduces Pater's actual appearance.[5] The book version, however, consistently uses

3. The first version was a series of sketches in the London magazine *Belgravia* 29–31 (June–December 1876), in which Mr. Rose's role is proportionately larger than in the book. After a process of substantial expansion and revision, the book version appeared in the first week of March 1877, when it seems to have driven Pater out of the race for the poetry professorship. Both these versions were published anonymously, Mallock's name not appearing until the third edition of the book, dated 1878, but coming out in late autumn of 1877. It is difficult to know what to make of Oscar Browning's claim — for he is typically a malicious and unreliable informant — that J. A. Symonds corrected proofs of Mallock's book in January of 1877 (*Memories* 229). Symonds, who knew both Mallock and the Oxford personalities Mallock was satirizing, would have made a particularly competent proofreader, and likely would have relished the discomfiture of Pater, then his rival for the poetry professorship, which was occasioned by Mallock's attack.

4. See the note reprinted from *London* published in Max Patrick's edition of *The New Republic*: "Here is a list that should enable the veriest Philistine to feel at home in such goodly and aesthetic company: . . . Rose, Mr. Walter H. Pater; Leslie, Mr. Hardinge" (xxxv). As there were a number of Mr. Hardinges extant at the time, however, the identification has mystified such later commentators as Patrick. That Mallock meant Leslie specifically for William Money Hardinge is nonetheless made clear by Raffalovich ("Giles" 25–26), who had his information about the Pater-Hardinge affair from Annie Thackeray Ritchie. Cf. also Mallock, *Memoirs*: "My characters in *The New Republic* were *all* portraits, though each was meant to be typical; but the originals of some — such as Lady Ambrose, the conventional woman of the world — were of no public celebrity, and to mention them here would be meaningless" (87; my emphasis).

5. Whether or not Mallock had ever met Pater is disputed: Levey judges no (143) and Wright yes, Wright conceding, however, that Mallock probably "derived most of his material from a young man who had been one of Pater's pupils" (2:12). Despite his general unreliability with regard to Pater, Wright may reasonably be trusted here. He had been in correspondence with Mallock in 1904 as he prepared to write his biography of Pater, and his own assumption that Mallock and Pater *did* meet appears to have gone uncontradicted by Mallock at a time when Mallock was otherwise disposed to minimize the connection between his characters and their real-life originals. The "young man" Wright mentions may conceivably have been Hardinge, especially if Hardinge went outside of Balliol to coach with Pater at Brasenose. In any case, all three men were regular devotés of the salon of the Lincoln College rector's wife, Emilia Pattison — the Lady Grace of *The New Republic* — and would have seen, and could have met, each other there.

Mr. Rose's own fondness for specific classical allusions as a way of suggesting his pagan sexual preferences,[6] a homoeroticism Mallock shows extending unmistakably to Mr. Rose's urgent present-day interest in "a boy of eighteen — a youth of extraordinary promise, I think, whose education I may myself claim to have had some share in directing" (*New Republic* 171), and whose febrile sonnet Mr. Rose insists on reading aloud. Mr. Rose's paiderastic education of "youth" thus is shown to represent merely an extreme form of the Socratic "corruption" Jowett's liberal education principles have already brought about in Oxford undergraduates. Mallock repeatedly depicts Dr. Jenkinson as irritated to exasperation by the languid pronouncements of Mr. Rose, who so uncannily manages to reproduce in an aesthetic register all Jenkinson's own religious syncretism and relativism.[7]

6. Rose eagerly celebrates such figures as Bathyllus, the Roman pantomime actor who notoriously impersonated Leda (*New Republic* 166), and the passionate pairs of Harmodius and Aristogeiton, Achilles and Patroclus, Socrates and Phaedrus (121). This ethos of Greek paiderastia may also be why Mallock in the earlier anonymous editions of the book describes Mr. Rose's voice as "like a lonely flute." For flutelike is how Socrates' voice is famously described by his pupil and *erōmenos* Alcibiades in *Symposium* 215b when the younger man describes the ravishing and enchanting effect of Socrates' words on men's souls, and tells Socrates, "you produce the same effect [as Marsyas, the gifted flute-player] with your voice only, and do not require the flute" (Jowett trans. 2:66). That Mallock meant this ostensibly slight detail to allude to Socrates and Pater and their "corruption" of youth is suggested by his decision to suppress the detail in the third edition when he published the book under his own name, as well as by this remark he has his spokesman, Laurence, make concerning the knowledge of books as books: "How it enriches conversation, by enabling us to talk by hints and allusions, and to convey so many more meanings than our actual words express" (*New Republic* 129). Mallock made a number of such changes to moderate his portrayal of Pater for the third edition, and they were noticed at the time.

7. Cf. Mr. Rose: "It will matter nothing to us whether [architectural styles] be pagan or Catholic, classical or mediaeval. We shall be quite without prejudice or bigotry" (*New Republic* 170). Furiously intent on distinguishing his own position from Rose's, Dr. Jenkinson repeatedly finds himself in inextricable difficulties, pausing in one such attack only because he suddenly recollects that "he might thus seem to be rooting up the wheat of his own opinions along with the tares of Mr. Rose's" (178). A persistent rumor about the estrangement between Jowett and Pater, recorded by Benson, maintained that it was Mallock who had put the damaging "Yours lovingly" letters into Jowett's hands which afterward gave Jowett such power over Pater (see Seiler 258). One possible reconstruction: Mallock took the incriminating letters to Jowett in order to confront and embarrass

Mallock's portrait of Mr. Rose, however, was to have several unintended consequences of the greatest significance for late-Victorian culture, not least of which would be its contribution to the constitution of homosexuality as a positive social identity at Oxford and beyond. For with the reductio ad absurdum embodied in his portrait of Mr. Rose Mallock would implicitly accept the basic premise from which Pater had begun — that male love had the capacity to initiate powerful cultural change — and the very brilliance of his satire would unwittingly serve to drive the premise home.

Mallock's conscious aim, of course, was to portray Pater's Hellenism as precisely a change toward cultural *dissolution*, Mr. Rose's Hellenism working along with Jenkinson's higher criticism and Storks's evolutionism and Saunders's atheism to tear down culture rather than to regenerate it, as Mill and the liberals had claimed. Yet simply in portraying Hellenism in this way, Mallock could not avoid underwriting its claim to lie at the heart of the new, to be the wave of the future. Thus, for instance, writing from the perspective of an older classical republican discourse, Mallock means to humiliate and discredit Pater by representing Mr. Rose with effeminate traits — as when Mr. Rose declares, "when I go to ugly houses, I often take a scrap of some artistic crétonne with me in my pocket as a kind of aesthetic smelling salts" (165).[8]

Yet the portrait of Mr. Rose is meanwhile underwritten at a deeper level by Mallock's own unconscious acceptance of the role of Hellenism and Aestheticism in the Arnoldian ideal of "culture." For throughout the commentary of Mallock's spokesman, Laurence, there runs a reluctant awareness that modern modes of thought have indeed evolved,

---

him with inescapable proof of the literally demoralizing effects of liberal teaching at Oxford, for which Jowett, who had in the past recommended Pater to Balliol pupils as a private coach in philosophy, might be held responsible.

8. In the same way, it is a classical republican perspective on virility as martial capacity which underlies Mallock's satiric point when Mr. Rose murmurs that to the men of the new aesthetic movement, "the boyhood of Bathyllus is of more moment than the manhood of Napoleon. Borgia is a more familiar name than Bismarck" (*New Republic* 166). Mallock in this way suggests that in the aftermath of the Franco-Prussian War (1870–71), rising German power may yet pose a greater danger to Britain than the ancient threat of France if the aestheticizing youth of England continue to prefer collecting cretonnes to more warlike activities.

bringing with them strange new modes of feeling which are, as Laurence says, "more sensitive, and more highly organised" (179). In such a moment as this Laurence, despite all his sharp nostalgia for the certitudes of his early childhood faith, finds himself agreeing with Mr. Luke and Mr. Rose, as he says, "that all our feelings have developed" (179). In no lesser degree does Laurence find himself aligned, even against his will, with the rising generation of those "choicer souls" (164) whom Mr. Rose, using a Platonic word, calls the *kharientes*, the men of taste, refinement, and education who form "the movement," and whose number, as Rose notes complacently, "is on the increase" (167, 166).

At such moments as these, in short, Mallock finds himself — without knowing it — of the devil's party, the party of Luke and Rose and Jenkinson, unintentionally imparting the dark glamour of a cultural vanguard to the aesthetic Hellenism he had meant instead to crush with ridicule. In the same way, precisely as Mallock plays with the intellectual positions of Jowett, Pater, and the rest does he brilliantly enact the very Balliol manner he so despises. Skillfully dramatizing these various positions in order to expose their devastating consequences for the hopeful young, Mallock displays even more clearly his own superb mastery of what Oscar Wilde would later call the "Oxford temper," the effortless deftness in intellectual matters of "one who could play gracefully with ideas" (*Letters* 426).

To see the specific antagonism in the caricature of Pater as Mr. Rose is thus to understand how Mallock's general attack on the tenets of Oxford liberalism was to function in an unforeseen way — exposing and publicizing the homoerotic subtext of Victorian Hellenism, and translating the hitherto abstruse cultural preoccupations of the Oxford elite into the ordinary language of Victorian middle-class aspiration. As he simplifies Pater for the purposes of satire, Mallock unintentionally makes Paterian Hellenism just that much more accessible, so that his picture of Mr. Rose ends by contributing to the sense of young Hellenists and aesthetes throughout England that they indeed belong to a cultural vanguard, a new "movement" of "choicer souls." *The New Republic* in this way operates as a translator mechanism between academic and public sectors, through which the claims to cultural regeneration — the spiritual procreancy of homoerotic Hellenism — now achieve a new currency and glamour in the eyes of its younger readers: "Decidedly clever," declared Wilde, who read the *Belgravia* number as soon as he could obtain it (*Letters* 20).[9]

Just as the Oxford of Jowett and Pater had provided the target of Mallock's conscious or intended satire in *The New Republic*, the book's wholly unintended glamorization of a new cultural avant-garde would, as though through some compensatory irony, first take root at Oxford as well. No episode more symbolic of its impact on the Oxford undergraduates of the day could be sought, perhaps, than that in which a poem offered by Mallock in *The New Republic* as an exaggerated parody of the vapidities of "aesthetic" undergraduate verse comes to supply in 1880 the epigraph for the Oxford pamphlet *Boy-Worship*, a wholly serious defense of pederasty as a mode of male romantic attachment (Inman, *Reading-2* 236).[10] In the longer run, *The New Republic* would become a

---

9. Wilde, who is writing from Ireland in a letter of 26 July 1876 (*Letters* 20–21), is probably responding to the first installment (June 1876) of the *Belgravia* version. This letter makes it clear that an identification key to Mallock's satiric characters was already available. Mallock's parody of Wilde's own poem would not appear until the September number. Wilde owned a copy of the book version of *The New Republic* as well, Ellmann reporting that it is now held by the library of King's College, University of London (599n).

10. These are the "dear lines" Mr. Rose insists on reading aloud:

> Three visions in the watches of one night
> Made sweet my sleep — almost too sweet to tell.
> One was Narcissus by a woodside well,
> And on the moss his limbs and feet were white;
> And one, Queen Venus, blown for my delight
> Across the blue sea in a rosy shell;
> And one a lean Aquinas in his cell,
> Kneeling, his pen in hand, with aching sight
> Strained towards a carven Christ; and of these three
> I knew not which was fairest. First I turned
> Towards that soft boy, who laughed and fled from me;
> Towards Venus then; and she smiled once, and she
> Fled also. Then with teeming heart I yearned,
> O Angel of the Schools, towards Christ with thee!
>
>   (*New Republic* 171)

In this poem, as a number of critics have noticed over the years, Mallock seems to be parodying the specific insipidities of the undergraduate Wilde (see Symons 264 and

kind of textbook of Oxford aestheticism which would be consulted by undergraduates into the 1920s. In the shorter term, its most momentous consequence would be its impact on the professorship of poetry election from which Pater would be compelled, in circumstances somewhat mysterious, to withdraw his candidacy in mid-March of 1877.

The professorship of poetry election, as we already have seen, becomes a symbolic episode within Oxford's institutional life, repressed afterward but at the time representing nothing less than a referendum on Oxford liberalism. For the election itself further exposes and embitters the breach Mallock had already so mercilessly abraded with his *Belgravia* version of the satire. Under the pressure of Tyrwhitt's attack on Hellenism in February 1877 and the exasperating reappearance of Dr. Jenkinson and Mr. Rose in the book-length version of *The New Republic* in early March, Jowett now abandons his pledge not to interfere in the election and, hoping to save something for the liberals, throws his influence behind J. C. Shairp, a Scots cleric and Balliol man, who is unanimously elected.

Yet this apparent victory for Balliol liberalism has only been won at a high ideological cost. For the election of this safe, dull, unpoetical Scots cleric — the candidate of that same Jowett who had been renowned among undergraduates as the great friend and protector of Swinburne himself — only intensified the sense among undergraduates of the rupture within liberalism. The Jowett who had been such an undergraduate hero for his dogged and principled resistance to the persecution of the High Church party during the 1850s and 60s was now disappearing into

---

Ellmann 89), who at this point in his Oxford career had not yet met Pater but admired his work extravagantly. Mallock's witty premise here is to convert the threefold vision of Wilde's sonnet "A Night Vision" (which Mallock would have had to have read in MS; see Mason 1:95) into a Hellenized Choice of Hercules. In classical republican discourse this choice is always the stern and taxing one youth must make between virtue and pleasure, the theme becoming a set topic in school and college exercises (see McLachlan). Here, by contrast, Mallock has modern Oxford youth deciding among three aesthetico-sensuous experiences: boy-love, girl-love, and the celibate frissons of Anglo- or Roman Catholicism. In the phrase "Angel of the Schools" there is a glancing reference to the Oxford "Schools," the all-important reading and examination system. For Mallock's influence on Wilde at Oxford, see Atkinson. For Wilde's early and unfinished Oxford poem "Choir Boy," see Fong 24.

the Master of Balliol, solidifying his power even as he dwindled by degrees into the role of consummate wire-puller in late-Victorian Oxford.

The craven cautiousness and compromise involved in the liberals' backing of Shairp for the poetry chair, however, contrasted too forcibly with their principle of intellectual fearlessness — Mill's great and enormously energizing call to follow the conclusions of the intellect wherever they might lead — for this retreat not to be highly visible and controversial in undergraduate eyes. Poor Shairp, the unwitting pawn in a larger institutional conflict, was confounded by the antagonism of his younger listeners. Even his friends conceded he was "out of touch with the rising generation, and his words, I fear, too often fell upon rebellious ears" (Knight 337). Struggling in the face of open and vociferous partisanship for the new aesthetic school, Shairp tried to tip the balance back again to early Victorian values by giving the Newdigate Prize (for which he was an official judge) to more "manly" poems. Instead, he found that the weaker, more "effeminate" side now had the stronger poets: indeed, he was forced to present his first Newdigate to none other than Oscar Wilde.

Against this defining background the Oxford undergraduate enthusiasm for aesthetic furnishings and Keatsian poetry, John Ruskin's road building and Pater's prose, Ritualism and Hellenism assumed the dimensions of a daring new movement — daring because presenting itself as the genuine realization of a liberalism that otherwise seemed to be faltering and losing heart. With Ruskin, the eloquent spokesman for an older aestheticism, in the Slade professorship issuing incomparable hymns to visual beauty, and undergraduate magazines filled with contentious debates between the aesthetes and the Philistines,[11] the time had

11. Cf. Wilde's letter of November 1881 to George Curzon: "[Oxford] must not be given entirely over to the Philistines. They have Gath and Ekron and Ashdod and many other cities of dirt and dread and despair, and we must not yield them the quiet cloister of Magdalen to brawl in" (*More Letters* 37). Curzon had attacked the Oxford Union for its crass rejection of the copy of Wilde's *Poems* which the union secretary had himself solicited from Wilde for its library. The contention within undergraduate Oxford over Aestheticism at this time may be indicated by the results of the full union membership poll on the question of accepting Wilde's book: for acceptance, 180; against, 188 (Ellmann 146).

at last arrived, or so it seemed to the moving spirits of an entire generation of Oxford undergraduates, for an end to what Pater in 1867 had so unforgettably called the "crucifixion of the senses" ("Winckelmann" 48).

The rebellion against this crucifixion of the senses would be given symbolic expression, most significantly, in the Oxford cult of "boy-worship" which was already beginning to surface, as we have seen, by the time of William Johnson's classic paean to romantic paiderastia, *Ionica* (1858). With its rites of admiring contemplation and pursuit — whether at Magdalen Chapel or the nude male bathing spot called Parson's Pleasure — and its attendant conventions of epistolary address — by which the fervors of public-school romance merged into the headlong emotional avowals of Tractarian friendship[12] — the cult of boy-love would find its literary expression in "Uranian" poetry. This poetry, celebrating that Uranian or "heavenly" love between males described in Plato's *Symposium* 180e, first appeared at about this time in Oxford[13] and, as Timothy d'Arch Smith has so extensively documented, would continue to be written there and elsewhere in England into the 1930s.

12. It is an index to the transformations within Oxford homosociality that "Yours lovingly" — the closing phrase Pater used with Hardinge which so alarmed Jowett in 1874 — had been routinely used by William Morris and his Oxford friends in the early 1850s when Tractarian modes still echoed resonantly throughout the university. See DeLaura, "O Unforgotten Voice." For the constitution of a distinct Oxford ethos under the Tractarians, see Nockles.

13. Cf. the letter of November 1886 sent by Norman Moor to J. A. Symonds in response to Symonds's question about youths being misled into pederasty by reading Plato: "I *can* tell you of a single instance that way. He went up from us [i.e., Clifton College] as a scholar to Balliol, and before he had been long at Oxford he declared himself a paederast, and went so far as to publish or at all events write and get printed an '*Apologia peri paiderastias*'—which contained a defence of the habit, i.e. of the ideal *paiderastia*— the purely spiritual views. I do not think that he for a moment contemplated any such cohabitation as the Greeks permitted themselves under certain conditions — it was all up in the clouds as the love of the beautiful. This youth was sent down from Balliol, and sent on a voyage round the world, much as one sends an invalid round the world to get rid of a disease. This boy was 'hurt'" (Symonds, *Memoirs* 296). Since W. M. Hardinge attended Clifton before going up to Balliol but was not elected Scholar, and C. E. Hutchinson, the author of *Boy-Worship*, matriculated at Brasenose, it is conceivable Moor is referring to still another boy-worshiping Oxford undergraduate author. For one survivor's nostalgic view of this epoch at Oxford, see Mackie.

To the end, Uranian poetry would be in some degree able to represent itself as belonging to that wider intensification of sensuous culture which in Foucault's analysis is so constitutive an element in the nineteenth-century middle-class hegemony.

Yet the most radical claim of the new Uranian poetry would always be that it sang the praises of a mode of spiritual and emotional attachment that was, at some ultimate level, innocent or asexual. Uranian poetry was able to give voice to a counterdiscourse of spiritual procreancy underwritten by the authority of Oxford Hellenism to precisely the degree it was able to represent itself as superior to the blind urgencies of a merely animal sexuality, either the imperatives of heterosexual reproductivity or, in the language of ancient social and religious taboo, the bestial degradation of sodomy as anal copulation. This pure and intellectual dimension of Uranian love would allow Wilde to defend it so fearlessly from the Old Bailey witness box, and would persuade even the largely cynical Oscar Browning that there had been something more at stake in Aestheticism than a convenient blind for carnal appetite.[14]

The degree of sexual innocence associated by the Uranians with the vision of spiritual procreancy derived from Socrates and Plato can

---

14. Cf. the private letter Browning wrote long after the 1870s, quoted by Anstruther: "Few people know that the aesthetic movement which had so much influence in England from Ruskin to Oscar Wilde had as one of its characteristics a passionate desire to restore 'Greek Love' to the position which its votaries thought it ought to occupy. They believed that bisexual love was a sensual and debasing thing and the love of male for male was in every way higher and more elevating to the character. I was interested, but did not agree with them and, as I was at that time a schoolmaster, it was absolutely impossible that I should take their view of things" (59). Browning was dismissed as an Eton master in 1875 precisely because of his overly amorous interest in one of his pupils, George Curzon (59). Whatever Browning's pederastic transgressions may have been, his departure from Eton, as one of the younger pupils was to recall, "dealt a severe blow to the intellectual life of the place for the simple reason that it was natural to him to seek the society of intelligent boys, and to talk to them on terms of equality about the things which interested him. No one ever attempted the same thing on the same scale, or with the same socratic enthusiasm. He encouraged shy boys to discuss bigger ideas, he put books in their way, and, best of all, he loved and practised leisurely talk. The same thing had been done before by William Johnson, who had an almost greater inspiration [cf. the Dorian *eispnēlās*, "inspirer"], and a similar power of meeting boys on perfectly equal terms" (Gilbert Coleridge 245).

scarcely be overestimated, however craven or absurd it was to appear to the later generations tutored by Freud who would derisively dismiss it as "the higher sodomy." It was this dimension of sexual innocence which allowed Oxford Hellenism to serve until Wilde's catastrophe in 1895 as a legitimating discourse for male love, one capable of enlisting within its discursive structures even conscious opponents of homoeroticism. Thus, for instance, it happens that someone like Edward Cracroft Lefroy, who was writing essays in the *Oxford and Cambridge Undergraduate's Journal* about the contest for the Oxford professorship of poetry, and condemning "Pater-paganism and Symonds-sophistry" for encouraging "the worst passions and most carnal inclinations of humanity" (Symonds "Lefroy" 92, 93), could yet himself defend, without any sense of inconsistency, the cultural work performed by precisely the sort of "aesthetic" Oxford tutor Pater had become.[15] The same idealist impulse prompted Lefroy to write the poems in praise of athletes' beautiful bodies which would in subsequent years draw the admiration and advocacy of exactly Symonds himself.[16]

As each successive Oxford controversy — over the poetry chair, over

15. Cf. Lefroy: "The cultured College Tutor, especially when he is a clergyman, often does good work by inspiring a select circle of men with something of his own spirit. Guide and director at once of the spiritual and intellectual faculties, old enough to be a philosopher, young enough to be a friend, he wields a potent influence over his pupils. Whether he speak with authority from the high platform of the pulpit, or familiarly amid the Morrisian oranges and sage-green leaf-clusters which decorate his rooms, he is equally a diffuser of sweetness and light; his contemplative philosophy and quiet humour possess a fascination even for 'our young barbarians,' because it lies so completely outside the range of their experience" (81).

16. Lefroy died in 1892 at the age of thirty-five before Symonds could write or meet him, although the older man was able to publicize Lefroy's poetry within Uranian circles by means of a sympathetic essay. In it, Symonds gently indicated — by quoting Lefroy's own words — the straining tension between Lefroy's resistance to " 'that Hellenic revival which some Oxford teachers desire' " ("Lefroy 90) and the Hellenic desires felt by Lefroy himself: "'In most football teams I can find one Antinous, sometimes two or three. And surely it is very beautiful to see the rapid movement of a perfect animal, &c. Some folk would say it was a mark of sickly or diseased sentimentalism to admire any but feminine flesh. But that only proves how base is the carnality, which is now reckoned the only legitimate form. The other is far nobler, unless it be vilely prostituted: and were I painter, sculptor or poet, I would teach the world so. Platonic passion in any relationship is better than the animalism which will go to all extremes'" (91).

boy-worship, over the lodging-house question,[17] over Pater's "Conclusion" — thus relays and translates its energies during the mid-1870s along the already densely reticulated network of local attitudes and institutional forms laid down in previous decades, Oxford becomes visible less as a concrete educational entity — a collection of Gothic quadrangles and traditions — than as "Oxford," a symbolic site upon which are felt to converge a multiplicity of discrete and competing power relations, constantly shifting and entering into new strategic combinations. In this context the Oxford to which Sir William Wilde sent his son may be said to have simply ceased to exist as a specific set of towers and tutors, becoming instead intelligible only as the already symbolic projection of certain of Newman's sermons and Arnold's poems and Jowett's tutorials and so on through the whole invisible but palpable range of preexisting, only partially recoverable texts.

As Wilde was to declare in *De Profundis*, one of the two great turning-points of his life occurred "when my father sent me to Oxford" (*Letters* 469). Everything he encountered there seems to have been charged with a palpitating vibrancy of signification — such that Wilde could not regard the Cumnor hills, for instance, without imagining Arnold's Scholar-Gipsy or consider the river Isis without seeing Socrates and Phaedrus beside the Ilissus—an aura of implication which was only to intensify for him in later years. Arriving in Oxford in the autumn of 1874, at the very moment Pater's "Conclusion" was being denounced from the university pulpit of St. Mary's, Wilde took up this fatal book —

17. The lodging-house question flared up into national attention in 1876 when a former vicar of St. Mary's, Oxford — John Burgon, Dean of Chichester — published a pamphlet charging that allowing undergraduates to lodge outside college walls led to sexual profligacy with housemaids. Writing as an undergraduate, Lefroy denied there had been any particular deterioration in sexual morality at Oxford, but the question was nonetheless widely and salaciously canvassed throughout England. J.E.C. Bodley recalled that it was Burgon who had denounced as vicious Wilde's aesthetic affectations in these terms: "When a young man says not in polished banter, but in sober earnestness, that he finds it difficult to live up to the level of his blue china, there has crept into these cloistered shades a form of heathenism which it is our bounden duty to fight against and to crush out, if possible" (Ellmann 45).

the book, as he was so memorably to tell Lord Alfred Douglas from prison, "which has had such a strange influence over my life" (471) — and committed to heart its intoxicating command to end the crucifixion of the senses and begin the renaissance of joy.

Yet the impact on Wilde of Mallock's *New Republic* as the unintended handbook of a new Oxford aestheticism was only slightly less intense. For Mallock's extraordinary succès de scandale — achieved (as was widely believed) when he was still an Oxford undergraduate — represented to Wilde precisely the image of his own ambitions after literary and social success, here stunningly realized as fact. Learning from Mallock that an Oxford undergraduate could become a significant figure in English cultural life by writing a witty and scandalous book, Wilde then grasps the possibility, to be so brilliantly realized in his own later works, of rewriting Mallock's *New Republic*, as it were, from the inside out — of portraying the English social and artistic world with all the elegant and cynical verve of a Robert Leslie.

It is in this sense that the distinguishing characteristics of the brilliant public personae deployed by Wilde in the world beyond Oxford during his later life and in his literary works would always be meant to invoke the imprimatur and sanction of the Oxford Greats school as precisely the most Oxonian and prestigious institution at Oxford. Greats, as Wilde himself declared, was "the only fine school at Oxford, the only sphere of thought where one can be, *simultaneously*, brilliant and unreasonable, speculative and well-informed, creative as well as critical, and write with all the passion of youth about the truths which belong to the august serenity of old age" (*More Letters* 33). The flexible comprehension of opposing viewpoints, the full appreciation of the "play of ideas," and the fearless pursuit of all questions beyond any prematurely closed conclusions had been inculcated as a mental discipline under the liberal regime of Jowett, Pattison, and the tutors teaching under their influence. It is, in turn, just this "Oxford temper" — this power of insouciant, apparently effortless play with ideas — which Wilde, after suitably enlarging its antinomian dimension — was to erect as his imperious standard in all intellectual and artistic matters.[18]

18. Wilde defines the "Oxford temper" in *De Profundis*, in the course of rebuking Lord Alfred Douglas for his utter lack of it, Douglas having left Oxford without taking a degree.

This is why we are able to see Wilde's later personae, and that movement of free play which was so brilliantly to characterize the movement of his critical dialogues, already taking form in his Oxford notebooks. Keeping such a commonplace book was a recommended and standard practice for honors candidates preparing for the Greats exam. Wilde's notations are unusual, however, in the way they continually strive to translate the conceptual language of one author or thinker into the intellectual system of another — so Darwin is brought to bear on Hegel, and Plato is made to confront Herbert Spencer.[19] Here we see commencing in rough outline the process that would culminate in *Decay of Lying* and *Critic as Artist*, when Wilde was to translate the Platonic doctrine of Ideas into the theory of aesthetic ontology which would later have such far-reaching consequences for twentieth-century literature and criticism.

At any such moment as this, Wilde is not so much studying Greek dialectical thinking as actively engaging in it, enacting its logic of discursive conflict repeatedly on the page. This he does, in turn, with a consciousness of the erotic tension shaping the Greek dialectic from within — in such discussions, as Wilde observes, "we wrestle to embrace, and embrace to wrestle."[20] To read Wilde's notations on Greek thought

---

Its importance to Wilde may be judged indirectly by reading Robert Ross's essay "The Brand of Isis," the amusing protest of a Cambridge man at the Oxford ascendancy. The battle of the two universities was a convention in the friendship between Ross and Wilde, and is alluded to in *The Portrait of Mr. W. H.*: "Yes, I am aware that Cambridge is a sort of educational institute," Wilde's narrator murmurs dismissively. "I am glad I was not there" (216). "I always fancied," recalled Robert Sherard, who had matriculated at New College, Oxford, "that the fact that I did not take my degree seemed to [Wilde] to draw a line between us. There were certain subjects on which he would not listen to me; and when other graduates were present, a vague feeling of exclusion from his confidence communicated itself to me" (74–75).

19. See, for example, Wilde's *Oxford Notebooks* 148–49, where he quotes from the long passage about the Platonic eros, cited above in Chapter 3, from Jowett's introduction to Plato's *Symposium*. I follow the editors' dating of Wilde's college notebook and commonplace book to the period of 1874–79.

20. Wilde is copying this phrase into his Oxford notebook from an essay by W. K. Clifford. Cf. also Wilde's notation: "*Erōs* and *dialektikē* as two sides of the same thing: *erōs*, the impassioned search after truth, as well the romantic side of that friendship so necessary for philosophy, because *discussion* was the primitive method" (*Notebooks* 146–47).

OSCAR WILDE in Greece, 1877.
(Photo in the Hyde Collection, Somerville, N.J.)

or Athenian education is thus to be constantly aware of his own excited sense of discovery, to see in his cognition an emergent self-recognition of the same sort that overtook Symonds when he first read the *Phaedrus* and the *Symposium*. "Philosophein met' erōtos," Wilde writes in his commonplace book (115), using the phrase so central to Pater. "Philosophein met' erōtos!" exclaims the narrator of Wilde's *Portrait of Mr. W. H.*, "How that phrase had stirred me in my Oxford days!" (211).

At the same time, it is clear how fully embedded these materials of the emergently homosexual legitimation strategy yet remain within the ideological matrix of Oxford liberalism. For even as Wilde meditates in the familiar Paterian cadences upon "the refinement of Greek culture coming through the romantic medium of impassioned friendships, the freedom and gladness of the palaestra" (*Notebooks* 115), his eye has been led to these embracing dyads of Greek wrestling or paiderastia by the diversity ideal of Victorian Hellenism. Flexibility, versatility, many-sidedness — all that had been enunciated so compellingly by Pericles in the Funeral Oration as to have become some twenty-three centuries later the central authorizing text for the liberalism of Jowett and Arnold, Grote and Mill — are now hailed familiarly in Wilde's notebook as "eutrapelia" (115).[21]

21. Wilde strikes this characteristic Millian-Grotean note of Oxford liberalism again when he declares in his undergraduate essay *Hellenism* that "this intense individuality, if one might use the term, of each city saved the Greeks from the mediocre sameness of thought and feeling which seems always to exist in the cities of great empires" (7). For the development of Wilde's Hellenism at Trinity College, Dublin, under the tutelage of the noted Greek scholar J. P. Mahaffy, see Stanford and McDowell; Pine; and Ellmann 27–30. Mahaffy was able to prevail upon a not unwilling Wilde to delay returning to Oxford in April 1877 and to visit Greece instead ("I stood upon the soil of Greece at last!" as the speaker of Wilde's "Impression de Voyage" exclaims in triumph [Fong 66]). "Seeing Greece," Wilde announced to the Dean of Magdalen whose permission he needed for a late return to the college, "is really a great education for anyone and will I think benefit me greatly and Mr. Mahaffy is such a clever man that it is quite as good as going to lectures to be in his society" (*Letters* 35). After his return to Oxford, Wilde's Catholic friends became convinced he was changed by this experience, "become Hellenized, somewhat Paganized," as one of them, David Hunter-Blair, would later say (Mikhail 1:9). Nor did the effect of Greece in providing an alternative source of transcendental value to Wilde seem to diminish with time. Writing in October 1880 a letter now held in the Robert H. Taylor Collection of the Princeton University Libraries and quoted here by permission, the actor Kyrle Bellew told Wilde bluntly, "I am a Catholic — you would have been one too had you been spared Greece."

In this context as well even those passages from Wilde's maturer works which from a twentieth-century perspective seem so obviously engaged with modern forms of forbidden experience — as when Eve Sedgwick, for instance, associates Wilde's recurrent use of "curious" and "subtle" in *Dorian Gray* with drug experimentation (*Epistemology* 174) — demand further to be seen deriving in direct terms from the Oxford liberal agenda of such writers as Arnold and Pater. For the literary genealogy of "curious," which Sedgwick reasonably enough traces back to Pater, does not begin there. Instead it passes quite beyond Pater to originate in specific terms with Arnold's *Function of Criticism* (1865),[22] and more generally in the urgent conviction among Victorian liberals that such new capacities as "curiosity," "individuality," and "diversity" — all Mill had meant when he called for "variety not uniformity" — quite simply demanded to be developed as the best hope for national survival amid the crisis of the new social and industrial modernity.

As we have already seen, the Greats school as it had been reshaped by Jowett and Pattison and the other university reformers represented the translation of exactly those theoretical arguments of Victorian liberalism into specific institutional terms. The great complaint about the reformed Literae humaniores school had always been that it taught very young men how to sound fluent and plausible on the basis of very little experience or thought — to "write with all the passion of youth," as we have heard Wilde say, "about the truths which belong to the august serenity of old age." This sort of showmanship, however, was precisely the mode in which Wilde himself, who was gifted with a sumptuous power of intellect as well as an extraordinary memory, could perform brilliantly. Even had he never worn an aggressively elegant coat cut like a violoncello or attempted to live up to his blue china, Wilde would have

---

22. Cf. Arnold: "It is noticeable that the word *curiosity*, which in other languages is used in a good sense, to mean, as a high and fine quality of man's nature, just this disinterested love of a free play of the mind on all subjects, for its own sake, — it is noticeable, I say, that this word has in our language no sense of the kind, no sense but a rather bad and disparaging one. But criticism, real criticism, is essentially the exercise of this very quality" (*Function* 268). Arnold was thinking of Ernest Renan's praise of curiosity in *Averroës et averroeisme* (1852). Pater emphasizes curiosity in the Leonardo essay of *The Renaissance* and, more especially, in the postscript to *Appreciations* (1889).

been famous beyond Oxford for his Newdigate and his Double First. As it was, his First was widely known to have been the best of his year (Ellmann 98), and supremely confident to begin with, Wilde was to launch his overwhelming personality upon the world from the uttermost pinnacle of Oxford celebrity.

By the time Wilde had completed his Oxford experience, ready to step forth as the most fearlessly original — even eccentric[23] — Oxonian of his time, the categories of Greek thought and literature would have become structuring categories of his literary and social imagination. Saturated in the language and literature of ancient Greece, Wilde would repeatedly grasp his own life in the terms supplied by such ancient Greek forms as the life of Socrates or the plays of Aeschylus — which were ever to him a reality more compelling than the lurid implausibilities published in the daily newspapers. This is why, when his anxious friends watched in bewildered suspense as the nets of the prosecution closed around him just before his arrest for sodomic indecency, they sensed in Wilde's puzzling inaction the inevitability of a Greek dramatic destiny.[24] Or why when Wilde summoned himself in prison to write the *De Profundis* letter to Douglas, it was the story of the lion cub from Aeschylus's *Agamemnon* which determined his understanding of his own relationship with this unreflectingly ferocious young man, whose fury at his own father had so recklessly and utterly destroyed Wilde's life and art (*Letters* 431).

23. Wilde's flamboyant self-presentation derived most immediately from his own personality and from his mother, with Ireland as an influence no very distant third. All these, however, need to be read within the larger sociocultural context established by the liberal sanction of eccentricity expressed so compellingly in Mill's *On Liberty*: "In this age the mere example of nonconformity, the mere refusal to bend the knee to custom, is itself a service. Precisely because the tyranny of opinion is such as to make eccentricity a reproach, it is desirable, in order to break through that tyranny, that people should be eccentric. Eccentricity has always abounded when and where strength of character has abounded; and the amount of eccentricity in a society has generally been proportional to the amount of genius, mental vigour, and moral courage which it contained. That so few now dare to be eccentric, marks the chief danger of the time" (269).

24. Cf. this reminiscence by an anonymous woman writer: "It was, as I believe, his sense of the Greek that carried him through [the trial], as it had brought him to its cause. He felt himself Socrates perhaps; but it is easier to drink hemlock than to return from prison" (Reade 52n).

In this sense the conventions of Greek life—*paiderastia, symposia, dialektikē*—would assume the status of lived categories for Wilde, ostentatiously flourished by him on the level of public presentation as a sign of his high Hellenic culture and Oxford credentials, yet simultaneously experienced by him on the level of ordinary existence as elements scarcely more remarkable than air or wine. "Between his mind and mine," as the young Wilde reports to one Oxford friend about another, "there is no *intellectual friction to rouse me up to talk or think*, as I used with you" (*Letters* 32; Wilde's emphasis), and beneath all the patent flattery of such a remark, we glimpse the Socratic ideal of mental intercourse between male friends. "You are the only one I would tell about it," Wilde writes the same friend concerning an episode of boy-worship he has chanced to witness, "as you have a philosophical mind" (35), and in the word "philosophical" we hear the rich manifold of accents—ironical, historicist, liberal, etymological—which were comprehended in Oxford Hellenism.

In the same way, the conventions of Greek paiderastia as mediated through the Oxford Greats school would visibly shape such literary works as *The Portrait of Mr. W. H.* There, in a long excursus on what Wilde calls the "soul" of neo-Platonism—by which he means the Platonic identification between "intellectual enthusiasm and the physical passion of love" (184)—he portrays the progress of this "soul" from Ficino to Shakespeare to the Romantics and beyond as the same metempsychosis of cultural renewal which Pater had once so suggestively traced: homoerotic friendship repeatedly becoming "a vital factor in the new culture, and a mode of self-conscious intellectual development" (183).

The great significance of Dorian Gray's given name becomes, in turn, the way it implicitly summons, with an elegantly offhand gesture of allusion, the legitimating authority of K. O. Müller's *Dorians* and, beyond it, a world of learned historical *Wissenschaft*—that "solid bedrock of classical scholarship," as Paul Cartledge has called it (10), upon which Wilde's seemingly airy Hellenism ultimately rests. This submerged body of Hellenic implication continuously operates in concert with other more visible systems of signification, as when Lord Henry Wotton, for instance, meditates upon the deep satisfaction he gains from influencing Dorian. For even as Wotton invokes experimental science and artistic creation as models for the pleasure he feels, the underlying basis for his desire to "project one's soul into some gracious form, and let it tarry there for a moment; to hear one's own intellectual views echoed back to one with all the added music of passion and youth" (*Dorian* 33) always remains, as Cartledge has reminded us, precisely the erotic and pedagogical pleasure generated within the hearer/inspirer relationship of Dorian paiderastia. So, too, does Lord Henry's "low, musical voice" always remain that of the Socratic corruptor of youth (20).[25]

Even to glance at recent gender criticism on *Dorian Gray* or Symonds or the Uranian poets is to see how fully such late-Victorian invocations of Hellenism and ancient Greece have by now been understood as legitimating gestures on behalf of "homosexuality," an appeal, as Sedgwick has justly characterized it, "to the virilizing authority of the Greeks" (*Between* 208). Yet such late-Victorian allusions to "Greek love" or Plato or Dorianism are further to be understood, on this account, as functioning within an ideological economy of repression, displacement, and resistance — Foucault's discarded law and sovereignty model of power here making its silent reappearance — by which reprobated ideas or expressions are suppressed outright or translated into forms that are the least intolerable to the socially dominant orders or, yet again, boldly redeployed against the prohibiting power itself.

In recent years, this critical approach has supplied a predictable interpretive context in which Wilde's failure in *Mr. W. H.* or *Dorian Gray*, for instance, to *name* the "love that dare not speak its name" as "homosexuality" or "inversion" or some other name will always be found to constitute either the sign of his ideological erasure from a dominant discourse that denies public forms of expression to male love or, alternatively, the sign of his opposition to that very discourse, the play of indeterminate or deferred naming in *Mr. W. H.*, for instance, constituting in Lawrence Danson's view "a necessary act of resistance" (997). Yet not to see that Wilde's very lack of specificity may itself constitute an aesthetic choice wholly independent of the mechanics of

---

25. Raffalovich notes that by 1895 the word "musical" had attained a special Uranian inflection (*Uranisme* 188–89).

Oscar Wilde in aesthetic costume, 1882.

repression and resistance is to make the mistake of reductionism — as if Basil Hallward, to take one salient instance, employs such a phrase as "the visible incarnation of that unseen ideal that haunts us artists like an exquisite dream" simply because he somehow lacks a language of properly "homosexual" denotation.

By contrast, only when we reembed such phrases as Hallward's in their originary context of Oxford Hellenism is their genuine expressiveness thrust into view. For Hallward's phrase in this case marks a double allusion to Greek culture by treating the Platonic doctrine of eros as if it were operating according to the Platonic doctrine of reminiscence (*anamnēsis*) — homoerotic friendship as a remembered dream, "as though in some antenatal experience I had lived the life of a philosophical Greek lover," which had proved, as we have seen, so moving to Pater and Symonds alike. In the same way, such suggestive phrases of Lord Henry Wotton's as "the Hellenic ideal" or "the aim of life is self-development" become fully intelligible only when they are understood — not as evasions or euphemisms — but as perfectly expressive, in their unspecific amplitude of implication, of precisely that imaginative richness, that many-sidedness and "variety" so central to the sociocultural agenda of Victorian Hellenism.

This is not to say that certain homosexual apologists did not feel the contemporary limits on homoerotic expressiveness as a heavy further penalty. For indeed nothing more clearly represents this sense of expressive constraint, perhaps, than the case of Symonds. Even after his removal with his wife and daughters to Switzerland — far from either the disapprobations of Mrs. Grundy or the depredations of those professional blackmailers ("renters") whose career paths had been opened by the 1885 Criminal Law Amendment Act later to be used to prosecute Wilde — Symonds chafed under these iron constraints as if they were, in the words of Lord Alfred Douglas's memorial tribute to him, "chains on the limbs of lovers and burdens on the wings of poets" (d'Arch Smith 17).[26]

---

26. Cf. Symonds's letter to Edmund Gosse of March 1890: "I must even sit down upon the ground & complain to heaven that Mrs Grundy's tyranny deprives us of the natural enjoyment of such works of art as [Gosse's poetic sequence "The Taming of Chimaera"]. . . I feel very bitter about this. Quoque tandem Domine? How long are souls

At the same time, the problem posed by Symonds in this context demands to be understood as less a problem in expressive prohibition than one of excess expressive capacity. In fact, Symonds's sharpest sense of constraint arises only when he himself rejects the very language of the Platonic eros which had once served him as a medium of homoerotic self-revelation. For as Symonds establishes long-term and fully sexual relationships with working-class men outside of England in the 1880s, he begins to regard the nongenital or nonphysical eroticism of the Platonic doctrine of eros with a deepening mistrust. It is then that a Platonic love denying or devaluing or indefinitely deferring all genital release[27] becomes for him "a deeply rooted mysticism, an impenetrable Soofyism" ("Dantesque" 71) — an iridescent web or maze into which such susceptible young men as himself had been led until they found themselves utterly lost. "It is a delusion to imagine," as Symonds declared in the 1890 essay that represents nothing less than his farewell to Platonic love, "that the human spirit is led to discover divine truths by amorous enthusiasm for a fellow-creature, however refined that impulse may be" (85).

With this realization, Symonds comes to a bitter new assessment of his old teacher Jowett, as though Jowett's Socratic "corruption" had somehow consisted in tempting suggestible young men down the delusive path to spiritual procreancy rather than fleshly excess. Writing from Davos in 1889, Symonds confronts his old tutor across a crevass of ancient and mutual misunderstanding into which the bitter sufferings of thirty years now pour. When young men in whom the homoerotic passion is innate come into contact with the writings of Plato, as Symonds now tells Jowett, "they discover that what they had been blindly groping after was once an admitted possibility — not in a mean

---

to groan beneath the altar, & poets to eviscerate their offspring, for the sake of what — What shall I call it? — an unnatural disnaturing respect for middleclass propriety. — I find no phrase for my abhorrence" (*Letters* 3:450–51).

27. Foucault, characterizing the principle of "indefinite abstention" in the Platonic doctrine of eros as "the ideal of a renunciation, which Socrates exemplifies by his faultless resistance of [Alcibiades'] temptation [in the *Symposium*]" and which "has a high spiritual value by itself," has argued that such an asceticism served the Greeks as a means "of stylizing [the love of boys] and hence, by giving shape and form, of valorizing it" (2:245).

hole or corner — but that the race whose literature forms the basis of their higher culture, lived in that way, aspired in that way. . . . derived courage, drew intellectual illumination, took their first step in the path which led to great achievements and the arduous pursuit of truth" (*Letters* 3:346). Symonds is making explicit here his sense of the cruel pedagogical contradiction within Oxford Hellenism which had harried him for so many years — his instruction in Platonic thought by the same teachers of Hellenism who denounced erotic relations between men as "unnatural": "those very men who condemn him, have placed the most electrical literature of the world in his hands, pregnant with the stuff that damns him" (3:347).

Such a young man has learned the lesson of Oxford Hellenism only too well, trained to regard Plato as "*the greatest uninspired writing,*" as if it were indeed the surrogate scripture that can save him from an outworn Christian orthodoxy now imploding from the combined effects of superstition and science. Such a student now reads his *Symposium* or his *Phaedrus*, Symonds tells Jowett, "as you would wish him to read his Bible — i.e. with a vivid conviction that what he reads is the life-record of a masterful creative man-determining race, and the monument of a world-important epoch" (3:347). Yet what in the end has been the result of all this deeply engaged, brilliantly historicist education? A class of perversely susceptible young men have been "injured" and "incriminated," raised up helplessly as victims to a Victorian Hellenism that works "by ensnaring the noblest part of them — their intellectual imagination" (3:346).

No wonder Symonds in concluding *A Problem in Modern Ethics* (1891), the last of the homosexualist apologias he was to have printed during his lifetime, should suggest that those who insist on punishing homosexuals at law would do better instead to "turn their attention to the higher education" being carried on in English public schools and universities. For it was just there that the "best minds of our youth are . . . exposed to the influences of a paederastic literature at the same time that they acquire the knowledge and experience of unnatural practices" (112).

Nor is it strange that Symonds, upon learning that Jowett lay gravely ill, should experience "the deepest strangest dreams of him," in which the Master of Balliol "came to me, and was quite glorified, and spoke to me so sweetly and kindly—as though he understood some ancient wrong he had not fathomed in me before" (*Letters* 3:620). Jowett had known of Symonds's sexual "inversion" ever since the Shorting scandal in the early 1860s. Symonds's sense of an "ancient wrong" between them must therefore be understood to represent his desire that his own miseducation at Jowett's hands be at last acknowledged and righted—Jowett, the translator of Plato who had for so long denied what Symonds had come to know as a burning truth, that "Greek love was for Plato"—and much more painfully, "for modern students of Plato"—not a mere figure of speech but nothing less than "a present poignant reality" (3:347).

To glimpse Symonds in these last years, then, is to see him struggling to free himself and the English Uranians from one half of the inheritance of Oxford Hellenism while retaining the other half of its powerful ideological support. Attempting to discard the crippling sexual sublimations of the Platonic eros, Symonds fights at the same time to preserve the ideal of Dorian comradeship first discovered in K. O. Müller's *Dorians*, the ideal that so powerfully contested the ancient slur of "effeminacy" invariably raised in England and America against men who loved men. Dorian comradeship, especially as this ideal had been unconsciously but completely realized by Whitman in the "Calamus" poems of *Leaves of Grass*, could strengthen the foundation, as Symonds believed, upon which "to regenerate political life and to cement nations" (*Whitman* 97), by imparting to the amorphous old dreams of democratic "fraternity" a new basis in men's bodily experience.

The more immediate significance of Greek comradeship to Symonds, however, is its tremendous force as a counterweight to contemporary medical and psychiatric opinion. For by the early 1890s Symonds realizes that through a peculiar discursive irony, masculine love is in danger of being imprisoned by what once had seemed to be the means of its own liberation: the medical "science" Symonds had hoped to use to legitimate male love was in fact working to consign it to the category of disease. Such terms as "inverted sexual instinct" or "homosexuality" or "male sexual morbidity," for all their useful neutrality, possessed their own autonomous discursive life, projecting new theoretical models of pathology and abnormality which would become, as Symonds now recognizes, no less crippling for the individual lives formulated within them than the religious and social models of sin and vice currently being repudiated by "science." The theory of morbidity is "more humane," Symonds declares, "but it is not less false, than that of sin or vice" (*Letters* 3:694).[28]

Against this solidifying consensus of the "so-called scientific 'psychiatrists'" (3:693), Symonds now urgently asserts that the historical study of ancient Greece could prove "absolutely essential to the psychological treatment of the subject" (3:691) because it would confront the investigators of sexual "abnormality" with the inescapable historical evidence of precisely the broad and sane and socially enriching *normality* of Greek comradeship. Such psychiatrists fatally err, Symonds tells Havelock Ellis in 1892 when seeking him as a collaborator on the book that would become *Sexual Inversion*, "by diagnosing as necessarily morbid what was the leading emotion of the best and noblest men in Hellas." "Casper-Liman, Tardieu, Carlier, Taxil, Moreau, Tarnowsky, Krafft-Ebing" — the massive ignorance of all these men, Symonds insists, "is only equalled to their presumption. They not only do not know Ancient Greece, but they do not know their own cousins and club-mates" (3:694).

Yet Symonds knows he cannot effectively intervene in the scientific discourse without the discursive permission of the scientists themselves — "Alone," as he tells his Uranian friend Edward Carpenter, "I could make but little effect — the effect of an eccentric" (3:797). He needs "somebody of medical importance to collaborate with" — and Havelock Ellis possesses an M.D. It is, however, precisely in his capacity *as* medical "scientist" that Ellis would in the end redirect the emphasis of *Sexual Inversion* away from Symonds's historical dimension centered

28. Symonds's rising dismay at the medical transformation of masculine love was soon to be echoed by Wilde. Not the least part of the social extinction Wilde felt after his release from prison was his knowledge that such works as Max Nordau's *Degeneration* had reduced his genius and personality to the banal statistical nullity of a "problem": The "fact that I am also a pathological problem in the eyes of German scientists," Wilde would say in 1897, "is only interesting to German scientists: and even in their work I am tabulated, and come under the law of *averages! Quantum mutatus!*" (*Letters* 695).

in the Greeks and toward the pole of neuropathy and morbidity and "science." The 1883 essay on Greek ethics which had constituted so momentous a step in Symonds's career as a homosexual apologist he now urged Ellis to install as the central core of their collaborative project. But driven first by the discursive momentum of "science" and later by the maelstrom of the Wilde catastrophe, Symonds's Greek essay would be pushed to the margins of *Sexual Inversion* — appearing as chapter 3 in the German translation (1896), as an appendix of the first English edition (1897), and in the second edition disappearing without a trace (Koestenbaum 47).

We tend today, almost inevitably, to interpret Symonds's struggle to develop a persuasive language of homosexual legitimation in light of the event we know is to come, the tragedy of Oscar Wilde. Yet in the cultural moment before the Wilde disaster there was no implication of an impending doom, only the gradual emergence into visibility of a new system of values and attitudes, associated with a variety of movements in art and society, having in common their relation to the inchoate counterdiscourse of "homosexuality." This is the moment in which "homosexuality" in the modern sense begins to be visible as such: the activities of a reprobated but largely invisible minority, given publicity by such scandals as the 1889 Cleveland Street affair, are at the same time being given positive status in various legitimated modes of action and expression. In the aesthetically charged atmosphere of the earlier 1890s the criminal homosexual subculture, with its houses of assignation, its cruising grounds in Leicester Square and Piccadilly,[29] and the "renters" whose activity had only been stimulated by the Criminal Law Amendment Act of 1885, are swept up in the momentum of a larger social and artistic movement that was, under Wilde's leadership, so energetically taking over the language of French avant-gardism to realize Pater's goal of cultural renaissance.

29. This association provides the larger context for W. S. Gilbert's celebrated line about the effeminate aesthete Bunthorne in the comic opera *Patience* (1881): "If you walk down Piccadilly with a poppy or a lily in your medieval hand." The line appears in the stanza celebrating "An attachment à la Plato."

This is why, from a twentieth-century perspective, the Yellow Nineties, lasting as a cultural epoch a mere five years, has always seemed so pronouncedly a moment in which the distinctions between dominated and dominant sexual cultures, especially among the young — and "nobody," as Graham Robertson said, "was very old in the early 'nineties" (233) — have blurred in a great onrush of aesthetic and social innovation. So it would happen, for instance, that the first-night audience at Wilde's *Lady Windermere's Fan* could include a score or more young men displaying green-carnation boutonnieres while totally unaware that the mystic green blossom had become the emblem of French homosexuals (Gagnier 164). Similarly, the young French poet Pierre Louÿs, writing home about his visits to the new English "school" gathered around Wilde, seems to be expressing a characteristic fin de siècle delight in the sexually transgressive when he reports that "These young people are most charming. . . . You cannot imagine the elegance of their manners. . . . the first day I was introduced to them, X, to whom I had just been presented, offered me a cigarette; but, instead of simply offering it as we do, he began by lighting it himself and not handing it over until after he had taken the first drag. Isn't that exquisite?" (McCormack 91).

Here we encounter the Victorian fin de siècle which so much contemporary writing about homosexuality has wanted to see as a privileged world of momentarily permeable sexual categories, where Wilde can safely consort with his male prostitutes at public restaurants, even as such "cultural inverts" as John Gray, Max Beerbohm, Ernest Dowson — men uninterested in masculine love as a sexual outlet yet drawn to the ethos of its subculture — can safely, or with a lack of safety less dangerous than merely stimulating — consort with Wilde himself. Yet as John Stokes has recently made clear, the truth remains that this view of the 1890s is a modern construction, a myth produced in our own cultural moment and made persuasive only as it succeeds in projecting an as-yet-unthought-of polarization of "homosexual" versus "heterosexual" — Barthes's "binary prison" in its newest guise — backward upon an indeterminate welter of late-Victorian psychosocial categories. And the reason we now so readily impose our own categories on fin de siècle culture is not far to seek. For these dimensions of late-Victorian erotic experience — "ego-mania" and "zooerast" and "urolagnia" quite as much as "Urning" and "Uranian" and "inversion" — are precisely what so abruptly vanish in what Sedgwick has memorably called the "sudden, radical condensation of sexual categories" (*Epistemology* 9) which was to be precipitated by the Wilde catastrophe.

By the early twentieth century, such fossils of pre-Wildean Victorian discourse as "invert" and "zooerast" would thus seem merely incoherent or, in light of the growing influence of Freudian theory, crudely prescientific. Thus the genuine richness and complexity of late-Victorian psychocultural experience, that world of vanished categories to which George Chauncey has recently recalled our attention, become once again intelligible only when we gaze upon it in the moment before its condensation into any modern opposition between "homosexual" and "heterosexual." For it was only a counterdiscourse composed as much of "male adhesiveness" and "Uranianism" as of "homosexuality" which had been able, given the exigencies of the cultural moment, to enter seamlessly into such late-Victorian formations as "the new" and "the artistic" and "the perverse," assuming, in Foucauldian terms, a thickening depth of discursivity.

Here may be glimpsed the roots of the modern homosexual identity, for during just this period the notion of Greek paiderastia made so vivid by Oxford Hellenism persuaded many late-Victorian "inverts" that the homoerotic emotions they themselves had felt in fearful isolation or confused disgust might instead belong to human experience in its fullest historicity and cultural density. And here we may begin to understand why, as well, it would become so crucial that the earlier tradition of Uranian love, now being eclipsed by a more generalized fin de siècle avant-gardism, had undertaken to deploy against the notion of a merely carnal homoeroticism certain ideals of undiseased psychological complexity and noble emotionality in male love.

Before these ideals would once again become available to "homosexuality" as a positive social identity, however, the Uranian modality of male love would be rejected by the avant-garde itself as an outworn fashion. This is the paradox: even as its ideals of spiritual procreancy and nongenital eroticism went on silently expanding the dimensions of intentionality and inwardness necessary to constitute "homosexuality" as a positive social identity, the Uranian ideal could in the early years of the twentieth century be contemptuously dismissed by such influential voices as that of Lytton Strachey as nothing more than a weak attempt to deny that physical desire now pronounced by Freud and others to be universal and all pervasive — as, in short, nothing more than "the higher sodomy."

In this sense Lionel Johnson's angry reaction to Symonds's call for a frankly genital view of male love — Johnson declaring Symonds "an absolute Priapus" (Fletcher 184), or André Raffalovich's searching condemnation of Wilde in *Uranisme et unisexualité* (1896) — may be said to constitute events in the prehistory of "homosexuality" rather than mere occurrences in late-Victorian literary relations. The problem posed by such a remark as Johnson's, we might ordinarily say, is its disabling degree of self-hatred and its hypocrisy masquerading as moral criticism. Yet not to understand that Johnson is writing from within the Oxford tradition of pederastic Hellenism is to make the mistake of regarding his phrase "an absolute Priapus" as a simple expression of phobic detestation for the male body and the genital sexuality which Symonds himself regarded as "the central reality of human life" (*Whitman* 78). Instead, nothing more clearly illustrates the enriching complexity of these late-Victorian homoerotic and homosocial filiations, perhaps, than the moment in which Johnson of New College, Oxford, dismisses Symonds of Balliol or, again, applauds and then denounces Wilde of Magdalen — for Johnson's Latin poem praising the "creator" of Dorian Gray (1891) was soon followed by his searing poetic rebuke to Wilde as "To the Destroyer of a Soul" (1892).

To grasp the all but obliterated contextual situation out of which a poet such as Johnson writes is thus to locate him not simply within that rising generation of Oxford undergraduates — of Lord Alfred Douglas, Charles Sayle, Theodore Wratislaw, and J. F. Bloxam — whose contributions to such Uranian publications as *The Spirit Lamp*, *The Artist*, and *The Chameleon* seem so obviously to confirm Symonds's own sense of these young men as his successors in the struggle to legitimate masculine love. Nor is it to place Johnson within that still more famous and tragic generation of Rhymers' Club poets which Yeats was so sumptuously to enamber in literary myth. It is rather to situate him at the conjunction of both these formations precisely as they engage Oxford Hellenism, with its traditions of Tractarian friendship, Socratic education, spiritual procreancy, and cultural renewal.

This is in turn why Johnson can both praise Wilde in a witty Latin poem for the "sweet sins" of Greek love portrayed in *Dorian Gray* and yet execrate him so bitterly in another poem a few months later as the "destroyer" of Lord Alfred Douglas's soul: "Call you this thing my friend? this nameless thing? / This living body, hiding its dead soul?" (74).[30] For the sustaining tradition of Oxford Hellenism within which Johnson is working both approves the spiritual procreancy represented by any such creator of fictions as Wilde and at the same time reprobates the failure of an erotic teacher such as Wilde genuinely to educate his beloved friend. Whatever his own feelings toward these two men may have been, Johnson is using the language of the Uranian ideal to condemn the betrayer of that ideal. For Wilde in his relation to Douglas has become in Johnson's eyes something hideously akin to Socrates' "nonlover" of *Phaedrus* 239 — a man to whom the "defects of mind and more in the beloved are bound to be a source of pleasure . . . if they do not exist already as innate qualities, he will cultivate them" (Hamilton and Cairns ed. 486). Here we see that Johnson, with the line "This living body, hiding its dead soul," is implicitly comparing his friend's changed

---

30. Johnson's own erotic conduct is now difficult to trace with any certainty (see Fletcher's account in his edition of Johnson, xxxvi–xxxviii and 301), but that he loved men, and perhaps specifically loved Douglas — his intimate friend, to whom he introduced Wilde — has always been suggested by a poem, dedicated to Douglas and published in 1890, praising youthful love in these terms:

> Their eyes on fire, their bright limbs flushed,
> They dominate the night with love:
> While stars burn and flash above,
> These kindle through the dark such flame,
> As is not seen, and hath no name:
> Can night bear more?
> Can nature bend
> In benediction without end,
> Over this love of friend for friend?
> (Fletcher, "Decadence" 185)

The "nameless" love and "dark flame" here both point forward in unmistakable terms to two of the most famous 1890s poems of Uranian provenance — Douglas's "Two Loves" ("I am the love that dare not speak its name") and Johnson's own "Dark Angel."

nature to Dorian Gray's unapparent yet radical inward ruin. For Johnson's larger point will always be that the real perversion involved here
has little to do with the outward physical transactions of male love: the
destruction of his friend has come instead through the sodomic evacua-
tion of the soul from the body.

The great significance of Johnson's work as a Uranian poet thus
becomes his attempt to defend the older tradition of pederastic Hellenism in the face of the newer sexual realism in male love being asserted
in the earlier 1890s by such writers as Symonds and Wratislaw and
indeed by Douglas himself. This is why Pater had come to represent such
a hero to Johnson, who hails his part in inspiring the new culture in a
memorial poem to Pater which employs all Pater's own exquisite etymological care for words:

> Momentous things he prized, gradual and fair,
>   Births of passionate air:
>   . . . . .
> Some delicate dawning of a new desire,
>   Distilling fragrant fire
> On hearts of men prophetically fain
>   To feel earth young again:
>   (L. Johnson 226)

Pater is so eminently "Worthy Uranian song," as Johnson says (226),
because the "births of passionate air" he prized are precisely the art and
thought born of the spiritual procreancy of male love — "momentous" in
arising *in* a moment and "simply *for* those moments' sake," as Pater
himself had so unforgettably said in the "Conclusion" to *The Renaissance*, but "momentous" as well in their far-reaching significance for
culture. At the same time, there runs through Johnson's poem the
wistful, valedictory note of a larger farewell. For by the time of Pater's
death in 1894 it was already becoming clear to Johnson just how
impotent Oxford Hellenism might prove in any contest that pitted
Oxford Greats culture against the clamorous sensuality of an urban
modernity — against "these surging cries, / This restless glare!" as he says
in his poem "Plato in London" (7).

There is no question that Pater himself had sensed this shift in the aesthetic and erotic atmosphere. In the last story he published before he died — "Apollo in Picardy" — for instance, Pater traces with an extraordinary subtlety of reference the doubtful fate of the Uranian love that had been bred out of Oxford Hellenism. Re-creating the fictional situation Symonds had depicted when he wrote his allegory of Jowett's Oxford in *Gabriel*, Pater describes in "Apollo in Picardy" a small community of monks, "creatures of rule" (156) whose severe life is transformed by the arrival of a handsome, pagan stranger whom they decide to call Apollyon. Commentators on Pater's fiction have from the first pointed to the homoerotic dimension of Apollyon's relationship with the young novice Hyacinth, for the youth's accidental death occurs in exactly the same manner as that of his famous Greek namesake — while playing quoits with his lover Apollo.

Yet this obvious parallel with the classical myth of Hyacinthus represents merely the superficial aspect of the homoerotic tradition Pater is drawing upon here. For when he says that in meeting Apollo/Apollyon both Hyacinth and the prior "come in contact for the first time in their lives with the power of untutored natural impulse, of natural inspiration" (156), Pater means that both men engage with Greek culture under its homoerotic aspect — the word "natural" having by now come to signify "Greek" as automatically in the Oxford tradition of pederastic Hellenism as "inspiration" signifies the "hearer/inspirer" relationship of Greek *paiderastia*. This ancient pederastic ethos explains why Hyacinth is able to assume all the physical grace and "immense gaiety" (156) of Greek athletes when Apollyon teaches him wrestling and archery. Nonetheless, it is the older monk, the prior Saint-Jean — so often dismissed in modern Pater criticism as a repressed or maddened or even "homophobic" figure — who is even more deeply transformed by the pagan erotic energies flowing out of Apollo/Apollyon.

Here we glimpse the great significance of the pedagogical scene between the prior and Apollyon. For it is the ostensible teacher — the prior — who is in fact taught or inspired "at the contact of this extraordinary pupil or fellow-inquirer" (164). In this moment the prior's relationship to his own knowledge is totally transformed: now he comprehends the old dry facts as living totalities, grasps the previously unimaginable as simple actuality, passing from a conventionally Ptolemaic view of the cosmos to a new vision of "the earth . . . moving round the sun" (164).[31] His mind illuminated by "this beam of insight, or of inspiration!" (164), the prior turns to write the last volume of his twelve-volume treatise on mathematics. Diverging radically from the earlier volumes, the argument of the new book is convulsed "as with the throes of childbirth" (143–44), its pages fill with "line and figure bending, breathing, flaming, into lovely 'arrangements'" (144–45) until the prior is declared mad by his monkish colleagues, and he breaks off the work to die.

It is precisely here that Pater shows Uranian love menaced by cruel incomprehension — as when the monks mistake the prior's homoerotic possession by Apollo/Apollyon for ordinary madness, or when the officers of justice mistake the outcome of Apollo/Apollyon's own homoerotic *mania* — the accidental death of Hyacinth — for the result of what they suppose to have been a "fit of mania" in the prior (170). In such misprisions as these Pater allows us to see his larger fears for homoerotic Hellenism. Quite simply, everything about what Socrates had called in the *Phaedrus* erotic "madness" (*mania*) — "the best of all forms of divine possession" — has been misunderstood in this monkish and unimpassioned world so like Oxford's own: Apollo is mistaken for Apollyon, the angel of the bottomless, sodomic pit; a dream of soft wintry auroras — "a low circlet of soundless flame, waving, licking daintily up the black sky, but harmless, beautiful" — is misinterpreted by the prior himself as "hellfire!" (147); the prior's childbirth-like throes of intellectual, spiritual procreancy — those "births of passionate air" — are taken by his fellow monks for the convulsions of a diseased mind; and all the stir and ferment of genuine cultural renewal in medieval Picardy — the barn architecture changing from Gothic to neoclassical, the Gregorian chants "turned to real silvery music" (161) — are dismissed as mere excesses owing to the winter solstice. This is doubtless why the silently flaming auroras that so continually reappear in "Apollo in Picardy" upon the prior's page as in the night sky, and foretell precisely what Lionel Johnson would call "Some delicate dawning of a new desire"

31. See Monsman, *Pater's Portraits*, 187–88, and the Keefes, *Gods*, 140–43, for the Copernican and Keplerian dimensions to the prior's vision of a heliocentric system.

about to be kindled in culture and the individual life by the ardent flame of the Platonic eros, are instead so repeatedly mistaken both within the story by Pater's characters and beyond the story by Pater's critics.[32]

All the painful burden of Pater's own experience at Oxford thus presses into view here — the intoxicating education, the fiery friendships, the hopes for cultural regeneration and a more liberal way of life, followed by the cold incomprehension, the hatred, the stony exile. Pater had made a celebrated career out of simultaneously uncovering and reveiling the homoerotic text within the cultural ideal of Victorian liberalism. Driven by scandal and satire at Oxford into a self-protective posture of covert resistance, "Mr. Rose" had had to begin again, in the beautiful, laborious historical fiction of *Marius the Epicurean* (1885), to attempt to vindicate himself and express the case for the cultural power of male love through all the elegant indirections of aesthetic humanism. Yet as this late story and some of his scattered remarks in the collected Oxford lectures known as *Plato and Platonism* (1893) repeatedly suggest, Pater never ceased to realize that the danger to homoerotic Hellenism might in fact come not from the predictably uncomprehending barbarians alone but also from the Greeks themselves: Socrates' teaching had been corrupted by Alcibiades, his own had been mistaken by Wilde.[33]

When the Wilde scandal first erupted in March of 1895, Pater had been dead less than a year, Symonds less than two. The scandal, with its

32. Richard Dellamora, for instance, imagines that the prior's dream of "a circlet of soundless flame, waving, licking daintily up the black sky, but harmless, beautiful, closing in upon that round dark space in the midst, which was the earth" represents the prior's "sexual fantasies of anilingus and anal copulation. The 'flame . . . licking daintily' refers to tongue and/or penis; 'the round dark space in the midst,' to the opening sphincter." Though the reading has been to some degree controversial, it is perhaps possible to agree with Dellamora that, in whatever case, all this "is a figment not just of the prior" (190).

33. Cf. Pater's characterization of the "rhapsodist" in Plato "whose sensitive performance of his part is nothing less than an 'interpretation' of it, artist and critic at once" (*Plato* 131) — Wilde, of course, was known for his rhapsodies and *contes parlés* — and his critical dialogue *Critic as Artist* had appeared in 1891. Pater's discussion of Plato's Alcibiades also bears on his own relationship to Wilde: "the winning brilliancy of the lost spirit of Alcibiades . . . the nature of one by birth and endowments an aristocrat, amid the

sordid arrests, trials, testimony, and incarcerations, assured that the hopes Pater and Symonds had once cherished for male love as the agent of personal and cultural transformation — for that "delicate dawning of a new desire" — were eclipsed in the ensuing controversy, completely overwhelmed by an extraordinary, lurid publicity. In this moment of March 1895 all the expanded scope Symonds had so cautiously, Pater so covertly, and Wilde so carelessly endeavored to win for homoerotic imagination and experience would seemingly vanish overnight. Yet even as it vanished, the apparent mechanism of its repression — the Victorian state apparatus of police and courts and prisons — would simultaneously be operating, as Foucault has taught us to understand, as a steady incitement to speech, the prosecution of the "love that dare not speak its name" impelling more people to speak more garrulously than ever before of this new thing now to be known as "homosexuality."

From the first moments of the scandal, Wilde was engulfed in a maelstrom of competing and meretricious fictions. Lord Alfred Douglas, Douglas's father the marquis of Queensberry, the lawyers, the newspapers — all the official and unofficial participants in the first trial sought to manipulate the available languages of legitimation to vindicate themselves and destroy their opponents. Queensberry, a poisonous atheist, debauché, and bully, fought to appear before the British public, as Wilde himself realized, "in an entirely new character, that of the affectionate father . . . a champion of purity," even as he transformed his son into "the good young man who was very nearly tempted into wrong-doing by the wicked and immoral artist, but was rescued just in time" (*Letters* 498). This ludicrously untrue yet deeply satisfying fiction would take on an autonomous life, becoming the version, as Wilde was to protest in *De Profundis*, that "has now actually passed into serious history: it is quoted, believed, and chronicled" (*Letters* 456).

When Wilde in turn was arrested and charged with gross indecency in the second trial, Queensberry's role as the defender of the innocent youth and the public interest was taken up by the Crown prosecutor,

---

dangers to which it is exposed in the Athens of that day — the qualities which must make him, if not the saviour, the destroyer, of a society which cannot remain unaffected by his showy presence. *Corruptio optimi pessima!* (130).

who sought to safeguard society, as we have already heard him say, from a sodomic sore upon the body politic "which cannot fail in time to corrupt and taint it all." In Wilde's third trial, the prosecutor would marshal a still richer rhetorical display of invective, so effective a set of forensic fictions — "like a thing out of Tacitus, like a passage in Dante, like one of Savanarola's indictments of the Popes at Rome" — as to convince even Wilde himself, who would remember "being sickened with horror at what I heard" (502).

On trial for his life — "All trials," as he was to declare in *De Profundis*, "are trials for one's life" (509) — Wilde, with the masterful peroration we have heard him pronounce, would call upon the language of Oxford Hellenism to contest and disarm the enormous residual power of the ideological traditions so massively marshaled against him. Charged with corrupting youth, Wilde invokes Plato's pedagogic eros. Confronted with the sordid evidence of sodomic indecency, he appeals to a "pure" procreancy of the spirit. Condemned as effeminate and degenerate, he shows the intellectual fearlessness and commanding flexibility of mind so celebrated in Victorian liberal Hellenism as the only vitally regenerative powers still capable of saving England.

In the brief moment remade by his overwhelming personality, when the profound silence of the Old Bailey courtroom is broken by loud applause, Wilde thus realizes in his own person all that Symonds had ever said about the revelation of reading Plato — he reveals masculine love as dwelling "not in a mean hole or corner" but at the very heart of "the race whose literature forms the basis of [our] higher culture." When Wilde speaks, the discourse of Oxford Hellenism speaks through him, and in this dire moment of its compelling authority claims in the name of an undeformed humanity a hearing for a masculine procreancy to which culture itself owes an inextinguishable debt.

Yet the full measure of Wilde's achievement in the witness box finally becomes clear only when we read his meditation on his own life in *De Profundis* and realize how much he had despised Douglas's vapid phrase about "the love that dare not speak its name." For as Wilde realized, Douglas had indolently borrowed the notion of "two loves" for his poem of the same title from the Platonic doctrine of the Uranian and Pandemic eros — where its subtle axis is poised between a telos of intellectual aspiration and a telos of physical appetite. Douglas then transferred the notion of "two loves" to a banal new polarity organized around sexual object choice — of "true Love," as Douglas says, filling the "hearts of boy and girl with mutual flame" (*"Two Loves"* 1) versus an antagonistic "Love that dares not tell its name," as Wilde would slightingly misquote the line (*Letters* 441). When Douglas's poem is cited in court as evidence of a spreading sexual indecency at Oxford and elsewhere, Wilde, loyal to him even in this extremity, summons himself to defend Douglas's lame verse. Speaking his mighty peroration, Wilde briefly embodies the power of a mind saturated in Greek thought and Oxford Hellenism to stave off the invading horror, to overcome another man's intellectual indolence and imaginative vulgarity, and to transfigure even vapidity into something eloquent and fine.

As Richard Ellmann's magisterial biography has made clear, the categories of Hellenic thought and experience which had so deeply informed Wilde's experience at Oxford — intensifying his pleasure, as we have heard him say, in *"intellectual friction to rouse me up to talk or think"* — never released their hold upon him. When some years after going down from Oxford, he was first seduced into homosexual practices by Robert Ross, Wilde understood their intercourse as proceeding along the Platonic ladder of love, passing from pandemic physical delight to Uranian intellectual friendship. With Ross, the Platonic ideal of an erotic procreancy of the spirit generating thought and art, as well as the frank Greek practice of "embracing to wrestle and wrestling to embrace," seemed to issue in a perfect fulfillment of Hellenism, for it was out of his conversation with Ross that Wilde achieved the ideas for both *Mr. W. H.* and *The Decay of Lying.*[34]

---

34. Ross's extensive collaboration with Wilde and other writers such as Siegfried Sassoon and Robert Graves has gone unnoticed in much recent work on male literary collaboration. He was, however, "one of the most *indirectly* creative [of] men," as Arnold Bennett told Sassoon (Margery Ross 11–12). Wilde's dedicatory inscription to Ross — "To the Mirror of Perfect Friendship: Robbie" (*Letters* 783n) — written years after Wilde's release from prison in February 1899, shows that his belief in the Platonic ideal of Uranian love continued even after he had ceased to look for anything more for himself than "Passion with the mask of Love" (766). Deriving from *Phaedrus* 255 d–e: "his lover is as it were a mirror in which he beholds himself . . . that counterlove [*anterōs*] which is the image of love" (Hamilton and Cairns ed. 501), the notion of the male lover as ethical

ROBERT ROSS.
(Photo in the
Hyde Collection,
Somerville, N.J.)

JOHN GRAY in 1893.
(Photo used by permission
of the Prior Provincial
of the Dominican Order,
St. Dominic's Priory,
London.)

In the same way, the beauty and homage of younger men genuinely inspired Wilde, as when admiring groups of undergraduates at Oxford or Cambridge would call upon him for "Early Church" or some other of his *contes parlés* — "bright young faces, and grey misty quadrangles, Greek forms passing through Gothic cloisters" (*Letters* 181). Roused within the radiant circle of their admiration, Wilde would then begin to weave one of his entrancing verbal arabesques. Even Wilde's frankly commercial relations with male prostitutes were conducted within the transforming frame of the Socratic eros. Frank Harris's wonderful tale of finding Wilde at the Café Royal discoursing on the Olympic Games with two Cockney youths of dubious aspect — "talking as well as if he had had a picked audience" — achieves, for all its improbability, the deeper truth of fiction: "'Did you sy they was niked?' 'Of course,' Oscar replied, 'nude, clothed only in sunshine and beauty'" (90, 146).

The full dimensions of his own catastrophe would become apparent to Wilde only as he wrote *De Profundis* during the final months of his prison term. For it was then, as the world he had lost yet remained intact to him — preserved in suspended animation by memory, and undiminished by the sordid world of social extinction, penury, and sickness which would rise around him once he was released — that Wilde was able to see his life with Alfred Douglas in its true relation to the ideal of Greek love. Cut off from the outside world, he writes his long letter to Douglas through a power of inertial momentum, drawing on the deep reserves of memory and imagination laid down in him by his Oxford experience: no other work of Wilde's, as Richard Jenkyns has reminded us, is so full of Greek echoes and quotations as *De Profundis* (97). With his acute suffering in prison now illuminating his own earlier suffering at Douglas's hands — misery once all but invisible to him in the blaze of the

---

mirror would come to be represented by the figure of Narcissus, a symbol that, emptied of its classical ethical content, would in turn come to represent male love — Wilde and Mallock, as we have seen, both deploy it in this way. This form of the Narcissus figure would later assume a new and pathological meaning as "narcissism" within Freud's psychoanalytic account of homosexuality. Pater had given the title "Anteros" to chapter 10 of his unfinished work *Gaston de Latour*. See Monsman "Unpublished Chapters." For the origin of the Anteros figure in the athletic and pederastic rituals of the Greek *palaestra*, see Böttiger.

younger man's beauty and his own triumphant success — *De Profundis* becomes in this context a moral epistle or essay on male friendship in the classical tradition of Cicero's *De Amicitia* or Aristotle's *Politics*.[35]

Beyond the very real likelihood that Wilde was convicted, as Ellmann has argued, for sexual acts Douglas had actually committed,[36] Wilde's overriding concern in the letter has little to do with sexual acts, which he regarded as trivial — "Sins of the flesh are nothing" (*Letters* 452). It is only as Douglas's own relentless interest in buggering boys approached "appetite without distinction "desire without limit" (463), only as his obsessive talk about boys and buggery drove out everything else, that Wilde recognized that the younger man's appetite for "the

35. Cf. *De Profundis*: "Guildenstern and Rosencrantz are as immortal as Angelo and Tartuffe, and should rank with them. They are what modern life has contributed to the antique ideal of friendship. He who writes a new *De Amicitia* must find a new niche for them and praise them in Tusculan prose. . . . Of course I do not propose to compare you. There is a wide difference between you. What with [Rosencrantz and Guildenstern] was chance, with you was choice" (*Letters* 505). As Wilde's warder at Reading Gaol was to recall, "He was no good for anything — except writing, and that as a rule has small place inside a prison. . . . He was so unlike other men. Just a bundle of brains — and that is all" (Jackson, *Aristotle* xiii).

36. Ellmann assumes that Douglas, in informing Wilde's counsel of certain information prejudicial to himself, and offering to testify, was taking responsibility for the incidents of buggery established in the trial through the evidence of stained bedsheets, since, as Ellmann says, "Wilde did not practice this" (461). Unable to refer to such a matter directly in a manuscript controlled by the prison authorities, Wilde himself appears to be referring to it guardedly in *De Profundis*: "The sins of another were being placed to my account. Had I so chosen, I could on either trial have saved myself at his expense, not from shame indeed but from imprisonment. Had I cared to show that the Crown witnesses — the three most important — had been carefully coached by your father and his solicitors, not in reticences merely but in assertions, in the absolute transference, deliberate, plotted, and rehearsed, of the actions and doings of someone else on to me, I could have had each one of them dismissed from the box by the Judge. . . . I could have walked out of court . . . a free man" (*Letters* 452).

Wilde presents his reproach here as arising not from the excruciating cost to himself of this sacrifice but from Douglas's complete moral obtuseness and ingratitude about it: "You had the sympathy and the sentimentality of the spectator of a rather pathetic play. That you were the true author of the hideous tragedy did not occur to you. I saw that you realised nothing of what you had done" (448). In this context Douglas's charge that the government had engaged in a criminal conspiracy to convict Wilde becomes intelligible as a displacement of or psychic defense against his own complicity in Wilde's ruin.

mire" had become a genuinely shameful "sin of the soul." As Wilde tells Douglas, "It was only in the mire that we met, and fascinating, terribly fascinating though the one topic round which your talk invariably centred was, still at the end it became quite monotonous I was often bored to death by it" (432).

For Wilde, the great and salient fact about their love thus becomes that "during the whole time we were together I never wrote one single line. Whether at Torquay, Goring, London, Florence or elsewhere, my life, as long as you were by my side, was entirely sterile and uncreative" (426). Here is the unmistakable language of the Platonic eros and spiritual procreancy, the native idiom of the high ideal which Wilde once believed, with the *anamnēsis* of the Oxford homoerotic imagination, had been miraculously reincarnated in Douglas, the Greek and gracious boy whom he so repeatedly hailed as "Hyacinth" and "Hylas" and "Narcissus." In *De Profundis* Wilde's genuine lovers, by contrast, are seen to have been such younger men as Robbie Ross, with whom Wilde shared both literary and sexual secrets, or Pierre Louÿs and John Gray, with whom he shared his art and probably nothing more: "My real life, my higher life was with them and such as they" (*Letters* 426).

As the corrupting instructor of Dorian Gray, Lord Henry Wotton represented, Wilde knew, all that the world imagined Wilde to be in his relation to Douglas. Yet the grotesque truth of their actual relationship would always remain that the "corruption" and fatal influence of "personality" had in fact worked all the other way. It was not Wilde who had ruined the younger man.[37] It was instead the younger man who had

37. Initiated into homosexual practices at Winchester, Douglas first sought out Wilde for help in dealing with a "renter" who was blackmailing him at Oxford. As Wilde tells him in *De Profundis*, "Your defect was not that you knew so little about life, but that you knew so much. . . . The gutter and the things that live in it had begun to fascinate you" (*Letters* 425). Nor was Wilde alone in this opinion. George Ives, the poet and homosexual apologist whose immense and earnest diary provides a view into the Uranian half-world of the 1890s, regarded Douglas as the foremost activist for "the Cause" at Oxford ("he has made Oxford what it is") but was unnerved by Douglas's "difficult character, swayed by passion, shaken by impulse" (Stokes, "Ives" 179, 178). After Douglas spent the night with Ives on 24 August 1894, and more especially after the Wilde trials, Ives came to regard him as "that miserable traitor . . . I knew he had faults and more or less insanity all along, but I thought him rather the victim than the villain he proved to be" (179).

ruined Wilde with "an unintellectual friendship, a friendship whose primary aim was not the creation and contemplation of beautiful things," a bond "intellectually degrading to me" (425, 426), destroying the conditions for his art, and insisting upon the ruinous suit against Queensberry which had made public such evidence that the authorities could not in the end avoid prosecuting Wilde.[38]

38. Cf. *De Profundis*: "Do you think I am here on account of my relations with the witnesses in my trial? My relations, real or supposed, with people of that kind were matters of no interest to either the Government or Society. . . . I am here for having tried to put your father into prison" (*Letters* 456). Ellmann has presented a compelling case for regarding Wilde's prosecution as more the result of grotesque accident and miscalculation than of specific judicial or social persecution.

Wilde himself trusted that the *De Profundis* letter would eventually vindicate him, telling Robert Ross in 1897, "When you have read the letter you will see the psychological explanation of a course of conduct that from the outside seems a combination of absolute idiocy with vulgar bravado. Some day the truth will have to be known: not necessarily in my lifetime or in Douglas's: but I am not prepared to sit in the grotesque pillory they put me into, for all time" (*Letters* 512).

The motives behind Wilde's prosecution have been central to much recent commentary on him and Victorian "homosexuality" generally (see, for example, Gagnier 205–207 and, following her, Dellamora 208–12). Responding to assertions by Jeffrey Weeks and others that the legal position of such "homosexuals" as Wilde greatly deteriorated in the later Victorian period as a result of changes in the law covering sodomy, attempted sodomy, and related offenses, Arthur Gilbert has argued that these historians have typically focused on the sodomy and attempted sodomy laws to the exclusion of the *application* of those laws. Gilbert's own studies of court records in the earlier nineteenth century have convinced him that the 1826 change in the sodomy statute (eliminating the requirement that emission as well as penetration be proved in sodomy cases, thereby making convictions easier to obtain) was followed by, if anything, a decrease in the number of sodomy convictions. With regard to the Labouchere amendment, under which Wilde was tried for "gross indecency," Gilbert has similarly found no evidence that the new law brought about any substantial increase in actual prosecutions (Review 215).

Proposing instead an explanation of English sodomy prosecutions and convictions as arising from a sense of imminent social catastrophe, Gilbert has argued that the historical record of England during the period 1749–1814 "seems to show that fear of disaster may be far more significant in general and in specific situations" than more general concerns about marriage, gender identity, and procreation ("Sexual Deviance" 100). He notes in particular that the 1749–92 period in London and Middlesex County saw only one execution for sodomy, whereas during the much shorter Napoleonic Wars period of 1803–14 seven men were executed. Indeed, the rate of prosecutions for attempted sodomy spiked in 1810—the year of the "Vere Street conspiracy" involving the patrons

The most damning of the evidentiary texts used to prosecute Wilde was a letter of fantastic literary conceits ("I know Hyacinthus, whom Apollo loved so madly, was you in Greek days" [326]), a letter that could "only be understood," as he now says to Douglas, "by those who have read the *Symposium* of Plato, or caught the spirit of a certain grave mood made beautiful for us in Greek marbles" (440). Its Uranian phrases caught from the Greats tradition, and gilded by Wilde's extravagant wit, such a letter was a Uranian eulogy to youthful beauty and promise which Wilde would have written "to any graceful young man of either University who had sent me a poem of his own making, certain that he would have sufficient wit or culture to interpret rightly its fantastic phrases" (440–41). Carelessly misplaced by Douglas, and later stolen by one of Douglas' male sex partners, the letter entered the economy of extortion, of "renters" and blackmail victims and police, where it circulated as "an infamous letter," and "every construction but the right one is put on it" (441), Douglas using it to taunt his dangerously inflammable father. So in the end the inescapable irony would always be not that the prosecutors or the respectable Victorian public could not understand what Wilde meant by a "pure" Platonic love or a "higher life" of spiritual procreancy, but that the Oxford Hyacinthus, Douglas himself, could not. "You had not yet been able to acquire," as Wilde now told him, "the 'Oxford temper' in intellectual matters, never, I mean been one who

---

of a male brothel — which was precisely the most difficult year of England's war with France.

The interpretation advanced in the present study argues that, beyond the search for scapegoats in times of national catastrophe posited by Gilbert, the intensified prosecution of suspected sodomites in times of war or danger represents a crisis response at the level of archaic civic consciousness as it identifies male weakness and "effeminacy" with the martial collapse of the collectivity. Amid the alarm over the Vere Street conspiracy, for instance, the *Morning Chronicle* could be heard invoking the familiar vocabulary of classical republicanism — Machiavelli's pervasive idiom of *corruzione* and *rovina* — when that newspaper called on the English to join those "zealously disposed to stemming a torrent of corruption that threatens to involve us in the gulf of infamy as well as ruin" (Crompton 168). A more recent sign of the remarkable persistence and residual power of the ancient civic response identifying male effeminacy with martial failure may be glimpsed in the American controversy over admitting declared homosexuals into the U.S. military.

could play gracefully with ideas but had arrived at violence of opinion merely" (426).

This is why Wilde has undertaken to write to Douglas the long letter of reproach and forgiveness that is *De Profundis* in the first place: to restore the true relations between older lover and younger beloved, *erastēs* and *erōmenos*, which had been so inverted in their actual friendship, returning it to the "hearer/inspirer" dyad of Dorian and Platonic love. For only by genuinely hearing what his lover now teaches will Douglas be rescued, so that the mean-spirited and hate-filled young man, whose golden beauty had once seemed to promise Wilde the very perfection of Greek love,[39] might at last, although with an appalling belatedness, truly realize himself as a man. "The only vice is shallowness," Wilde now counsels Douglas, appealing repeatedly to the presiding ideal of liberal Germano-Hellenism, to *Bildung* and human development in its richest diversity: "whatever is realised, is right." If Wilde, following his release from prison, was briefly to return to and live with Douglas on the old degraded terms of graceless excess and thankless exploitation, it is, as Ellmann has suggested, largely because his real life had ended in Reading Gaol ("I died in prison," "Something is killed in me," as Wilde would tell his remaining friends), and he was now condemned to relive all his past existence, but this time as a failure.

The symbolic point of rupture would thus always remain the trials for Wilde's life of April–May 1895, when the discourse of Oxford Hellenism still spoke so powerfully through him that it compelled an unwill-

---

39. This valorization of male bodily beauty derives its ethical claims from the passage in *Symposium* 212a noted earlier, where Diotima instructs Socrates that "it is only when he discerns beauty itself through what makes it visible that a man will be quickened with the true, and not the seeming, virtue." Wilde's own visual sensitivity bordered on hyperaesthesia — cf. *De Profundis*: "There is not a single colour hidden away in the chalice of a flower, or the curve of a shell, to which, by some subtle sympathy with the very soul of things, my nature does not answer. Like Gautier I have always been one of those *pour qui le monde visible existe*" (*Letters* 509). Robert Sherard considered Wilde's delight in visual beauty and corresponding horror at physical ugliness to have been entirely sincere if excessive: "I have heard him refuse to meet people who were ugly, however sympathetic to him, because of the real distress which their appearance caused to him. I have heard him excuse himself on such occasions in accents which left no doubt of his sincerity. 'I cannot do it — I really cannot'" (55–56).

OSCAR WILDE and LORD ALFRED DOUGLAS in 1892. (Photo reproduced by permission of the William Andrews Clark Memorial Library, University of California, Los Angeles, the Estate of Oscar Wilde, and the Lord Alfred Douglas Literary Estate.)

ing assent from the men in the Old Bailey courtroom. As they listened to a superbly confident expositor of the supremely confident tradition of Oxford Hellenism, these men recognized in Wilde's voice the language of their own aspiration — an aspiration that had been shaped for Victorians by Mill and Grote, Jowett and Arnold, Gladstone and Pater out of the tumult of the mid-Victorian cultural crisis.

To regard any such symbolic moment as this one is to see that Victorian Hellenism has here become powerful enough as a legitimating discourse to counter and momentarily to silence the ideological constructions of an ancient classical republicanism — *effeminatus* and "effeminacy," *virtus* and "corruption" — which had for so long determined so much that was now being discursively reconfigured as "homosexuality." It is, perhaps, one measure of the ideological potency of Victorian liberal Hellenism that it can in this moment speak without loss of persuasive power through the medium of precisely the most notorious dandy-aesthete-effeminatus of the day, a man who had flourished specifically those modes of dress, mannerism, and speech which had since the time of Pope's Sporus and Smollett's Whiffle signaled to the English that effeminacy and civic incapacity have once again minced forward within the polity and now threaten it with utter ruin.

Yet even as Wilde speaks his mighty peroration, Victorian Hellenism has already begun to slip into equivocality, a semantic shift we may hear beginning when Swinburne calls Simeon Solomon, the Pre-Raphaelite painter arrested 1873 for soliciting in a London urinal, "a Platonist" and a "translator . . . of Platonic theory into Socratic practice" (2:261); and accelerating, when Benjamin Jowett tells Hallam Tennyson in 1892 that his father's feeling for Shakespeare's sonnets constituted "a sort of sympathy with Hellenism" (Tennyson 340); and approaching completion when George Ives, the secretive agitator for homosexualism, declares himself in 1903 to be "a cold disciplined Hellenist" (Ellmann 454).

Above all in later years, it would be Wilde's own hapless and sordid catastrophe that was to seem in the public imagination to have entered into indissoluble combination with the cultural values asserted by Pater and Symonds and the English Uranians, reducing any invocation of a high and "gracious" Hellenism to something half ridiculous and partially suspect.[40] It is because a writer such as Compton MacKenzie would ultimately be able to summon up a whole late-Victorian epoch at Oxford and Eton and such other "Arcadian" venues in the murmurous, flutelike speech of a single Hellenizing invert in *Sinister Street* (1913), or because G. Lowes Dickinson's little handbook on Greece would come to serve as much as a source of information about paiderastia as about hubris or helots or the agora for generations of desperately ignorant English and American homosexual young men, that such recent defenders of Greek studies as Richard Jenkyns have only been able to regard the inheritance of Pater's Hellenism or Symonds's and Wilde's with a deeply angry dismay.

In the same way, Wilde's late twentieth-century heirs have been able to see, as Eve Sedgwick has said, nothing more than "Oscar Wilde" — a largely empty, almost arbitrary name onto which law and journalism, medicine and theology, prejudice and ignorance would so ceaselessly project their theories and loathing and fears. But today, as Wilde is steadily becoming audible once again as a cultural hero rather than merely a homosexual martyr, it is the supreme confidence and the Dorian "manliness" of Oxford Hellenism which lifts his voice to be heard. For it is only now, perhaps, a century after the tragedy of Wilde's fall, that we are at last able to hear in the demand for a nonmedical or nonpsychiatric or unpathologized account of "homosexuality" — as a normality unencumbered by norms — precisely the recovery of a perspective that had originally entered Anglo-American consciousness

---

40. Cf. E. F. Benson's remark in his memoir *As We Were* (1930) that Wilde believed "he was realizing for a drab world the ancient Greek ideal of the joy and beauty of life. Nothing could have been less like what he was doing, for the Greek genius for exquisite living was founded on physical fitness and moderation in all things, while he based it on the unbridled gratification of animal appetites" (206). An intimate friend of Alfred Douglas (who had by this time renounced all sodomy and Uranian themes), Benson sounds a note Wilde himself had taken up in *De Profundis* and in his post-prison letters: "I do not accept the British view that Messalina is better than Sporus: these things are matters of temperament, and both are equally vile, because sensual pleasures wreck the soul: but all my profligacy, extravagance, and worldly life of fashion and senseless ease, were wrong for an artist" (*Letters* 594). Although Wilde here is addressing an aesthetic former-clergyman, and hence is inclined to exaggerate his new regard for *sōphrosynē*, the theme recurs even with such correspondents as Ross from whom Wilde had little to hide.

through the spiritual procreancy ideal of Oxford Hellenism. If it has been inordinately difficult for late twentieth-century homosexual apologists to see this idealist dimension of Hellenism either in the formative moment of Victorian "homosexuality" or in Wilde, it is precisely because the salient forces fostered by that discourse — self-development, diversity, "liberty of the heart" — so completely survived the wreck of Wilde's life and art as to have become quite invisibly what we are.

WORKS CITED

Abbott, Evelyn. *The Life and Letters of Benjamin Jowett, M.A., Master of Balliol College, Oxford*. Vol. 2. London: John Murray, 1897.

Anstruther, Ian. *Oscar Browning: A Biography*. London: John Murray, 1983.

Aristotle. *The Politics*. Trans. T. A. Sinclair. Harmondsworth, Middlesex: Penguin, 1962.

Arnold, Matthew. *Culture and Anarchy*. In *Prose Works*, 5:87–256.

———. *The Function of Criticism at the Present Time* (1865). In *Prose Works*, 3:258–85.

———. *The Prose Works of Matthew Arnold*. Ed. R. H. Super. 11 vols. Ann Arbor: University of Michigan Press, 1960–77.

Arnold, Thomas. "Inaugural Lecture." In *Introductory Lectures on Modern History*. 2d ed. 1–33. London: B. Fellowes, 1843.

———. "The Social Progress of States" (1830). In *Miscellaneous Works*, 306–27. New York: Appleton, 1845.

Atkinson, G. T. "Oscar Wilde at Oxford." *Cornhill Magazine* 66 (1929): 559–64.

Bayley, C. C. *War and Society in Renaissance Florence: The "De Militia" of Leonardo Bruni*. Toronto: University of Toronto Press, 1961.

Benson, A. C. *Walter Pater*. London: Macmillan, 1906.

Benson, E. F. *As We Were: A Victorian Peep Show*. London: Longmans, Green, 1930.

Berlin, Isaiah. "Two Concepts of Nationalism: An Interview with Isaiah Berlin." *New York Review of Books*, 21 November 1991, 19–23.

Best, G. F. A. "The Protestant Constitution and Its Supporters, 1800–1829." *Transactions of the Royal Historical Society* 8 (1958): 107–27.

Blackwood's Edinburgh Magazine. "The Cockney School of Poetry, I" 2 (October 1817): 38–41; II, 2 (November 1817): 194–201; III, 3 (July 1818): 453–56; IV, 3 (August 1818): 519–24; V, 5 (April 1819): 97–101; VI, 6 (October 1819): 70–76; VII, 12 (December 1822): 775–81; and "Letter from Z. to Mr. Leigh Hunt" 2 (January 1818): 414–17 and 3 (May 1818): 196–201.

Bloomfield, Samuel Thomas, trans. *The History of Thucydides.* 3 vols. London: Longman, Rees, Orme, Brown and Green, 1828.

Böttiger, Karl August. "Eros und Anteros." In *Kleine schriften archäologischen und antiquarischen Inhalts,* 1: 159–63. 3 vols. Dresden: Arnold, 1837–38.

Bolingbroke, Henry St. John, Viscount. *The Craftsman* (1726–36). 14 vols. London: printed for R. Francklin, 1731–37.

Bowden, John Edward. *The Life and Letters of Frederick William Faber, D.D., Priest of the Oratory of St. Philip Neri, 1814–63.* London: Thomas Richardson, 1969.

Brake, Laurel. "Judas and the Widow: Thomas Wright and A. C. Benson as Biographers of Walter Pater: The Widow." *Prose Studies* 4 (1981): 39–54.

Bray, Alan. *Homosexuality in Renaissance England.* 2d ed. London: Gay Men's Press, 1988.

Brendon, Piers. *Hurrell Froude and the Oxford Movement.* London: Paul Elek, 1974.

Brown, Horatio F. *John Addington Symonds: A Biography.* 2 vols. London: John C. Nimmo, 1895.

Brown, John. *Estimate of the Manners and Principles of the Times.* 2d ed. London: printed for L. Davis and C. Reymers, 1757.

Browning, Elizabeth Barrett. *Aurora Leigh,* ed. Margaret Reynolds. Athens: Ohio University Press, 1992.

Browning, Oscar. *Memories of Sixty Years, at Eton, Cambridge, and Elsewhere.* London: Lane, 1910.

Buchanan, Robert. *The Fleshly School of Poetry and Other Phenomena of the Day.* London: Strahan, 1872.

Burrow, J. W. "Introduction." In Wilhelm von Humboldt, *The Limits of State Action,* vii–xliii. Cambridge: Cambridge University Press, 1969.

———. *Whigs and Liberals: Continuity and Change in English Political Thought.* Oxford: Clarendon, 1988.

Campbell, Lewis. *The Life and Letters of Benjamin Jowett, M.A., Master of Balliol College, Oxford.* Vol. 1 London: John Murray, 1897.

Carpenter, Edward. "Homogenic Love" (1894). In Reade, *Sexual Heretics,* 324–47.

Cartledge, Paul. "The Importance of Being Dorian: An Onomastic Gloss on the Hellenism of Oscar Wilde." *Hermathena* 147 (1989–90): 7–15.

Cassidy, John A. "Robert Buchanan and the Fleshly School Controversy." *PMLA* 67 (1952): 65–93.

Cecil, Algernon. *Six Oxford Thinkers: Gibbon, Newman, Church, J. A. Froude, Pater, Lord Morley of Blackburn.* London: John Murray, 1909.

Chauncey, George, Jr. "From Sexual Inversion to Homosexuality: Medicine and the Changing Conceptualization of Female Deviance." *Salmagundi* 58–59 (1982–83): 114–46.

Chitty, Susan. *The Beast and the Monk: A Life of Charles Kingsley.* London: Hodder and Stoughton, 1974.

Church, R. W. *The Oxford Movement: Twelve Years, 1833–1845.* London: Macmillan, 1891.

Clark, J. C. D. *English Society 1688–1832: Ideology, Social Structure, and Political Practice during the Ancien Regime.* Cambridge: Cambridge University Press, 1985.

Cockburn, Henry. *Memorials of His Time, 1779–1830.* Edinburgh: T. N. Foulis, 1910.

Coleridge, Gilbert. *Eton in the Seventies.* London: Smith, Elder, 1912.

Coleridge, Samuel Taylor. *A Lay Sermon* (1817). In *Coleridge's Writings on Politics and Society,* ed. John Morrow, 97–151. Princeton: Princeton University Press, 1991.

Collini, Stefan. "The Idea of 'Character' in Victorian Political Thought." *Transactions of the Royal Historical Society,* 5th ser., 35 (1985): 29–50.

———. "Introduction." In *Collected Works of J. S. Mill,* 21:vii–lvi.

———. *Public Moralists: Political Thought and Intellectual Life in Britain 1850–1930.* New York: Oxford University Press, 1991.

Crackenthorpe, Mrs. *The Female Tatler by Mrs. Crackenthorpe, a Lady That Knows Everything.* London: sold by A. Baldwin, 1709.

Croker, John Wilson. *Essays on the Early Period of the French Revolution.* London: John Murray, 1857.

Crompton, Louis. *Byron and Greek Love: Homophobia in 19th-Century England.* Berkeley: University of California Press, 1985.

Culler, A. Dwight. *Imperial Intellect: A Study of Cardinal Newman's Educational Ideal.* New Haven: Yale University Press, 1955.

Dale, Henry. *Thucydides: The History of the Peloponnesian War Literally Translated.* 2 vols. London: George Bell, 1891.

Danson, Lawrence. "Oscar Wilde, Mr. W. H. and the Unspoken Name of Love." *ELH* 58 (1991): 979–1000.

d'Arch Smith, Timothy. *Love in Earnest: Some Notes on the Lives and Writings of English 'Uranian' Poets from 1889 to 1930.* London: Routledge and Kegan Paul, 1970.

de Grazia, Sebastian. *Machiavelli in Hell*. Princeton: Princeton University Press, 1989.

DeLaura, David J. "The Context of Browning's Painter Poems: Aesthetics, Polemics, Historics." *PMLA* 95 (1980): 367–88.

——. *Hebrew and Hellene in Victorian England: Newman, Arnold, and Pater*. Austin: University of Texas Press, 1969.

——. " 'O Unforgotten Voice': The Memory of Newman in the Nineteenth Century." *Renascence* 43 (1990–91): 81–104.

——. "Reading Inman Rereading Pater Reading: A Review-Essay." *Pater Newsletter*, no. 26 (1991): 2–9.

Dellamora, Richard. *Masculine Desire: The Sexual Politics of Victorian Aestheticism*. Chapel Hill: University of North Carolina Press, 1990.

Detienne, Marcel. "La phalange: Problèmes et controverses." In *Problèmes de la guerre en Grèce ancienne*, ed. J.-P. Vernant, 119–42. The Hague: Mouton, 1968.

Dickinson, G. Lowes. *The Greek View of Life*. 3d ed. New York: McClure, Phillips, 1906.

Douglas, Alfred. "A Port in the Aegean." *The Artist and Journal of Home Culture*, no. 167 (October 1893): 311.

——. *"Two Loves" and Other Poems: A Selection*. East Lansing, Mich.: Bennett and Kitchel, 1990.

Dover, K. J. *Greek Homosexuality*. Cambridge: Harvard University Press, 1989.

Dunton, John. "The He-Strumpets: A Satire on the Sodomite Club." In *Athenianism*, 2:93–99. London: printed for T. Darrack, 1710.

Dyer, John. *The Ruins of Rome*. In *Minor Poets of the Eighteenth Century*, 315–28. London: J. M. Dent; New York: E. P. Dutton, 1930.

Ellmann, Richard. *Oscar Wilde*. New York: Knopf, 1987.

Engel, A. J. *From Clergyman to Don: The Rise of the Academic Profession in Nineteenth-Century Oxford*. Oxford: Clarendon, 1983.

Epstein, Julia. "Either/Or — Neither/Both: Sexual Ambiguity and the Ideology of Gender." *Genders* 7 (1990): 99–142.

"Essays and Notices: *The New Republic*." *Contemporary Review* 30 (November 1877): 1098–1100.

Faber, Frederick W. *The Cherwell Water-Lily and Other Poems*. London: J. G. F. and J. Rivington, 1840.

Faber, Geoffrey. *Jowett: A Portrait with Background*. London: Faber and Faber, 1957.

——. *Oxford Apostles: A Character Study of the Oxford Movement*. London: Faber and Faber, 1933.

Fletcher, Ian. "Decadence and the Little Magazines." In *Decadence and the 1890s*, ed. Ian Fletcher, 172–202. London: Edward Arnold, 1979.

Fong, Bobby. "The Poetry of Oscar Wilde: A Critical Edition." Ph.D. dissertation, University of California, Los Angeles, 1978.

Forbes, Duncan. *The Liberal Anglican Idea of History.* Cambridge: Cambridge University Press, 1952.

Foucault, Michel. *The History of Sexuality.* Trans. Robert Hurley. 3 vols. New York: Vintage, 1980–88.

Francis, Elizabeth A. "Tennyson's Political Poetry, 1852–1855." *Victorian Poetry* 14 (1976): 113–23.

Freeman, E. A. "Oxford after Forty Years." *Contemporary Review* 51 (June 1887): 609–23.

Froude, Hurrell. "On State Interference in Matters Spiritual" (1833). In Parsons, *Religion in Victorian Britain,* 3:4–8.

Fyffe, Charles Alan. "Study and Opinion in Oxford." *Macmillan's Magazine* 21 (December 1869): 184–92.

Gagnier, Regenia. *Idylls of the Marketplace: Oscar Wilde and the Victorian Public.* Stanford: Stanford University Press, 1986.

Gallagher, Catherine. "Response." In Neil Hertz, *The End of the Line: Essays on Psychoanalysis and the Sublime,* 194–96. New York: Columbia University Press, 1985.

Garrick, David. *Miss in Her Teens: or, The Medley of Lovers.* London: printed for J. and R. Tonson and S. Draper, 1747.

Gibbon, Edward. *The Autobiography of Edward Gibbon.* Ed. Dero Saunders. New York: Meridian, 1961.

Gilbert, Arthur N. Review of *Coming Out,* by Jeffrey Weeks. *Journal of Homosexuality* 6 (1980–81): 214–16.

———. "Sexual Deviance and Disaster during the Napoleonic Wars." *Albion* 9 (1977): 98–113.

Gladstone, William Ewart. "The Place of Ancient Greece in the Providential Order of the World." In *Gleanings of Past Years, 1843–79,* 7:31–96. New York: Charles Scribners, 1879.

Goodman, Jonathan. *The Oscar Wilde File.* London: Allison and Busby, 1988.

Gosse, Edmund. "Walter Pater." In *Critical Kit-Kats,* 241–71. New York: Dodd, Mead, 1897.

Greenberg, David F. *The Construction of Homosexuality.* Chicago: University of Chicago Press, 1988.

Grosskurth, Phyllis. *Havelock Ellis: A Biography.* New York: New York University Press, 1985.

Hamilton, William. "English Universities: Oxford." *Edinburgh Review* 54 (December 1831): 478–504.

———. "The Universities and Dissenters." *Edinburgh Review* 60 (January 1835): 422–45.

Hardinge, William Money. "Some Personal Recollections of the Master of Balliol." *Temple Bar* 103 (October 1894): 173–85.

Harrington, James. *The Commonwealth of Oceana*. In *The Political Works of James Harrington*, ed. J. G. A. Pocock, 156–359. Cambridge: Cambridge University Press, 1977.

Harris, Frank. *Oscar Wilde*, ed. Lyle Blair. East Lansing: Michigan State University Press, 1954.

Harvie, Christopher. *The Lights of Liberalism: University Liberals and the Challenge of Democracy, 1860–86*. London: Lane, 1976.

Hinchliff, Peter Brigham. *Benjamin Jowett and the Christian Religion*. Oxford: Clarendon, 1987.

Honan, Park. *Matthew Arnold: A Life*. Cambridge: Harvard University Press, 1983.

Hopkins, Gerard Manley. *The Journals and Papers*. Ed. Humphry House and Graham Storey. London: Oxford University Press, 1959.

Hutchinson, Charles Edward. *Boy-Worship*. Oxford: privately printed, 1880.

Hyde, H. Montgomery. *Lord Alfred Douglas: A Biography*. New York: Dodd, Mead, 1985.

——. *The Trials of Oscar Wilde*. London: William Hodge, 1948.

Inman, B. A. "Estrangement and Connection: Walter Pater, Benjamin Jowett, and William M. Hardinge." In *Pater in the 1990s*, ed. Laurel Brake and Ian Small, 1–20. Greensboro, N.C.: ELT Press, 1991.

——. *Walter Pater and His Reading, 1874–1877*. New York: Garland, 1990.

——. *Walter Pater's Reading, 1858–1873*. New York: Garland, 1981.

Jackson, John Wyse. *Aristotle at Afternoon Tea: The Rare Oscar Wilde*. London: Fourth Estate, 1991.

Jackson, William Walrond. *Ingram Bywater: The Memoir of an Oxford Scholar, 1840–1914*. Oxford: Clarendon, 1917.

Jenkyns, Richard. *The Victorians and Ancient Greece*. Cambridge: Harvard University Press, 1980.

Johnson, Lionel. *The Collected Poems of Lionel Johnson*. Ed. Ian Fletcher. Rev. ed. New York: Garland, 1982.

Johnson, Samuel. "Letters to Mrs. Thrale." Quoted in *Boswell's Life of Johnson*, ed. George Birkbeck Hill and L. F. Powell, 3:428–30. Oxford: Clarendon, 1934.

Johnson, William. *Extracts from the Letters and Journals*. Ed. Francis Warre Cornish. Oxford: Hart, 1897.

——. *Ionica* (1858). London: George Allen and Unwin, n.d.

——. *Plato: A Poem*. Cambridge: n.p., 1843.

Jowett, Benjamin, trans. *Thucydides*. 1st ed. 2 vols. Oxford: Clarendon, 1881.

Kains-Jackson, Charles. *The New Chivalry* (1894). In Reade, *Sexual Heretics*, 313–19.

Keefe, Robert, and Janice A. Keefe. *Walter Pater and the Gods of Disorder*. Athens: Ohio University Press, 1988.

Kinglake, Alexander William. *The Invasion of the Crimea: Its Origin and an Account of Its Progress Down to the Death of Lord Raglan*. 8 vols. Edinburgh: William Blackwood, 1868.

Kingsley, Charles. "Alexander Smith and Alexander Pope." *Fraser's Magazine* 48 (October 1853): 452–66.

——. "Froude's *History of England*, Vols. VII and VIII." *Macmillan's Magazine* 9 (January 1864): 211–24.

——. *The Saint's Tragedy, or True Story of Elizabeth of Hungary, Landgravine of Thuringia, Saint of the Roman Calendar*. London: John W. Parker, 1848.

——. "Thoughts on Byron and Shelley." *Fraser's Magazine* 48 (November 1853): 568–76.

——. "Why Should We Fear the Romish Priests?" *Fraser's Magazine* 37 (April 1848): 467–74.

Kingsley, Frances. *Life and Works of Charles Kingsley*. 19 vols. London: Macmillan, 1901–3.

Knight, William. *Principal Shairp and His Friends*. London: John Murray, 1888.

Koestenbaum, Wayne. *Double Talk: The Erotics of Male Literary Collaboration*. New York: Routledge, 1989.

Lancaster, Nathaniel. *The Pretty Gentleman: or, Softness of Manners Vindicated from the False Ridicule Exhibited under the Character of William Fribble, Esq.* (1747). Edinburgh: privately printed, 1885.

Lattimore, Richmond, trans. *Greek Lyrics*. 2d ed. Chicago: University of Chicago Press, 1960.

Lauritsen, John, and David Thorstad. *The Early Homosexual Rights Movement* (1864–1935). New York: Times Change, 1974.

Lefroy, Edward Cracroft. "Aestheticism." In *Undergraduate Oxford: Articles Reprinted from the Oxford and Cambridge Undergraduate's Journal, 1876–77*, 74–82. Oxford: Slatter and Rose, 1878.

Levey, Michael. *The Case of Walter Pater*. London: Thames and Hudson, 1978.

Levinson, Marjorie. *Keats's Life of Allegory: The Origins of a Style*. Oxford: Blackwell, 1988.

Macaulay, Thomas Babington. "Civil Disabilities of the Jews" (1831). In *Critical Essays*, 2:307–23.

——. *Critical, Historical and Miscellaneous Essays*. 6 vols. Boston: Dana Estes, n.d.

——. "Machiavelli" (1827). In *Critical Essays*, 1:267–320.

McCormack, Jerusha Hull. *John Gray: Poet, Dandy, Priest.* Hanover, N.H.: University Press of New England for Brandeis University Press, 1991.

McGann, Jerome J. "Tennyson and the Histories of Criticism." In *The Beauty of Inflections: Literary Investigations in Historical Method and Theory,* 173–203. New York: Oxford University Press, 1988.

Machiavelli, Niccolò. *Discorsi sopra la Prima Deca di Tito Livio* in *Tutte le Opere Storiche e Letterarie di Niccolò Machiavelli,* ed. Guido Mazzoni and Mario Casella, 55–262. Florence: G. Barbera, 1929.

McIntosh, Mary. "The Homosexual Role." *Social Problems* 16 (1968): 182–92.

MacKenzie, Compton. *Sinister Street.* 2 vols. London: Martin Secker, 1913.

Mackie, Gascoigne. *Charmides, or Oxford Twenty Years Ago.* Oxford: Blackwell, 1898.

McLachlan, James. "*The Choice of Hercules:* American Student Societies in the Early 19th Century." In *The University in Society,* ed. Lawrence Stone. 2 vols., 2:449–94. Princeton: Princeton University Press, 1974.

Mallet, Charles E. *A History of the University of Oxford.* 3 vols. New York: Longmans, Green, 1924–28.

Mallock, W. H. *Memoirs of Life and Literature.* London: Harper, 1920.

———. "The New Republic." *Belgravia* 29 (June 1876): 514–43; 30 (July 1876): 48–73; 30 (August 1876): 133–51; 30 (September 1876): 343–60; 30 (October 1876): 434–49; 31 (November 1876): 46–65; 31 (December 1876): 189–209.

———. *The New Republic; or, Culture, Faith, and Philosophy in an English Country House* (1877). Ed. J. Max Patrick. Gainesville: University of Florida Press, 1950.

Mandeville, Bernard de. *An Enquiry into the Origins of Honour and the Usefulness of Christianity in War.* London: printed for John Brotherton, 1732.

Martin, Robert Bernard. *The Dust of Combat: A Life of Charles Kingsley.* London: Faber and Faber, 1959.

Mason, Stuart [Christopher Millard]. *Bibliography of Oscar Wilde.* 2 vols. London: Laurie, 1914; rpt. New York: Haskell, 1972.

Matthew, H. G. C. "Noetics, Tractarians, and the Reform of the University of Oxford in the Nineteenth Century." *History of Universities* 9 (1990): 195–225.

Maurice, Frederick Denison. *Towards the Recovery of Unity: The Thought of Frederick Denison Maurice.* Ed. John F. Porter and William J. Wolf. New York: Seabury, 1964.

Mikhail, E. H., ed. *Oscar Wilde: Interviews and Recollections.* 2 vols. New York: Barnes and Noble, 1979.

Mill, John Stuart. *Autobiography.* In *Collected Works* 1:1–290.

————. *The Collected Works of J. S. Mill.* 33 vols. Ed. John M. Robson. Toronto: University of Toronto Press, 1965–91.

————. "Grote's History of Greece [II]" (1853). In *Collected Works*, 11:307–37.

————. "Headnote to *The Protagoras*." In *Collected Works*, 11:39–61.

————. *On Liberty.* In *Collected Works*, 18:213–310.

Monsman, Gerald. "Old Mortality at Oxford." *Studies in Philology* 67 (1970): 359–89.

————. *Pater's Portraits: Mythic Pattern in the Fiction of Walter Pater.* Baltimore: Johns Hopkins University Press, 1967.

————. *Walter Pater's Art of Autobiography.* New Haven: Yale University Press, 1980.

————. "Walter Pater's Portrait of Marguerite of Valois, Queen of Navarre: The Hitherto Unpublished Chapters IX and X of *Gaston de Latour*" *Victorians Institute Journal* 20 (1992): 262–302.

Mozley, Thomas. *Reminiscences, Chiefly of Oriel College and the Oxford Movement.* 2 vols. Boston: Houghton Mifflin, 1882.

Müller, Karl Otfried. *Die Dorier: Geschichten hellenischer Stämme und Städte.* 3 vols. Breslau: Josef Max, 1824. Trans. Henry Tufnell and George Cornewall Lewis, *The History and Antiquities of the Doric Race.* 2d ed. 2 vols. London: John Murray, 1839.

Neville, Henry. *Plato Redivivus* (1681). In *Two English Republican Tracts*, ed. Caroline Robbins. Cambridge: Cambridge University Press, 1969.

Newman, John Henry. "Antony in Conflict" from *The Church of the Fathers* (1833). In *Essays and Sketches*, ed. Charles Frederick Harrold, 3:92–108. New York: Longmans, Green, 1948.

————. *Historical Sketches.* London: Basil Montagu Pickering, 1873.

————. "Medieval Oxford" (1838). In *Historical Sketches*, 315–35.

————. "Personal Influence the Means of Propagating the Truth" (1832). In *Fifteen Sermons Preached before the University of Oxford*, 75–98. London: Longmans, Green, 1892.

————. "The Rise and Progress of Universities" (1836). In *Historical Sketches*, 1–251.

————. "Tract No. 1" (1833). In Parsons, *Religion in Victorian Britain*, 3:9–10.

Newsome, David. *Godliness and Good Learning: Four Studies on a Victorian Ideal.* London: John Murray, 1961.

————. *On the Edge of Paradise: A. C. Benson the Diarist.* London: John Murray, 1980.

Nockles, P. B. "An Academic Counter-Revolution: Newman and Tractarian Oxford's Idea of a University" *History of Universities* 10 (1991): 137–97.

Paget, Stephen. *Henry Scott Holland: Memoir and Letters.* London: Murray, 1921.

Palmer, Roy. *A Ballad History of England from 1588 to the Present Day.* London: B. T. Batsford, 1979.

Parsons, Gerald, ed. *Religion in Victorian Britain.* 4 vols. Manchester: Manchester University Press, 1988.

Pater, Walter. "Apollo in Picardy" (1893). In *Miscellaneous Studies,* 142–71.

———. "Coleridge's Writings." *Westminster Review* 29 (January 1866): 106–32.

———. "Diaphaneitè." In *Miscellaneous Studies,* 247–54.

———. *The Letters of Walter Pater.* Ed. Lawrence Evans. Oxford: Clarendon, 1970.

———. *Miscellaneous Studies: A Series of Essays.* London: Macmillan, 1920.

———. *Plato and Platonism: A Series of Lectures* (1893). London: Macmillan, 1910.

———. "Postscript." In *Appreciations, with an Essay on Style,* 241–61. London: Macmillan, 1910.

———. *The Renaissance: Studies in Art and Poetry: The 1893 Text.* Ed. Donald L. Hill. Berkeley: University of California Press, 1980.

———. "Winckelmann." *Westminster Review* 87 (January 1867): 36–50.

Patmore, Coventry. *The Poems of Coventry Patmore.* Ed. Frederick Page. London: Oxford University Press, 1949.

Pattison, Mark. *Memoirs of an Oxford Don.* London: Cassell, 1988.

———. "Sermon V: 30 April 1865." In *Sermons,* 103–36. London: Macmillan, 1885.

Pine, Richard. *Oscar Wilde.* Dublin: Gill and Macmillan, 1983.

Plato. *The Collected Dialogues including the Letters.* Ed. Edith Hamilton and Huntington Cairns. Princeton: Princeton University Press, 1961.

———. *The Dialogues of Plato Translated into English with Analyses and Introductions.* Trans. Benjamin Jowett. 2d ed. 5 vols. Oxford: Clarendon, 1875.

———. *Opera Omnia,* ed. Gottfried Stallbaum. 2d ed. 10 vols. Gotha: Hennings; London: David Nutt, 1858.

Pocock, J. G. A. *The Machiavellian Moment: Florentine Political Thought and the Atlantic Republican Tradition.* Princeton: Princeton University Press, 1975.

Pope, Alexander. *Epistle to Arbuthnot.* In *The Poems of Alexander Pope,* ed. John Butt, 597–612. New Haven: Yale University Press, 1963.

Pulteney, William. *A Proper Reply to a Late Scurrilous Libel Intitled "Sedition and Defamation Displayed."* London: printed for R. Francklin, 1731.

Raffalovich, Marc-André. "Giles and Miles and Ysabeau." *Blackfriars Magazine* 9 (1928): 18–29.

———. *Uranisme et unisexualité: Etude sur différentes manifestations de l'instinct sexuel.* Lyons: A. Storck; Paris: Masson, 1896.

Reade, Brian. *Sexual Heretics: Male Homosexuality in English Literature from 1850 to 1900: An Anthology.* New York: Coward-McCann, 1970.

Report of Her Majesty's Commissioners Appointed to Inquire into the State, Discipline, Studies and Revenues of the University and Colleges of Oxford. London: W. Clowes for H. M. Stationery Office, 1852.

Richards, Jeffrey. "'Passing the Love of Women': Manly Love and Victorian Society." In *Manliness and Morality: Middle-class Masculinity in Britain and America, 1800–1940,* ed. J. A. Mangan and James Walvin, 92–122. New York: St. Martin's, 1987.

Ricks, Christopher, and Edgar Shannon. "'The Charge of the Light Brigade': The Creation of a Poem." *Studies in Bibliography* 38 (1985): 1–44.

Robertson, W. Graham. *Life Was Worth Living.* New York: Harper, 1931.

Robespierre, Maximilien. "Discours X." In *The Principal Speeches of the Statesmen and Orators of the French Revolution, 1789–95,* ed. Henry Morse Stephens, 2:421–66. Oxford: Clarendon, 1892.

Robison, John. *Proofs of a Conspiracy against All the Religions and Governments of Europe* (1797). 4th ed. London: printed for T. Cadell and W. Davies, 1798.

Ross, Margery. *Robert Ross: Friend of Friends.* London: Jonathan Cape, 1952.

Ross, Robert. "The Brand of Isis." In *Masques,* 33–46.

———. *Masques and Phases.* London: Arthur L. Humphreys, 1909.

———. "Mr. Benson's 'Pater.'" In *Masques,* 125–34.

Satan's Harvest Home. London: printed for the editor, 1749; rpt. New York: Garland, 1985.

Scarry, Elaine. *The Body in Pain: The Making and Unmaking of the World.* New York: Oxford University Press, 1985.

Schlesinger, Kathleen. "Fife." In *Encyclopaedia Britannica,* 10:331. 11th ed. New York: Encyclopaedia Britannica, 1910.

Sedgwick, Eve Kosofsky. *Between Men: English Literature and Male Homosocial Desire.* New York: Columbia University Press, 1985.

———. *Epistemology of the Closet.* Berkeley: University of California Press, 1990.

Seiler, R. M., ed. *Walter Pater: A Life Remembered.* Calgary: University of Calgary Press, 1987.

Shadwell, Charles Launcelot. "Preface." In Pater, *Miscellaneous Studies,* 1–2.

Sherard, Robert H. *Oscar Wilde: The Story of an Unhappy Friendship.* London: privately printed, 1902; rpt. New York: Haskell, 1970.

Shuter, William F. "Pater as Don." *Prose Studies* 11 (1988): 41–60.

———. "Walter Pater and the Academy's 'Dubious Name.'" *Victorians Institute Journal* 16 (1988): 129–47.

Smith, Goldwin. *The Elections to the Hebdomadal Council: A Letter to the Rev. C. W. Sandford, M.A., Senior Censor of Christ Church.* Oxford: Parker, 1866.

Smith, Sydney. "Essays on Professional Education by R. L. Edgeworth." *Edinburgh Review* 15 (October 1809): 40–53.

Smollett, Tobias. *The Adventures of Roderick Random* (1748). Ed. Paul-Gabriel Boucé. Oxford: Oxford University Press, 1979.

Stanford, W. B., and R. B. McDowell. *Mahaffy: A Biography of an Anglo-Irishman.* London: Routledge and Kegan Paul, 1971.

Stanley, Arthur. "The Oxford School." *Edinburgh Review* 153 (April 1881): 157–72.

Staves, Susan. "A Few Kind Words for the Fop." *Studies in English Literature* 22 (1982): 413–28.

Stephen, Leslie. *Life of Henry Fawcett.* New York: G. P. Putnam's Sons, 1886.

Sterling, John. "Simonides." *London and Westminster Review* 32 (December 1838): 99–136.

Stokes, John. *In the Nineties.* Chicago: University of Chicago Press, 1989.

———. "Wilde at Bay: The Diaries of George Ives." *English Literature in Transition* 26 (1983): 175–86.

Stone, Marjorie. "Taste, Totems, and Taboos: The Female Breast in Victorian Poetry." *Dalhousie Review* 64 (1984–85): 748–70.

Stout, G. D. "The Cockney School." *Times Literary Supplement,* 7 February 1929, 98.

Swinburne, Algernon Charles. *The Swinburne Letters.* Ed. Cecil Y. Lang. 6 vols. New Haven: Yale University Press, 1959.

Symonds, John Addington. "The Dantesque and Platonic Ideals of Love" (1890). In *Key of Blue,* 55–86.

———. "Edward Cracroft Lefroy." In *Key of Blue,* 87–110.

———. *Gabriel.* Ed. R. L. Peters and Timothy d'Arch Smith. London: Michael deHartington, 1974.

———. *In the Key of Blue and Other Prose Essays.* London: Elkin Mathews and John Lane, 1893.

———. *The Letters of John Addington Symonds.* Ed. Herbert M. Schueller and Robert L. Peters. 3 vols. Detroit: Wayne State University Press, 1969.

———. *Male Love: A Problem in Greek Ethics and Other Writings.* Ed. John Lauritsen. New York: Pagan, 1983.

———. *The Memoirs of John Addington Symonds: The Secret Homosexual Life of a Leading Nineteenth-Century Man of Letters.* Ed. Phyllis Grosskurth. Chicago: University of Chicago Press, 1986.

———. *A Problem in Greek Ethics* (1883). In *Male Love,* 1–73.

———. *A Problem in Modern Ethics* (1891). In *Male Love,* 75–113.

———. *The Renaissance: An Essay Read in the Theatre, Oxford, June 17, 1863.* Oxford: Henry Hammans, 1863.

———. *Studies of the Greek Poets*. London: Smith, 1873.

———. *Studies of the Greek Poets*. 2d series. London: Smith, 1876.

———. *Walt Whitman: A Study*. London: George Routledge; New York: E. P. Dutton, 1893.

Symonds, Richard. *Oxford and Empire: The Last Lost Cause?* London: Macmillan, 1986.

Symons, A. J. A. "Wilde at Oxford." *Horizon* 3 (1941): 253–64.

Tennyson, Alfred. *Tennyson: A Selected Edition*. Ed. Christopher Ricks. Berkeley: University of California Press, 1989.

Tholfsen, Trygve R. *Working Class Radicalism in Mid-Victorian England*. New York: Columbia University Press, 1977.

Thucydides. *Thucydidis Historiae*. Ed. Karl Hude. 2 vols. Leipzig: B. G. Teubner, 1901.

Tollemache, Lionel A. *Old and Odd Memories*. London: Edward Arnold, 1908.

Trenchard, John, and Thomas Gordon. *Cato's Letters; or, Essays on Liberty, Civil and Religious, and Other Important Subjects* (1720–23). 5th ed. 4 vols. London: printed for T. Woodward et al., 1748.

Trumbach, Randolph. "The Birth of the Queen: Sodomy and the Emergence of Gender Equality in Modern Culture, 1660–1750." In *Hidden from History: Reclaiming the Gay and Lesbian Past*, ed. Martin Bauml Duberman, Martha Vicinus, and George Chauncey, 129–40. New York: New American Library, 1989.

Tucker, Herbert F. *Tennyson and the Doom of Romanticism*. Cambridge: Harvard University Press, 1988.

Turner, Frank M. *The Greek Heritage in Victorian Britain*. New Haven: Yale University Press, 1981.

Tyrwhitt, Richard St. John. "The Greek Spirit in Modern Literature." *Contemporary Review* 29 (March 1877): 552–66.

———. *Hugh Heron, Christ Church: An Oxford Novel*. London: Strahan, 1880.

Vance, Norman. *The Sinews of the Spirit: The Ideal of Christian Manliness in Victorian Literature and Religious Thought*. Cambridge: Cambridge University Press, 1985.

Walpole, Horace. *Letters*. Ed. Mrs. Paget Toynbee. 16 vols. Oxford: Clarendon, 1903–5.

Ward Ned. "The Mollies Club." In *The History of the London Clubs or, the Citizens' Pastime*, pt. 2. London: J. Dutton, 1710.

Weeks, Jeffrey. *Coming Out: Homosexual Politics in Britain, from the Nineteenth Century to the Present*. London: Quartet, 1977.

Wells, J. "The Honour School of Literae Humaniores." In *Oxford: Its Life and Schools*, ed. A. M. M. Stedmann, 244–65. London: G. Bell, 1887.

Whitehead, William. *The Roman Father* (1750). In *Plays and Poems*. London: printed for J. Dodsley, 1774.

Wilde, Oscar. *Hellenism*. Edinburgh: Tragara, 1979.

———. *The Letters of Oscar Wilde*. Ed. Rupert Hart-Davis. New York: Harcourt, Brace and World, 1962.

———. *More Letters of Oscar Wilde*. Ed. Rupert Hart-Davis. London: Murray, 1985.

———. *Oscar Wilde's Oxford Notebooks: A Portrait of Mind in the Making*. Ed. Philip E. Smith and Michael S. Helfand. New York: Oxford University Press, 1989.

———. *The Picture of Dorian Gray* (1891). Ed. Donald L. Lawler. New York: Norton, 1988.

———. *The Portrait of Mr. W. H.* In *The Artist as Critic: Critical Writings of Oscar Wilde*, ed. Richard Ellmann, 152–220. New York: Random House, 1969.

Wolffe, John. *The Protestant Crusade in Great Britain, 1829–1860*. Oxford: Clarendon, 1991.

Wright, Thomas. *The Life of Walter Pater*. 2 vols. London: Everett, 1907; rpt. New York: Haskell, 1969.

INDEX

Hallam, Arthur Henry, 84
Hardinge, William Money, 100–102, 106–7
Harrington, James, 48
Harris, Frank, 145
Harrow School, 67, 86, 88
Harvie, Christopher, 84
Hegel, Georg Wilhelm Friedrich, 63, 64, 70, 73, 84, 90
Hellenism: as force for cultural renewal, 3–5, 31, 35–36, 59–66, 79–80, 90, 94, 96–97, 104, 109–10, 121–22, 135–36, 142–43; as "homosexual code," 3, 27–28, 35, 66, 91–99, 110, 135–40, 152–53; as study of ancient Greece, 35, 72–74, 129, 131–32
Hervey, John Lord, 9n
˙Hinchliff, Peter, 70n
Holland, Henry Scott, 44
Homer, 77
Homosexuality: as pathology, 3, 130–32; as positive social identity, 2–4, 27, 103, 109, 132–35, 141, 152–54
Homosociality, 35, 66, 81, 85–86, 114n. *See also* Friendship, male
Hopkins, Gerard Manley, 43
Hoplite warfare, 47–48
Horace (Quintus Horatius Flaccus), 22
Housman, A. E., 99
Humboldt, Wilhelm von, 60, 62n
Hunt, Leigh, 13, 15–16, 21–24
Hunter-Blair, David, 121n
Hyde, Montgomery, 3n

Inman, B. A., 81, 100–102, 106n
"Inspiration," and hearer/inspirer dyad, 83–84, 102, 115n, 138–39, 150
Ives, George, 147n, 152

Jenkyns, Richard, 4, 28, 72, 77, 145, 153
Johnson, Lionel, 135–37
Johnson, Samuel, 18
Johnson, William, 68, 69n, 87n, 115n; *Ionica*, 86–87, 114
Jowett, Benjamin, 43, 60, 64–66, 83, 95, 97, 99, 152; as Dr. Jenkinson, 105–8, 109n; as Master of Balliol, 91–92, 112–13; and Pater-Hardinge affair, 100–103; as tutor, 32–35, 68–70, 72–78, 80, 88–89

Kains-Jackson, Charles, 27, 29–31
Keats, John, 13, 15–16, 22–24
Keble, John, 37
Keefe, Janice, 139n

Keefe, Robert, 139n
Kingsley, Charles, 44–46, 48–50, 58
Kingsley, Henry, 44n
Koestenbaum, Wayne, 132

Lady Margaret Hall, Oxford, 85n
Lancaster, Nathaniel, 10
Lauritsen, John, 79n
Lefroy, Edward Cracroft, 116, 117n
Lessing, Gotthold Ephraim, 70
Levey, Michael, 107n
Levinson, Marjorie, 20
Lewes, George Henry, 14
Liberalism, 13–14, 26, 86–87; Victorian crisis of, 56–62, 66
Lincoln College, Oxford, 107n
Literae humaniores, 32, 64, 67–77, 80, 83–86, 101–2, 105, 118–19, 122, 124
Louÿs, Pierre, 133, 147

Macaulay, Thomas Babington, 6–7, 36–37, 55–56
McDowell, R. B., 121n
Machiavelli, Niccolò, 5–7, 10, 48, 52, 61, 149n
McCormack, Jerusha, 133
McGann, Jerome, 49
McIntosh, Mary, 11–12n
MacKenzie, Compton, 153
Mackie, Gascoigne, 114n
McLachlan, James, 112n
Magdalen College, Oxford, 88, 113n, 114, 121n, 135
Mallock, W. H.: *New Republic*, 104–12, 118
Mandeville, Bernard de, 7, 10
Mania, as erotic madness, 96, 139
"Manliness," 10, 36, 54, 58–59. *See also* Warrior ideal
Martin, Robert Bernard, 44n
Matthew, H. G. C., 37n, 70n
Maurice, Frederick Denison, 68, 69n
Michelet, Jules, 20, 84
Mikhail, E. H., 121n
Mill, John Stuart, 68, 75–76, 78, 85n, 90, 96, 113; *On Liberty*, 56–63, 76–77, 80, 84, 123n; *System of Logic*, 64, 85n
Milner, Alfred, 72
Molly, 11, 46
Monsman, Gerald C., 82n, 94n, 95, 139n, 145n
Montesquieu, Charles Louis de Secondat de, 10, 19
Moor, Norman, 89, 114n

Breinigsville, PA USA
06 January 2011

252812BV00001B/61/A